KT-232-760

COUNSELLING ADOLESCENTS

COUNSELLING ADOLESCENTS

THE PROACTIVE APPROACH

SECOND EDITION

Kathryn **Geldard** & David **Geldard**

SAGE Publications

Los Angeles • London • New Delhi • Singapore

© Kathryn Geldard and David Geldard 2004

First edition published 1999
Reprinted 1999, 2000, 2001, 2002, 2003 (twice)
Second edition published 2004

Reprinted 2005 (twice), 2006, 2007

Apart from any fair dealing for the purposes of research or
private study, or criticism or review, as permitted under the
Copyright, Designs and Patents Act, 1988, this publication
may be reproduced, stored or transmitted in any form, or by
any means, only with the prior permission in writing of the
publishers, or in the case of reprographic reproduction, in
accordance with the terms of licences issued by the
Copyright Licensing Agency. Inquiries concerning
reproduction outside those terms should be sent to
the publishers.

 SAGE Publications Ltd
1 Oliver's Yard
55 City Road
London EC1Y 1SP

SAGE Publications Inc.
2455 Teller Road
Thousand Oaks, California 91320

SAGE Publications India Pvt Ltd
B 1 /I/ 1 Mohan Cooperative Industrial Area
Mathura Road, New Delhi 110 044
India

SAGE Publications Asia-Pacific Pte Ltd
33 Pekin Street #02-01
Far East Square
Singapore 048763

British Library Cataloguing in Publication data

A catalogue record for this book is available
from the British Library

ISBN 978 1 4129 0234 2
ISBN 978 1 4129 0235 9 (pbk)

Library of Congress Control Number available

Typeset by C&M Digitals (P) Ltd., Chennai, India
Printed in Great Britain by TJ International Ltd, Padstow, Cornwall

Contents

PART ONE

UNDERSTANDING THE ADOLESCENT

1   The nature of adolescence

There are many professional counsellors who work exclusively with adolescents and gain success and satisfaction from their work. However, there are many other counsellors who are reluctant to work with adolescents. This may be because they find adolescents difficult to work with or are discouraged by outcomes. Although some adolescents are difficult to work with, counselling adolescents can be exciting, challenging and effective, provided that some basic principles are understood and respected. The principles and practices required for counselling adolescents are not complicated or difficult but are in many ways significantly different from those required for counselling either children or adults. It is only by recognizing the different approach required that satisfaction and success are likely to be achieved.

In order to help adolescents effectively we need to understand the nature of adolescence and the developmental processes which are involved. Once we have this understanding, we can use a counselling approach which is specifically designed to parallel the adolescent developmental process and to take account of normal adolescent communication processes. By doing this, there is synchrony between the counselling process and the adolescent's own experiences. This enables the counsellor to join appropriately with the young person to achieve a mutually beneficial working relationship.

In Part 1 of this book we will discuss the developmental processes which occur in adolescence and will consider the impact of a variety of internal and external stimuli on adolescent development. We will begin the discussion in this chapter by considering the question 'what is adolescence?', and then examine adolescent development. This book is not intended to be primarily a theoretical treatise, but a practical guide for counsellors who wish to work with adolescents. It is a companion book to *Counselling Children: A Practical Introduction* (Geldard and Geldard, 2002). Those readers who wish to review the theory of adolescent development in more depth may wish to refer to Dacey and Kenny (1997) who provide discussion of the contributions of a number of important theorists, including G. Stanley Hall, Sigmund Freud, Ruth Benedict, Margaret Mead, Albert Bandura, Robert Havighurst, Abraham Maslow, Erik Erikson and Richard Lerner.

What is adolescence?

The question 'what is adolescence?' is one of definition, and the precise nature of the definition is likely to vary from culture to culture. In this book we will consider adolescence to be the stage in a person's life between childhood and adulthood. It is the period of human development during which a young person must move from dependency to independence, autonomy and maturity. The young person moves from being part of a family group to being part of a peer group and to standing alone as an adult (Mabey and Sorensen, 1995).

Generally, in Western society, movement through adolescence from childhood to adulthood involves much more than a linear progression of change. It is multi-dimensional, involving a gradual transformation or metamorphosis of the person as a child into a new person as an adult. It is important to note, however, that the required changes in a young person during adolescence differ with culture. For example, in some cultures some of the roles played by children and adults are similar. Children may be expected to perform work-like tasks for the welfare of the family while quite young. Also, in some cultures the number of years spent in being educated before working is short. In such cultures the transition from childhood to adulthood is likely to be less challenging (Mead, 1975).

Adolescence involves a process which extends over a significant period of a person's life. However, there are individual differences, with some young people moving through adolescence much more quickly than others. Adolescence presents many challenges as physiological, biological, psychological and social changes are confronted. Important processes of change need to occur within the young person if these challenges are to be confronted adaptively and with success. When an adolescent is unable to confront and deal with a developmental challenge successfully there are likely to be unhelpful psychological, emotional and behavioural consequences. It is in dealing with these that counselling may be useful, with the counsellor helping the young person to find new ways to proceed adaptively along the required developmental journey.

As will be discussed more fully in Chapter 5, some young people are more successful than others at confronting and dealing with the challenges of adolescence; they are more resilient and have better coping strategies. This may be partly related to personality traits and partly to past history and the current environment. Adolescent development can be considered in terms of the following challenges which inevitably occur:

- biological challenges
- cognitive challenges
- psychological challenges
- social challenges
- moral and spiritual challenges

Biological challenges in adolescence

Adolescence begins with the well-defined maturation event called puberty. Puberty refers to the biological events which surround the first menstruation in girls and the first ejaculation in boys. These events signal the beginning of a process of profound physical change (Colarusso, 1992). Although this is a normal maturation process it can cause difficulties for the individual. This may particularly be the case where a young person is precocious in puberty or if puberty is significantly delayed. In these situations the adolescent may experience an uncomfortable level of stress. Consequences may be a lowering of self-esteem and self-concept with the person feeling awkward and lacking self-confidence. The biological changes of adolescence result in physiological changes, sexual changes and emotional changes.

Physiological changes

During adolescence major physiological changes take place. The young person grows in height, weight and strength, develops sexually, and changes in appearance. Girls develop breasts, boys' voices break, body hair grows, and changes occur in sexual organs. These physiological changes occur over a period of time. They happen at different ages and different rates for different young people. Consequently, there may be issues for the adolescent who may feel embarrassed, self-conscious, awkward and out of step with peers who are developing at a different rate. It is therefore not surprising that many adolescents become very anxious about their appearance.

Sexual changes

Significant and important increases in the production of sexual hormones occur during puberty. These result not only in changes to the body as described above but also trigger an increase in sexual arousal, desire and urge in both males and females. These changes are likely to cause discomfort for the adolescent. As sexual drive rises, the adolescent is confronted with issues of personal sexuality and sexual identity. These issues will influence the young person's decisions with regard to relationships. In early adolescence, young people tend to form close relationships with friends of the same sex because they feel secure with them (Blos, 1979). Additionally, this is a part of their process of movement away from dependence on their parents and family. During this time, some will become involved in sexual experimentation with their friends. However, for others the sexual feelings of early adolescence are managed through the use of fantasy and masturbation. The early stage of adolescence typically extends from the age of 11 to 14 years. From this stage the young person gradually moves into the later stage of adolescence which occurs typically from 15 to 18 years. The early stage and the later stage are differentiated by differences in cognitive, moral and social thinking (Dacey and Kenny, 1997).

By late adolescence, with the acceptance of the new physically and sexually mature body, there is a gradual move, in most young people, toward heterosexual relationships. According to Colarusso (1992), by late adolescence many young people are psychologically ready for an active sexual life which includes intercourse. Some young people may at this stage begin to explore their sexual preferences and to make decisions with regard to homosexuality. Because many in society tend to be homophobic, such explorations may be a source of anxiety, particularly if the decision is to choose a partner of the same sex (Mabey and Sorensen, 1995).

With regard to sexual development, some young people have difficulty progressing from the early stages of adolescence through to the later stages. This may be because they are unable to separate their own sexuality from their parents. As a consequence they may engage in unhelpful sexual fantasies which fail to direct them to appropriate non-incestuous partners (Colarusso, 1992). When assessing sexual development it is important to recognize that early sexual experience is not an indicator of rapid developmental progression. Indeed, it may be an indicator of childhood sexual trauma.

Emotional changes

During adolescence, the rise in sexual hormones may influence the young person's emotional state. It would, however, be a mistake to assume that hormones act in isolation and that they alone are the cause of mood changes. They act in conjunction with other major changes which are impacting on the young person, such as changes in social relationships, changes in beliefs and attitudes and changes in self-perception.

Biological changes clearly present the adolescent with major challenges. The adolescent has to cope with body changes which may be disturbing and worrying and with the emergence of sexual urges that drive the young person into the exploration of new relationships which themselves produce new social challenges.

Cognitive challenges in adolescence

While biological changes are occurring in the adolescent, cognitive changes are also taking place. The adolescent develops a capacity for abstract thinking, discovers how to think about relationship issues, discerns new ways of processing information and learns to think creatively and critically.

Development of abstract thinking

According to Piaget (1948/1966), during early adolescence young people typically make the transition from 'concrete operations' to the 'formal operations' stage. That is, they move from the limitations of concrete thinking to being able to deal cognitively with ideas, concepts and abstract theories. The adolescent is able to become passionately interested in abstract concepts and notions and is therefore able to discern what is real from what is ideal.

Flavell (1977) suggested a number of ways in which adolescent thinking progresses beyond that of childhood. Included among these were the ability to:

- imagine possible and impossible events
- think of a number of possible outcomes from a single choice
- think of the ramifications of combinations of propositions
- understand information and act on that understanding
- solve problems involving hypothesis and deduction
- problem solve in a wider variety of situations and with greater skill than in childhood.

The adolescent is challenged both in the development of these cognitive skills and in their use. As confidence is gained in using such skills, it is likely that they will be tried out in new situations, but not always with success. Clearly, learning through success and failure is part of the challenge.

Egocentric thinking

Adolescents are egocentric. This trait starts in early adolescence and develops more fully in mid- to late adolescence. They may have the idea that everyone is watching them as though they were on stage. Sometimes they will deliberately 'parade' themselves in front of others, exhibiting particular poses or behaviours to invite attention to themselves. Adolescents frequently make up stories about themselves which Dacey and Kenny (1997) refer to as *personal fables*. They may have dreams of success and may start to believe that these are true. They may have the idea that they are both unique and invulnerable (Elkind, 1967). They may at times feel omnipotent, all-powerful and that they cannot be hurt. This is all part of the complex process of becoming a separate unique individual on a journey which will lead to adulthood. Unfortunately, these beliefs, and in particular the sense of uniqueness, make it difficult for adolescents to believe that anyone else is capable of understanding them or how they are feeling. This has important implications for counsellors.

The ability to think about other people

Along with the sense of uniqueness or individuation comes the ability to think critically about other people and interpersonal issues. Adolescents learn how, from their own perspectives, to understand or 'make sense of' other people. This enables them to make decisions about how to interact with others.

New ways of processing information

During adolescence the ability of young people to perceive, comprehend and retain information seems to improve with age (Knight et al., 1985). Additionally, they progressively develop the ability to make better use of memory strategies and are more able to detect contradictions (Keil and Batterman, 1984). Thus older adolescents tend to have a greater ability than younger adolescents for dealing with complex social and ethical issues. They have a more complex level of information-processing. However, this information-processing ability is dependent on intelligence because, as described by Jensen et al. (1989), the ability to process information quickly is directly related to higher levels of intellectual functioning.

The ability to think critically

Adolescents develop the ability to think logically and to use their capacity for logical thinking to make judgements and decisions for themselves. They are able to recognize and define problems, gather information, form tentative conclusions and evaluate these to make decisions. Of particular importance to counsellors is that several studies suggest that adolescents can be taught to improve their capacity for critical thinking (Pierce et al., 1988). Thus, part of a counsellor's role may be to help a young person to find ways to do this.

The ability to think creatively

Creative thinking involves divergent thinking, flexibility, originality, the consideration of remote possibilities and the ability to consider a variety of solutions to the same problem. Adolescents develop the ability to think creatively and are consequently better able to understand and use metaphor (Dacey and Kenny, 1997). This latter ability can be particularly useful in a counselling situation where metaphor can be a powerful tool for producing change.

Psychological challenges in adolescence

The biological and cognitive changes which have been described not only present challenges directly, but also have a significant impact on psychological functioning. Additionally, there are major psychological challenges for the young person with regard to a central feature of adolescence which involves the formation of a new identity. The adolescent is no longer a child; a new person is emerging.

Forming a new identity

Perhaps the most important psychological task for the adolescent is the formation of a personal identity. Failure to achieve a satisfying personal identity is almost certain to have negative psychological implications. This is supported by Waterman (1992) who conducted an extensive review of research which showed a strong link between ego identity and effective psychological functioning. As discussed by Kroger (1996), major theorists including Erikson, Blos, Kohlberg, Loevinger and Kegan have written about the development of identity in adolescence using terms which are individual to themselves such as 'self', 'ego', 'I', and so on. Although they have used individual terms, they all seem to agree that 'personal identity', as we will call it, should be defined in terms of what is taken to be 'self' in contrast to what is considered to be 'other'. The means by which we differentiate ourselves from others is central to our experience of personal identity. The adolescent has the task of forming a personal identity which is unique and individual. However, during the process in which a conscious sense of individual identity develops there will also be an unconscious striving for continuity of the individual's personal character (Erikson, 1968). As personal identity develops, over time, maturation occurs, moving the adolescent towards adulthood.

Functions of personal identity

Adams and Marshall (1996), drawing on numerous analyses and studies of the self and identity, suggest the following as the five most commonly recorded functions of personal identity:

1 Providing the structure for understanding who one is.
2 Providing meaning and direction through commitment, values and goals.
3 Providing a sense of personal control and free will.
4 Enabling consistency, coherence and harmony between values, beliefs and commitments.
5 Enabling the recognition of potential through a sense of future possibilities and alternative choices.

Adams and Marshall (1996) believe that the search for identity is a continuing process which is not just restricted to adolescence. They indicate that personal identity can be altered through heightened self-awareness, and that there are sensitive points along the life-cycle, one of which is adolescence, where self-focusing and identity formation are heightened. Even though we agree that the search for identity is a process which continues throughout life, our observations of young people indicate that such self-focusing and identity formation are more pronounced in adolescence and are central characteristics of adolescence.

Individuation

Whereas a child is joined with parents and family, the adolescent moves away into a separate space becoming a separate individual. In other words, *individuation* occurs. The process of individuation involves the development of relative independence from family relationships, the weakening of ties to objects which were previously important to the young person when a child, and an increased capacity to assume a functional role as a member of adult society (Archer, 1997). The processes of establishing a personal identity and achieving individuation have implications socially. The adolescent can only construct concepts of self within the context of relations with others, yet is also seeking to establish separateness through boundaries. Thus the adolescent's process of socialization is based on a balance between individuation together with the formation of personal identity, on the one hand, and integration with society on the other (Adams and Marshall, 1996). Unless this balance is achieved, there are likely to be personal crises for the adolescent which may result in the need for counselling. For example, if an adolescent seeks a very high degree of individuation the consequence may be that relationships with peers are damaged. This may result in the young person being marginalized. In this situation adolescents will sometimes seek the company of other marginalized peers. Even so, there are likely to be consequences as the adolescent's sense of being valued by others may be reduced (Schlossberg, 1989).

Rather than seek a high degree of individuation, some adolescents do the opposite and seek extreme connectedness with others. This can leave adolescents prone to difficulties in adapting to new circumstances where they need to deal with situations on their own (Josselson, 1987).

Emotional responses

As adolescents progress on their journey of self-discovery, they are continually having to adjust to new experiences, encounters and situations, while at the same time adjusting to biological, cognitive and psychological changes. This is both stressful and anxiety-provoking for them. It is not surprising, therefore, that adolescents demonstrate a decreased ability to tolerate, assimilate and accommodate change (Shave and Shave, 1989). The adolescent developmental stage is therefore characterized by emotional reactivity and a high intensity of emotional response. This makes it difficult for adolescents to control and modulate their behavioural responses, which at times may be inappropriately extreme. Stimuli of relatively minor significance for most adults may result in significant mood swings for the adolescent who may respond with unexpectedly high levels of emotion including excitement, anger, sadness, depression and embarrassment. Adolescents clearly have a difficult time dealing with the heightened intensity of their emotions and reactions.

A major disruptive emotion of early adolescence is shame (Shave and Shave, 1989). Adolescents frequently experience feelings of ridicule, humiliation and embarrassment, and feel disgusted and ashamed of themselves. It is therefore understandable that they tend to develop strong defence mechanisms which may include disavowal, denial, projection and regression. These defence mechanisms play an important role in the way early adolescents react to situations and interact with others. Inappropriate behaviour may often be a consequence of these internal ego-defending mechanisms.

Ethnic identity and psychological adjustment

For adolescents who belong to ethnic minority groups there are special problems with regard to establishing personal identity. An important part of their personal identity is likely to involve their ethnic identity. Waterman (1984) has suggested a model of ethnic identity formation. In the first stage of ethnic identity development, minority adolescents accept the values and attitudes of the majority culture. This often includes internalizing negative views of their own group. Waterman (1984) believes that this first stage of ethnic identity development continues until individuals have an experience of racism or prejudice which forces them to see themselves as members of a minority group. This awareness then leads them to a personal ethnic identity search. The search involves efforts to learn about their own culture and is often likely to be highly emotional. In this stage, emotions such as anger and outrage may be directed towards the majority society. A satisfactory outcome of this ethnic identity process can then be achieved with individuals developing a deeper sense of belonging to a group.

Social challenges in adolescence

A major challenge for adolescents is concerned with their need to find their place in society and to gain a sense of fitting in that place. This is a process of socialization involving an adolescent's integration with society. This process occurs at the same time as the search for personal identity. In fact, the socialization process and the search for personal identity are strongly interrelated and interdependent. Socialization enhances the sense of personal identity, and the development of personal identity helps the adolescent to deal with society's expectations and standards.

The wider society, parents, family and peer groups all have expectations regarding the adolescent. These expectations are based on the appropriate assumption that the adolescent is now becoming capable of behaving differently. The combined expectations of society, parents and peers, together with newly acquired psychological and cognitive changes, challenge the adolescent to make changes in social behaviour.

Society's expectations

Society's expectations pose a challenge for adolescents and are valuable in helping them to progress along the path to adulthood. In communities where adults express consistent values and expectations, adolescents tend to develop a positive sense of self (Ianni, 1989). In contrast, in communities where family, school and community fail to offer consistent direction and positive goals, adolescents drift towards undesirable behaviours, tend to become confused and cynical and to experience a generally diffused sense of self.

The adolescent can only construct a personal identity in the context of relationships with others. Having relationships with others unquestionably involves respecting and responding appropriately to their expectations. Society in general has expectations about how adolescents should behave and these will often conflict with adolescent expectations. Hence, the adolescent's need to achieve individuation provides a conflictual challenge for the young person who is striving for personal identity and is, at the same time, exploring new ways of fitting into society. Consequently, there is likely to be marked ambivalence in many adolescents concerning issues of independence versus dependence, and with regard to expressing attitudinal and behavioural changes while maintaining social relationships (Archer, 1997).

Many of the tasks of adolescence involve strong social expectations. Havighurst (1951) believed that the mastery of the nine developmental tasks listed below were critical to adaptive adolescent adjustment:

1   Accepting one's physique and sexual role.
2   Establishing new peer relationships with both sexes.
3   Achieving emotional independence of parents.
4   Selecting and preparing for an occupation.
5   Developing intellectual skills and concepts necessary for civic competence.
6   Achieving assurance of economic independence.
7   Acquiring socially responsible behaviour patterns.
8   Preparing for marriage and family life.
9   Building conscious values that are harmonious with one's environment.

This list of tasks might seem daunting for many adolescents. Some will find the challenges overwhelming and will feel alienated from society because they are unable to achieve society's expectations.

As adolescents grow, they start to look like young adults and are able to communicate more maturely and effectively than children. Consequently, it is understandable that many adults expect adolescent behaviour ought to reflect the norms of adult behaviour. The expectation that adolescents will be responsible and will conscientiously set out to meet the developmental tasks of adolescence is unrealistic. The adolescent is in a process of growth and is dealing with new and previously unmet challenges, so is unlikely to stay focused on particular tasks and is sure to make mistakes. Adolescents who are overwhelmed by society's expectations may revert to anti-social behaviour, becoming involved in behaviours ranging from low-level delinquency to serious crime. Some will find ways of satisfying their needs through membership of delinquent gangs. By being in a gang they may experience the feelings of belonging that they need, along with expectations that they can meet.

The impact of society's stereotypical expectations for adolescents of both sexes has been clearly identified in the relevant literature (Schrof, 1995). In spite of the influence of feminism, girls may get messages that their primary role in life is to marry, have children and become good wives and mothers. This may play havoc with their selection of long-term goals and be damaging to some girls' self-esteem. Similarly, the ideas that teenage boys have about being an adult male can be psychologically destructive when they try to live up to them. For both girls and boys, problems ranging from addiction to violence may often have their roots in the adolescent's inability to cope with the demands of the socialization process.

Parental expectations

Most parents do not know what is normal and realistic with regard to their expectations of their adolescent children. As their children grow through adolescence many parents become worried, and at times distressed, by behaviours which are normal for adolescents. Rutter (1995) believes that most adolescents are not particularly difficult or troublesome but the problem, in Western society, is how parents respond to the adolescent phase. She argues that the parents' response may create negative feelings and catapult the adolescent into anti-social behaviour. In her discussion of the issues she draws on research by Steinberg (1990).

Steinberg's (1990) hypothesis is that when children reach puberty the combination of the adolescent phase of development and the behaviour and emotions of parents produces tremendous changes in the parents, with parents becoming increasingly distressed. This may often be accompanied by a decline in marital satisfaction, regret for missed childhood opportunities, recognition of the ageing process, emotional rejection and isolation from an independent adolescent, increasing criticism from challenging teenagers, decline in respect for previously accepted authority and guidance, powerlessness, loss of youthful appearance and doubt about their own sexuality. These changes, Steinberg and Steinberg (1994) believe, often result in parents disengaging from their adolescents at a time when they need continuing guidance and support. It is understandable, although unfortunate, that some parents withdraw from their adolescents at this time. Adolescents need to withdraw because becoming independent is central to their role. But this does lead to many parents feeling dismayed and abandoning them at a time when they need special care and attention because of the transitions they are making.

Even when there are tensions in family life, the family remains one of the most effective vehicles for promoting values in adolescence, enabling adolescents to be successful at school and to have confidence in peer relationships. Steinberg and Steinberg (1994) find that the common link between successful adolescents is that they generally have positive relationships with their parents. Thus an important challenge for adolescents is to maintain positive relationships with their parents while achieving their developmental goals, one of which, somewhat paradoxically, is to separate and detach from their parents. Clearly, this is hard to achieve.

Research discussed in *USA Today* (1997) shows that most children normally detach from their parents between the ages of 10 and 18. Although this may sometimes be the result of family dysfunction, it must also be recognized as part of the normal process for adolescents. There are gender differences: boys generally seem to spend less time with their families than girls. Also girls are more likely to talk about personal issues with parents than are boys.

Many parents become distressed because their adolescent children do not want to discuss personal issues with them. However, because adolescents are seeking independence they are more likely to talk to parents at a time which suits them rather than responding to parental enquiries at other times. Further, they are more likely to continue talking if they are allowed to take the lead. These traits of adolescents have important significance for counsellors.

Adolescent expectations

A question of importance for counsellors is what adolescents themselves believe are their major challenges. Adolescents believe that their major challenges revolve around relationship issues with peers and others and performance issues within society, school or college (Youniss and Smollar, 1985). There are some differences here with regard to age. School pressures have been identified by young adolescents as being the most problematic, whereas for adolescents of 14 years and older, parent–adolescent conflicts were identified as being the most problematic.

Issues concerning peer relationships were universally considered to present problems, although more so for the older adolescent (Spirito et al., 1991). Along with forming close relationships and friendships, most adolescents are interested in belonging to a group whose members share common attitudes and interests. Within these groups they have strong expectations that their friends will be trustworthy and loyal to them. They tend to be intolerant of disrespectful acts, moodiness, stubbornness, conceit, drinking too much and bragging. Such behaviours are most likely to cause conflict (Youniss and Smollar, 1985).

Moral and spiritual challenges in adolescence

Important to the processes of social development and the formation of a personal identity are issues relating to moral and spiritual development.

Moral development

During adolescence the young person is confronted and challenged by a wide range of moral decisions. There are a number of differing views concerning the process of moral development. Important contributors to theory in this field are Kohlberg (1984) and Gilligan (1983). Kohlberg (1968, 1984) suggests a model that outlines stages of moral development based on ways of thinking about moral matters. His stages of moral development are as follows:

Stage one: pre-conventional morality (aged 4–10 years). In this stage the child will do good or avoid wrong with a motive of either avoiding punishment or receiving a reward.

Stage two: conventional morality (aged 10–13 years). During this stage the child or adolescent learns to conform to the society in which they lives. The motives for doing good or avoiding wrong depend on the approval of older people. Additionally, there is an emphasis on conforming with law and order.

Stage three: post-conventional morality (aged 13 years onwards). During this stage the individual develops a sense of human rights and starts to develop a conscience. Being aware of human rights may involve thinking about changes in the law to strive for more acceptable conditions. Additionally, at this stage adolescents develop clear ideas about what they believe in and what they are prepared to stand up for. No longer does the individual act merely out of fear or the need for approval. Instead, moral principles are integrated within, and owned by, the individual.

Kohlberg (1984) is conscious that not all adolescents reach stage three. For some adolescents, morality and motives may be at a stage-one level. For them, morality is tied up with rewards or with not 'getting caught'.

Gilligan (1983) believes that Kohlberg's theory does not truly represent the moral development of females, and it must be acknowledged that much of Kohlberg's research was based on male subjects. Gilligan suggests that there are three distinct levels of female development as follows:

Level one: individual survival is the driving force for moral reasoning. The female is limited strictly by concern for herself.

Level two: the adolescent moves to a position of self-sacrifice and social conformity.

Level three: moral decisions in this stage are characterized by consideration for the woman's individual needs as well as those of others. There is an emphasis on not hurting others.

Gilligan (1983) believes that women often use the ethic of care in making decisions about their lives. She suggests that the ethic of care comes from the attachment of children to their mothers, and that through their mothers girls learn about the 'give-and-take' nature of relationships in which moral decisions are made. Comparison of Gilligan's and Kohlberg's theories of moral development suggests that there are differences between males and females in the development of moral decision-making. The development of moral reasoning may also be heavily influenced by the context in which the adolescent lives and is largely dependent on intellectual development which also occurs at this time (Lovat, 1991).

Spiritual development

As adolescents seek to establish their personal identity, they attempt to find meaning in their lives. They look within themselves to examine thoughts and feelings, and to reason about them. This leads many young people to seek answers to questions of a spiritual nature (Elkind, 1980). Conventional religious beliefs and participation in organized religious practices demonstrate aspects of spirituality. However, adolescent spirituality is often demonstrated in a more fundamental way through the adolescent's search for meaning in life's daily experiences.

Fowler (1981) believes that spirituality can develop only within the scope of the intellectual and emotional growth of the individual. He sees the spiritual beliefs of children from the ages of 5 and 6 as relying heavily on the verification of facts from authority figures such as parents and teachers. In early adolescence, the emphasis is on symbolism rather than knowing factual truth. Later in adolescence, personal experiences, symbols and rituals may play a major part in the development of spiritual beliefs. At this stage the young person is likely to recognize that other people might have different and equally valid ways of understanding and expressing their spirituality. Some adolescents find conventional religious systems problematic and inconsistent with their need to achieve some level of separation from their family's traditions and values. Those adolescents who are struggling with identity formation, and are striving to find their place in society, may be attracted to unorthodox religious cults and practices in order to explore their spiritual beliefs and values. Some adolescents will look to such cults to provide them with a deeper sense of the meaning of life. Unfortunately, they may then become involved in religious practices which are unacceptable in conventional society. This may lead to the adolescent being marginalized.

Involvement in Satanism is an example of an unorthodox way in which adolescents may seek to explore their spirituality. Tucker (1989) suggests that adolescents are deeply fascinated by the kind of experience found in the practice of Satanism. Unfortunately, Satanism can seem attractive for a number of reasons. It provides a sense of group identity and bonding, the opportunity to develop a self-perceived 'charismatic' personality, power because it engenders fear in others and freedom from the restrictions of conventional belief systems. It also offers the opportunity to reject mainstream religion openly. It is not surprising that some adolescents are attracted to this belief system.

In summary

Clearly, adolescence is a time of change and crisis which may be adaptively encountered by some but for others presents the possibility of undesirable psychological, social and emotional consequences. The primary goal of adolescence is to make the transition from childhood to adulthood. Adolescents need to do this while dealing with biological, psychological and social challenges. Further, reaching adulthood successfully and unscathed will be influenced by the childhood experiences, environmental stresses and environmental hazards discussed in Chapters 2, 3 and 4.

2   The influence of childhood experiences

In Chapter 1 we explored the biological, cognitive, psychological and social challenges which adolescents need to negotiate and overcome. These developmental challenges may be daunting and overwhelming for some. However, many adolescents are ready and keen to accomplish the tasks confronting them. In favourable circumstances, given support from loving parents, from understanding teachers and from the wider society, the transition through adolescence can be managed with relative ease, the outcome being a well-adjusted mature adult. Unfortunately, in reality, many young people will not experience a smooth, untroubled journey through adolescence. Difficulty may be attributed to a variety of factors, the most important of which may be the adolescent's personality and ability to cope. Other factors include the influence of early childhood experiences, external or environmental stresses, and current social conditions. All of these may interfere, at times, with the ability of the adolescent to proceed along the developmental journey towards maturity and adulthood.

In this chapter we will examine the influence of childhood experiences which may, if not resolved, interfere with a young person's ability to deal adaptively with the tasks of adolescence. We will discuss the effects of unresolved childhood issues related to each of the following:

- early attachment problems
- the influence of unhelpful parental behaviour
- the effects of abuse
- the effects of trauma
- genetic effects.

Early attachment problems

The word *attachment*, as used in developmental psychology literature, describes the tendency of a child to repeatedly seek closeness with a specific person, usually the mother, in order to reduce internal tension. Bowlby (1969) is a major contributor to the relevant theory. He believed that attachment is an enduring affectionate bond which has a vital biological function indispensable for survival, and that the relationship between a child and the attachment figure provides a secure base from which the child can explore and master the world.

Some children do not have the opportunity to form a secure attachment to one person. They may have neglectful or abusive parents, be subjected to hospitalization which separates them from a parent, lose their parents through accident or war, or be subjected to other repeated traumatizing events which prevent a secure attachment from forming. As a consequence, these children are likely to suffer from what is known as an attachment disorder which can have quite serious consequences for them.

The kind of attachment that a child develops with the primary care-giver may impact on that child's development throughout life. Young people who have relatively secure attachments experience fewer and less stressful events related to school, and less strain during college years, than those with less secure attachments. They also exhibit higher academic performance (Burge et al., 1997). Attachment to parents is also found to have a strong effect on self-image, particularly with regard to aspects that gain prominence during adolescence such as body image, vocational goals and sexuality (O'Koon, 1997).

Early attachment with primary care-givers seems to have an effect on much of an adolescent's later experiences and to influence the way in which the adolescent deals with stressful situations. Insecure or unsatisfactory attachments during childhood have been linked with later substance abuse (Gerevich and Bacskai, 1996; Burge et al., 1997), eating disorders (Burge et al., 1997; Salzman, 1997), early sexual activity and high-risk sexual behaviour (Smith, 1997) and poor self-image (O'Koon, 1997) in adolescents. It has been found that anxiety disorders were more likely to occur in adolescents who had anxious attachments to their mothers as infants when compared with those who had secure attachments (Warren et al., 1997).

Clearly, it is important for counsellors to recognize that some maladaptive behaviours in adolescence may be partly the result of poor attachment relationships with primary figures during childhood.

The influence of unhelpful parental behaviour

The family is the primary provider of the emotional, intellectual and physical environment in which a child lives. This environment will impact on that child's views of the world later in life and on the child's ability to cope with future challenges. Thus, family connectedness and structure will impact on an adolescent's adjustment. Clearly, the ability of a family to function healthily will depend on the parent or parents.

It is both obvious and trite to say that parents have a major influence over child and adolescent development. Even so, we need to remember the truth of this statement, and to recognize that many children have competent parents who enable them to grow up to confront the challenges of adolescence successfully. However, because this book is about counselling we will often be considering those factors that lead to problems for adolescents, so that these problems can be understood by the counsellor when devising proactive counselling strategies. When parents give their own needs priority without adequate regard for the needs of their children, family systems become dysfunctional (Neumark-Sztainer et al., 1997) and as a consequence children will be affected in a variety of ways, as described in this chapter.

Parents need to address unacceptable behaviours in their children and to encourage the development of socially appropriate behaviours. If they do not do this, there will be consequences, either in childhood or when the child reaches adolescence, with regard to social relationships. There is generally a developmental sequence in which anti-social and aggressive behaviours develop. Such behaviours often begin in early childhood and include arguing, bragging and demanding attention. Unless these behaviours are addressed appropriately by parents they are likely to develop in middle childhood into behaviours such as being cruel, fighting, lying and cheating, with consequent poor peer relationships. Destructiveness and stealing in the home may then begin to emerge. Antisocial and aggressive behaviours thus start in mild forms of unacceptable behaviour in children and develop in intensity, frequency and form as the child gets older.

Some parents engage in behaviours which are unacceptable to society, with consequent damage to their children. Unfortunately, when parents engage in anti-social and maladaptive behaviours they increase the possibility of their children doing the same (Kazdin, 1985). It has been consistently demonstrated that both criminal behaviour and alcoholism in parents, particularly in fathers, is related to adolescent anti-social behaviour (West, 1982). Thus, irresponsible behaviour by parents may result in anti-social and aggressive behaviours being passed down within a family to successive generations.

The effects of abuse

When children are abused there will be psychological and emotional consequences for them at the time that the abuse occurs, and also later when they reach adolescence. The psychological and emotional effects of abuse will almost certainly result in the development of maladaptive behaviours unless the child or adolescent is able to resolve related troubling issues satisfactorily. In considering the effects of abuse we will discuss the following:

- neglect
- emotional abuse
- physical abuse
- sexual abuse

Often the effects of different types of abuse overlap. In addition, the young person's responses may be affected by underlying factors such as genetic predisposition, poor early attachment relationships and dysfunctional family patterns of behaviour, as previously discussed.

Neglect

The impact of neglect on children has been the focus of numerous studies. Many children at risk of neglect come from low socio-economic environments and underprivileged or culturally deprived minority groups. Others come from dysfunctional families where there are psychological problems, alcohol and/or drug abuse or financial problems (Swanson, 1991). Neglect can result in behaviour problems, poor school attendance, weak academic grades and low achievement generally. Children who have been neglected demonstrate a higher risk of having a diagnosis later in life of anti-social personality disorder (Luntz and Widom, 1994).

When an adolescent has had a history of childhood neglect, the young person may carry angry feelings towards the neglectful carers, and is likely to have problems with regard to such matters as personal safety, the provision of essential needs, equity, fairness, trust and responsibility.

Emotional abuse

Emotional abuse is often combined with other types of abuse. McGee et al. (1997) examined adolescents' perceptions of maltreatment experiences including emotional abuse, physical abuse, sexual abuse, neglect and exposure to family violence. Of these various types of abuse, the adolescents in the study reported emotional maltreatment as the most potent type of maltreatment.

Some parents put their own needs first at times when their children and/or adolescents need assistance, affirmation and reinforcement for positive behaviour. By doing this, these parents absent themselves emotionally from their children. This is abusive. When these children reach adolescence they are likely to have unresolved issues with regard to their emotional needs. Consequently, it is highly likely that they will seek out new ways to meet these needs. They may, for example, become involved in substance abuse or join up with peers who are engaged in 'exciting' risk-taking delinquent behaviours.

Similarly, in families where substance abuse and/or chemical dependence is occurring, there may be a lack of communication between parents and children, inadequate and inconsistent discipline within the family, and an absence of close emotional support and attachment (Garcia, 1992). Children growing up in these families are likely to carry emotional scarring into adolescence and will consequently be prone to develop dysfunctional behaviours.

Adolescents who have experienced emotional abuse as children may often present in counselling with behaviour problems. It is the proactive counsellor's task to identify the underlying emotional issues and to help the young person to find resolution.

Physical abuse

Children who have been subjected to physical abuse are certain to carry psychological scars with them into adolescence. In many cases, they not only need to deal with painful experiences from their past, but also may have to deal with continuing abuse in the present. An important dynamic in physical abuse is the issue of power and control. Consequently, adolescents who have been abused as children are likely to have strong unresolved emotional feelings around the issues of power and control.

Abusive parents tend to have common characteristics such as not taking responsibility for their behaviour, blaming the child, being incongruent, saying one thing and doing another, needing to have power over the child, distrusting their children, being selfish and being over-concerned with their own needs. They tend to repeat their abusive behaviour compulsively (McEvoy and Erickson, 1990).

Often, physical abusers of children have developed strong beliefs about parenting and the use of physical control and corporal punishment of children as a way of shaping behaviour. They should not be confused with parents who are authoritative, rely on non-abusive methods of behaviour management and use adaptive communication strategies. Unfortunately, parents who rely solely on power approaches, such as using force, physical punishment and threats to deal with their children, are less likely to be successful with regard to developing their children's moral values (Hoffman, 1988). Parents who rely on praise, social isolation and withdrawal of affection for punishment seem to produce children with high levels of conscience development because their children internalize parental standards and values (Baumrind, 1971). Authoritative parents are most successful in producing children who are socially competent and responsible.

It has been found that children and adolescents exposed to physical abuse may develop symptoms similar to those of post-traumatic stress disorder (Glod and Teicher, 1996). These authors also observed that children who had been physically abused had activity profiles similar to those of children diagnosed with attention deficit hyperactivity disorder (ADHD). This could be confusing for counsellors and is of considerable importance to them. It would be easy to make incorrect assessments because of the similarities in presentation of physically abused and ADHD children and adolescents.

The parents of adolescents need to develop new skills if they are to make the transition from parenting a child to appropriate parenting of an adolescent.

Making this transition is stressful for some parents. Consequently, adolescents from drug and chemically dependent families and alcoholic families may be at risk of physical abuse because their parents may become frustrated by their changing behaviour. In addition, many chemically dependent and alcoholic parents have poor anger-management skills.

Adolescents who have been physically abused as children and suffer abuse which continues into adolescence commonly respond to such abuse in one of two ways. They may express their feelings by acting out in anti-social ways with high levels of aggression, or they may hold back and internalize their feelings with the consequent development of depression and suicidal ideation. Those who internalize their feelings may also withdraw and disengage from mainstream adolescent social contacts and become marginalized in socially disconnected peer groups (Schmidt, 1991).

A further problem for those adolescents who internalize their feelings and experience powerlessness as a consequence of childhood and/or continuing physical abuse is the risk of suicide. Suicide and suicide attempts are increasingly recognized as options by adolescents with poor coping strategies. Kaplan et al. (1997) found that the rate of suicide attempts increased in adolecents who had been physically abused as compared to adolescents who had not been abused. These adolescents were also different from the non-abused peers in that they demonstrated significantly greater risk factors for suicide; for example, depression, substance abuse and disruptive behaviour.

Sexual abuse

Sexual abuse occurring during childhood has been widely documented as contributing to later adolescent and adult adjustment problems. Further, sexual victimization prior to adolescence contributes to the risk of delinquency in adolescents (Widon, 1994). Studies examining the short-term effects of childhood sexual abuse indicate that symptoms of depression and anxiety are common. The victims may also suffer from other sequelae which may continue through adolescence, including sexualized behaviours, nightmares, social withdrawal, isolation, sleep difficulties, anger, acting-out behaviours, somatic problems and schooling difficulties.

Studies of the long-term effects of childhood sexual abuse reveal that, as adults, victims of such abuse tend to have a high level of mental health problems, including depression, anxiety disorder, substance abuse, sexual dysfunction and interpersonal difficulties (Browne and Finkelhor, 1986). Further, sexual abuse during childhood and adolescence has been documented as contributing to suicidal gestures and attempts (VanderMay and Meff, 1982; Bagley et al., 1997).

Garnefski and Diekstra (1996) noticed that sexually abused boys had considerably more emotional and behavioural problems, including suicidal behaviour, than their female counterparts. Their research suggests that there may be gender differences in the ways that young people respond to sexual abuse. Sexually victimized female adolescents often have feelings of inferiority or disgust about their femininity and sexuality. This may lead to concern about their body weight, shape and size (Oppenheimer et al., 1985). It is not surprising, therefore, that many sexually abused adolescents report disturbances in body image, seeing themselves as fat, ugly and unworthy. They may then develop eating disorders (Hall et al., 1989). Clearly, sexual abuse in childhood and body-image disturbance are related. Welch et al. (1997) discovered that adolescents who were diagnosed with bulimia nervosa reported previous life events, such as sexual abuse, which involved a threat to their sense of bodily integrity and safety. Additionally, Casper and Lyubomirsky (1997) showed bulimic eating behaviour to be significantly related to sexual abuse.

It is common for children to be sexually abused by someone they know and trust. Such abuse may last for several years and often continues into adolescence. According to Alexander and Kempe (1984), the most serious type of sexual abuse is incest between father and daughter. There is also a high incidence of sexual abuse between stepfathers and stepdaughters. Often a daughter will be manipulated into wrongly believing that the abuse is all her fault. In addition, she may be warned that if she talks to anyone about the abuse she will be seen as a bad person and may also be arrested and jailed. Sadly, the outcome of such a situation is often for the adolescent to withdraw socially or run away from the family. The adolescent may engage in truancy, sexual promiscuity and have difficulty with future relationships (Alexander and Kempe, 1984). Some will move towards prostitution. Unfortunately, adolescents with a history of childhood sexual abuse not only feel victimized, but also are at risk of victimizing others and of sexual offending themselves (McClellan et al., 1997).

Sexual abuse can often be found in the histories of adolescents with severe mental health disturbances. Atlas et al. (1997) document the presence of features of Dissociative Identity Disorder in adolescents with a history of sexual abuse. Sanders and Giolas (1991) also suggest that dissociative symptoms are associated with traumatic sexual abuse experiences in adolescence. Dissociative symptoms appear to be related to very frightening sexual abuse that leaves the adolescent highly fearful. A behavioural analysis of situations in which the child 'spaces out', loses track of time or appears unresponsive to external stimuli is essential in such cases.

The effects of trauma

Most of the research on post-traumatic stress disorder has looked at the treatment of symptoms in adults rather than children. Reports of children's responses to traumatic events suggest that they bear a close resemblance to those symptoms of post-traumatic stress disorder in adults. Some recent studies of the disorder in children have examined children exposed to natural disaster (Frederick, 1985; Earls et al., 1988), man-made disasters (Handford et al., 1986), war-related trauma (Arroyo and Eth, 1985), violent crimes (Nader et al., 1990) and traumas related to medical procedures (Stoddard et al., 1989). Findings from these studies support the validity of the existence of post-traumatic stress disorder in children where the traumatic events have resulted in physical harm to the child or injury or death of a significant other.

One of the most common forms of trauma experienced by children today is domestic violence. Typically, when domestic violence occurs there will be injury and sometimes death of adults, adolescents or children in the home. Even if children are not personally involved as victims, they will be traumatized by witnessing the violence and will suffer from post-traumatic stress.

As a result of post-traumatic stress, the traumatic event may be persistently re-experienced by the young person through recurrent and intrusive memories and/or dreams. They may experience dissociative flashback episodes where they find themselves acting or feeling as if the event was actually reoccurring. They may experience intense distress when internal or external cues that resemble an aspect of the traumatic event trigger off memories. They may persistently avoid stimuli associated with the trauma and may experience a general unresponsiveness or numbing. Numbing involves attempts to avoid thoughts or feelings associated with the trauma, an inability to recall and report aspects of the trauma, marked disinterest in or lack of participation in activities, and feelings of being detached. They may also have a restricted range of emotional affect (for example, be unable to have loving feelings). Sometimes they may have persistent feelings of arousal, hyper-vigilance, irritability and difficulty in concentrating (American Psychiatric Association, 2001).

Exposure to severe violence is highly associated with psychiatric disorders, specifically post-traumatic stress disorder (PTSD). In a study by Steiner et al. (1997) the prevalence of PTSD in incarcerated juvenile delinquents was assessed. One half of the subjects described witnessing interpersonal violence as their traumatizing event. Of those subjects diagnosed with post-traumatic stress disorder, all showed elevated distress, anxiety, depression and lowered restraint, impulse control and suppression of aggression. They had high levels of immature defences such as projection, somatization, conversion, dissociation and withdrawal.

Unfortunately, just as with sexual abuse where the victim may become an abuser, children subjected to, or witnessing, domestic violence are likely to become violent themselves. As evidence of this, strikingly high levels of severe violence, such as shooting or stabbing, have been found to be perpetrated by inner-city youths who witnessed severe violence themselves (Singer et al., 1995).

There are also long-term effects of trauma in adolescence. Desivilya et al. (1996) examined the long-term psychological symptoms and behavioural changes resulting from exposure to a terrorist attack during adolescence. Consequences included difficulties in intrapersonal and interpersonal relationships, significantly high levels of mental health problems, greater vulnerability to psychological difficulties triggered by war-like events, lower levels of intimacy with spouses, as well as a more unstable employment history than adolescents who had not been exposed.

Loss

Children and adolescents are frequently traumatized by loss. They may lose peers such as boyfriends and girlfriends through relocation, rejection, death or suicide. They may also experience loss of parents through rejection, abandonment, divorce or death. For homeless children there are a number of losses, a critical one being denial of an education (Eddowes and Hranitz, 1989).

Where children experience loss, the grieving process may extend into adolescence and may influence their emotional state and behaviours. It is becoming increasingly recognized as important for adolescents to work through the grieving process so that their developmental journey is not impeded by their grief. While depression during bereavement is normal, it is important to consider when depression becomes pathological. Adolescents suffering the loss of a friend who has committed suicide appear to be more likely to experience a major depression occurring as a complication of the bereavement (Brent et al., 1993). Adolescents may also develop an increased risk of suicide themselves after someone they loved has committed suicide. As youth suicide is becoming more prevalent in Western society, it has been noticed that bereavement after suicide is more complicated. Guilt plays a greater role in bereavement when death has been by suicide as compared with death by natural causes (Peters and Weller, 1994).

Adolescents who suffered the loss of a parent by death reported intense shock, disbelief and a sense of loss. These experiences were found to be more intense than those of adults who lost parents through death. Adolescents also reported more anger at the deceased, sleep disturbances, dream activity and irritability than the adults (Meshot and Leitner, 1993).

Genetic effects

When counselling adolescents we need to recognize that, in addition to the effect of life experiences, there may also be genetic predispositions to psychological and behavioural disorders in adolescence. Comings (1997) reviewed evidence to support the concept that many childhood and adolescent disruptive behaviours including attention deficit hyperactivity disorder, Tourette's syndrome, learning disabilities, substance abuse, oppositional defiant disorder and conduct disorder are part of a spectrum of interrelated behaviours and have a strong genetic component. Comings (1997) also suggests that the genetic components of these disorders have a number of genes in common which affect dopamine, seratonin and other neuro-transmitters.

In summary

In this chapter we have considered various factors relating to unresolved childhood issues which impact on the adolescent. It is essential that, when counselling adolescents, we examine the impact of their early childhood experiences on their ability to negotiate the developmental tasks of adolescence.

3   Environmental stresses for adolescents

Adolescence is a time of change where the young person is facing new experiences. The various environments in which the adolescent moves are likely to present new and unexpected situations and events which require responses which the adolescent may have never previously used. Dealing with the unexpected and being required to use new, untested responses is certain to raise anxiety and cause stress in the young person.

There are wide differences in the ways in which adolescents respond to stress (see Chapter 5). Some adolescents are particularly resilient and have high-level coping strategies, whereas others have difficulty attending to the requirements of the developmental process in which they are engaged. The following are a number of environments and situations which have an inherent potential for raising stress in adolescents:

- the family environment
- the educational environment
- the work environment
- changing relationships
- exposure to sexuality issues
- socio-economic pressures and unemployment.

Clearly, the adolescent is unable to escape exposure to these environments because being exposed to them is an inevitable part of living. Moreover, this exposure is needed as part of the process which enables the young person to make the transition from childhood to adulthood.

The family environment

There are a number of factors within the family environment which have the potential to cause stress for the adolescent. These include:

- the family's style of functioning
- parenting style
- the parental relationship
- separation and divorce
- blended family issues
- an alcoholic parent
- domestic violence
- cultural issues.

The adolescent clearly has no control over any of these factors. However, they make up an important part of the environment in which the adolescent has to learn new behaviours in moving from childhood to adulthood. Although the quality of the environment may have an influence on an adolescent's potential for successful movement towards adulthood, it is the adolescent's personal responses to the environment which will finally determine the extent of that success.

The family's style of functioning

As described by the McMaster model of family functioning (Epstein et al., 1980), families vary along different dimensions. Some families are very rigid and others *laissez-faire*; some families are very enmeshed and others are disengaged. In rigid families rules are clear and inflexible, with definite and specific consequences if they are broken. There is a strong commitment to maintain the status quo, and a low threshold for the tolerance of disagreement. Naturally, these families have great difficulty in times where change and growth are necessary. Consequently, they may find that adolescent experimentation with new behaviours which are individual may be unacceptable to the family and may cause conflict and disharmony. Also, since disagreement is not permitted, there is likely to be a lack of conflict resolution where there can be explicit negotiation of differences (Garralda, 1992).

Other families are *laissez-faire*, with very free and easy rules. These families may have fewer problems as the adolescent changes. However, adolescents from these families may experience difficulties adjusting in wider society and the workplace where different rules and expectations may apply. There could also be other difficulties for them: because of the absence of external control by parents they will need to rely almost entirely on their internal locus of control to avoid self-destructive behaviours which may seem attractive in adolescence.

In enmeshed families an adolescent may find the home environment over-protective and family members unwilling to accept the need for the adolescent to seek a level of separation and individuation. Thus, the young person's development of autonomy and independence may be retarded. Similarly, families where there is a high level of warmth and affection may find that it is hard to allow an adolescent to move away from the family to establish the necessary and required independence. Adolescents from disengaged families may have some advantages in seeking independence because family members already have high levels of independent functioning within clear individual boundaries. However, these young people may not receive the family support they need during the transition to adulthood.

It is clear from this discussion that, whatever the family style of interaction, there may be some problems for the young person. Adjusting to the changes of adolescence is difficult, regardless of the family environment. However, some families do provide helpful environments for adolescent growth and development. The emotional climate within a family is certain to have some influence on the ability of the adolescent to develop adaptively and with a minimum of stress. Optimum conditions for adolescents exist in families where the environment is harmonious, where there is a genuine level of warmth and caring, where there is acceptance of difference, a respect for others' needs, good communication and the ability to resolve conflict. It is to be expected that in families where the environment is coloured by discord and disharmony, where communication is poor, tolerance of others' behaviours is low, and conflict-resolution skills are absent that the adolescent may be subjected to levels of stress and anxiety which will make adaptive progression to adulthood more difficult.

Parenting style

Adolescents have little option but to cope with whatever style of parenting their parents choose to use. If the parenting style is one which inhibits change and tries to maintain the same structure that applied when the adolescent was a child, then the adolescent will struggle to make the changes which are required to move towards adulthood. The adolescent may respond with compliance, in which case normal adolescent development will be inhibited. Alternatively, there may be confrontation, in which case a high level of stress and conflict will be inevitable.

Although parents need continually to provide the adolescent with opportunities for change, they need to continue to exert a level of parental control, remembering that the adolescent is not yet an adult. This requirement is supported by Baumrind's (1991b) research. Baumrind suggests that adolescents tend to be higher in competence and self-esteem in families where the parents are supportive, encourage positive rational and interactive communication while they use firm and constant discipline. In other words, the parents are authoritative. The advantage in having such parents may be because the transition into adolescence is one which requires autonomy while avoiding self-destructive behaviour during an inherently demanding process of individuation (Searight et al., 1995).

Clearly, parenting communication styles are very important. Those parents who are able to communicate with their adolescents effectively, and to do this in a two-way process, so that both they and the adolescent get the opportunity to state their points of view, are more likely to enable the young person to develop adaptively.

Parental expectations are also important. Most parents have expectations of their adolescent with regard to behaviours, beliefs, attitudes, values and choice of friends. Their expectations may also extend to academic or employment performance. Clearly, these expectations will impact on the adolescent and may be helpful in promoting development or may be an impediment.

The parental relationship

The quality of the parental relationship, whether the parents are together, separated or divorced, is of major importance to the adolescent. Grossman and Rowat (1995) examined a number of families where the parents were married and living together, were separated or divorced. They found that low life satisfaction, a diminished sense of the future and high anxiety were related to the quality of the parental relationship, and not to the separated, divorced or married status of the family. Even so, it might be expected that adolescents will benefit from being in families where there are stable and adaptively functioning parental relationships. Such an environment is likely to provide the young person with feelings of security and safety during a period in life when much is changing. Additionally, a well-functioning parental relationship can provide modelling of suitable ways of relating in couple relationships for the adolescent.

Separation and divorce

At a time when the adolescent is trying to establish independence it can be very disturbing for the family to break up. Ideally, adolescents need to be able to determine their own independence without being concerned about the safety and security of their families. Unfortunately, where there is parental disharmony there are likely to be problems for the adolescent, as discussed, whether separation occurs or not.

There is a demonstrated association between parental divorce and adolescent depression (Aseltine, 1996). Additionally, separation and divorce create numerous secondary problems as a result of the altered life situation. Single parents and their adolescents are under potentially significant amounts of stress due to a combination of factors relating to the single-parent family structure and factors related to adolescent development (Houser et al., 1993).

Blended family issues

Some people have the view that divorce and subsequent remarriage involving the blending of two families adversely affects adolescent development. Certainly, there are issues for adolescents when parents separate and divorce, and there will also be issues when their parents join up with new partners. However, divorce and remarriage do not necessarily relate to difficulties in adolescent adjustment. What is more important is that adolescent adjustment is found to relate to the level of perceived family conflict. If harmony prevails, then the effect on the adolescent is likely to be diminished (Borrine et al., 1991).

An alcoholic parent

Parental alcoholism affects the way a family functions. Alcoholic parents tend to be emotionally detached from their children, and are often not available to them as a consequence of their drinking patterns. Alcohol abuse may also lead to other forms of dysfunctional behaviour such as physical and sexual abuse. Roles of family members often become rigid and set in families where there are alcoholic parents. Vernon (1993) describes a number of dysfunctional roles which evolve in alcoholic or chemically dependent families. Three of these roles are particularly relevant for adolescents. They are:

1   *The enabler*: this family member is usually the partner of the alcoholic person but may be an older adolescent child. This person's role is to soften the negative effects of alcoholism by covering up the alcoholic's drinking.
2   *The hero*: this is usually the oldest child in the family. The role is to provide hope and pride to the family through activities such as excelling in school.
3   *The scapegoat*: the scapegoat tends to get recognition from peers by engaging in acting-out behaviours. Typically, in adolescence, these young people develop at-risk behaviours such as early substance abuse.

An understanding of these roles, and others described by Vernon (1993), may be useful to the counsellor in helping adolescents from alcoholic families.

Research by Tomori (1994) suggested that adolescents with alcoholic parents have high levels of anxiety. However, although this anxiety may be partly due to being in an alcoholic family, it may also be related to a personality trait. Parental alcoholism is associated with a heightened incidence of child and adolescent symptoms of psychopathology. However, it is not true that a major portion of the population of children and adolescents from alcoholic homes will develop psychological disorder (West and Prinz, 1988). Chassin and Barrera (1993) discovered that adolescent children of alcoholics whose alcoholic fathers had discontinued drinking tended to understand the need for self-control in limiting drinking, recognized the risk of future drug problems and could see the negative effects of alcohol in others. They suggested that these adolescents might be deterred from substance abuse because of their beliefs.

Domestic violence

Domestic violence has a significant impact on adolescent development. Where adolescents have witnessed either parent–child violence or violence between parents there are negative effects on adjustment with consequent externalizing and internalizing behavioural problems (O'Keefe, 1996). Additionally, when adolescents witness violence in the home, they may come to accept this as a normal and acceptable part of family life.

Cultural issues

As contemporary Western society becomes increasingly multi-cultural we need to recognize the special problems of adolescents who belong to ethnic minority groups. There are likely to be problems for those adolescents who grow up in a society where their own family cultural background differs from the major cultural influences of their environment. Friedman (1993) argues that the meaning of adolescent social development differs with culture. He notes that different meanings for particular cultures are affected by the changing social environment, differing cultural patterns of social development in puberty and marriage, and issues of health and health promotion.

Major problems for adolescents growing up in cultures different from that of their families is stress due to conflicts in culturally determined social and moral values and exposure to conflicting beliefs, attitudes and behaviours. Adolescents in this situation not only have to cope with their normal developmentally changing beliefs, attitudes, values and behaviours but also have to consider how these fit within the present and future cultural contexts of their lives.

The educational environment

Adolescents find the pressures of school, college and university stressful. Both the risk and experience of failure, in an educational setting, are sources of psychosocial stress for adolescents. These stresses are likely to be intensified when there is conflict with parents. As a consequence, poor school performance is made worse when conflict occurs with parents about issues concerning scholastic achievement and educational plans (Hurrelman et al., 1992).

There are also other concerns for the adolescent at school or college. Generally, in educational environments, the student has little power or authority and those teaching the student have considerable power and authority. For the emerging adolescent, issues of power and authority are very salient. If adolescents are to learn to take responsibility in the way that adults do then they need to be able to have some level of control over what they do and how they do it. Educational environments may therefore be stressful for adolescents because they are disempowering.

School refusal

Some adolescents either refuse to go to school or truant. These adolescents are responding, in the best way they know how, to particular stressors. Although there can be many different reasons for school refusal, problematic family relationships have often been cited as the underlying cause of such behaviour. Kearney and Silverman (1995) have suggested that there are different types of families where adolescents refuse to go to school. These are:

1 *The enmeshed family*: the focus is on overinvolved parent–child/adolescent relationships, particularly mother–child relationships, where an affectionate but overprotective attachment has been fostered with the child.
2 *The disengaged family*: members are not sufficiently involved with one another's activities to attend to one another's thoughts and needs. Parents within these families may not be particularly vigilant about their child's activities or problems until they are readily apparent or severe.
3 *The isolated family*: characterized by little extra-familial contact, they tend to shun activities outside the home.

Unfortunately, school refusal among adolescents may lead to severe long-term dysfunction if left untreated.

The work environment

Many young people find part-time employment while still studying at school, college or university; others leave school to go into full-time employment. The employment environment is one in which adult behaviours are generally required. Consequently, experience in the workplace may impact on the adolescent developmental process.

In the workplace, adolescents learn to take responsibility for the completion of tasks assigned by supervisors, generally experience some level of autonomy, have to deal with conformity issues regarding workplace expectations and are subjected to a variety of relationship issues (Safyer et al., 1995). They are exposed to relationships with peers, with adults and with those in authority, in an environment which has structure and expectations. Clearly, such a situation provides opportunity for personal growth and movement towards adulthood. It also presents challenges which may result in stress for the adolescent.

Changing relationships

Adolescents continually face issues which are likely to be stressful for them concerning changes in relationships. As the adolescent matures, relationships with parents, siblings, peers and those in positions of authority will all undergo change. Additionally, there are likely to be romantic attachments involving sexual attraction and these relationships may well be temporary, unstable and vulnerable to change because adolescents are in a stage of exploration and experimentation. Most adolescents experience powerful feelings of romantic love. Consequently, they may suffer in self-esteem when rejected by the person they love and may feel confused if their feelings change and they become attracted to someone else.

The adolescent's relationship with parents needs to change as the adolescent assumes more responsibility and parents start to hand over responsibility. Many parents struggle with the issue of handing over responsibility, and may, either consciously or subconsciously, wish to retain control of their children because of their own attachment to them, coupled with fear that relinquishing control might lead to disaster. Typically a struggle will develop with the adolescent wanting more control over life decisions and the parents being reluctant to allow this to occur at a pace acceptable to the young person. When such a struggle occurs, communication between the adolescent and parents is clearly of paramount importance if conflict is to be avoided.

White (1996) discusses problems which arise when communication with parents is not satisfactory. Unfortunately, when adolescents perceive communication with their parents as less than satisfactory, they may be forced into the company of others who are more accepting of their views and opinions. If this happens, parental influence will be diminished.

Exposure to sexuality issues

Dusek (1996) points out that there are wide differences between cultures with regard to the sexual behaviours expected of adolescents. At one extreme, there are cultures where children and adolescents are expected to refrain from engaging in sex until married and adult. At the other end of the continuum, there are societies where sexual behaviour develops more gradually and may be allowed or even encouraged in young people with few restrictions. In contemporary Western society there are clearly wide individual differences in attitudes and behaviours, both culturally and because of belief systems. The adolescent may therefore be faced with difficult choices which need to be made on the basis of information coming from a variety of sources which offer differing opinions about what is appropriate.

Most importantly, Dusek (1996) draws on research findings to confirm that parental influences on adolescent sexual behaviour are minimal. Adolescents whose parents discuss sex with them or whose parents keep a tight rein on their activities are no more or less likely to engage in premarital sex (although some evidence indicates that greater maternal monitoring of activities is associated with reduced *unprotected* sex for females). Adolescents who have sexually active friends or believe their friends are sexually active are more likely to be sexually active themselves. These factors are stronger for older rather than younger adolescents and also for females rather than males. Risks associated with sexual activity for adolescents will be discussed in Chapter 4.

Socio-economic pressures and unemployment

In today's society, with television and the print media, there are high pressures placed on adolescents in terms of socio-economic expectations. The media continually display role models where those who are attractive seem to have a high level of material possessions (for example clothes). This is particularly unfortunate in a society where many young people find it difficult to obtain employment.

Research convincingly demonstrates that unemployed adolescents tend to suffer from a number of serious problems. Being unemployed is generally a negative experience for young people, whereas gaining employment is a positive experience (Patton and Noller, 1990). Moreover, unemployed youth report significantly more depression, negative mood and loss of behavioural and emotional control than the employed (Winefield and Tiggemann, 1990; Heubeck et al., 1995). Additionally, a number of studies show that unemployment is associated with increasing risks of psychological disorder among adolescents (Hammarstrom, 1994; Fergusson et al., 1997a; Meeus et al., 1997).

There is an association between unemployment and juvenile crime. In particular, being unemployed after leaving school may be associated with increased risks of juvenile offending. However, much of the association between unemployment and juvenile crime is likely to reflect common life-course processes and factors that make young people vulnerable to both unemployment and criminal offending (Fergusson et al., 1997b).

Although poverty tends to have a negative influence on adolescent development and behaviour, these effects have been found to be mediated by the organizational structure and cultural features of the neighbourhood (Elliot et al., 1996). It is clear that much depends on the local social system and the controls and influence which this has on the young person.

In summary

In this chapter we have considered the effects of a number of environmental stresses on adolescents. In Chapter 4 we will discuss specific hazards. During the normal developmental process the adolescent will be confronted by both environmental stresses and hazards. Some adolescents will cope with these adaptively; others will not and they may seek counselling. It is essential for a counsellor to recognize the significance of those situations, events and stimuli which present difficult challenges for the adolescent and to be able to find ways to enable the young person to deal with them effectively.

4   Hazards for adolescents

In Chapter 3 we dealt with some of the environmental stresses which impact on adolescents. There are also a number of specific hazards which are likely to confront them. During childhood, most young people live in an environment which is protected and structured and where parents or other adult carers are in control. During adolescence, young people tend to have less dependence on the protection of the family as they make new relationships and enter into situations which they have not previously encountered. Dealing with these new situations is part of the growing-up process. Because adolescents have not previously experienced similar situations, they have to devise ways of responding to them and this can be hazardous.

Adolescence is a time of experimentation and of trying out new behaviours in response to new situations. This is risky. Unfortunately, adolescents are inherently susceptible to engaging in excessive and unchecked risk-taking because they often have the egocentric belief that they are almost indestructible. In our discussion of hazards we will consider the following:

- the influence of parents and peers
- peer groups and gangs
- smoking, sniffing, alcohol and other drugs
- sexual behaviour
- risk-taking involving anti-social behaviour
- weight control.

The influence of parents and peers

During adolescence, parental influence should be expected to reduce and the influence of peers to increase. However, both the influence of parents and that of peers will be impacting on the adolescent. At times, these influences will conflict, and when they do they will inevitably create an internal struggle for the adolescent who may have a difficult time trying to work out how to respond.

The influence of parents

Even though parental control generally diminishes during adolescence, most parents continue to exert a significant influence in their children's lives and this will have an effect on the way in which the young person deals with the hazards which present themselves.

The process of adolescence requires the young person to strive for autonomy, and, ideally, in doing this to avoid self-destructive behaviours. This is difficult to achieve in what is an inherently demanding process of individuation. It is here that parents can help. Research suggests that supportive parents who encourage positive, rational and interactive communication while they use firm and consistent discipline (that is, authoritative parents) have adolescent children who are higher in competence and self-esteem and are better equipped to deal with hazardous life events (Baumrind, 1991a, 1991b).

Adolescents test limits and boundaries, and this is what they need to do so that they can gain a clear sense of how to respond to the world in which they will live as adults. During this testing period it is advantageous if parents provide boundaries for support, so that the adolescent has some sense of containment to foster the development of security at a time when there will be inner turmoil. What is best is for parents to set clear, consistent, non-punitive limits and boundaries, which also respect the young person's boundaries (Gaoni et al., 1994).

In order to feel good, adolescents need to believe that they have the approval of their families. Research confirms that both males and females have higher self-esteem in early adolescence if they perceive that they have approval and support from their families. However, there are gender differences, with young females being much more dependent on family approval and support than young males (Eskilson and Wiley, 1987).

The struggle between peer pressure and parental pressure

It is easy to understand how there may be tension between the expectations of a peer group and the expectations of parents. Adolescents are striving for individuation with some sense of separation from their families, while at the same time having a need for acceptance. This need for acceptance drives adolescents to join with peers and it is desirable that they should do so. Failure to develop good peer relationships can have unfortunate consequences with regard to behavioural and scholastic problems (Connor, 1994). In attempting to join with peers, there may be strong pressure to participate in undesired or undesirable activities as the price of acceptance. Those adolescents with high self-esteem and self-confidence are better able to resist negative peer pressure because they are more easily able to form and maintain friendships and to be accepted by others.

The struggle between family pressure and peer pressure will be influenced by the qualities of the family system. Where a family atmosphere is supportive of independence and does not press for achievement, early adolescents tend to use their peer group as a source of emotional support without a strong need to conform to group pressure. This is in contrast to early adolescents whose family life is characterized by conflict, emphasis on achievement and lack of support for individual development. In these families, the young person is likely to become more conformist to group pressure (Shulman et al., 1995).

The influence of peer pressure

Peers clearly do exert pressure on adolescents and this is often most noticeable in terms of the way in which adolescents present themselves. This can be disconcerting for many parents who become anxious when their adolescent children make changes to their personal appearance in ways which are not easily acceptable to them. They may correctly blame peer influences. However, it is important to recognize that such changes, although due to the influence of peer pressure and a need for acceptance by peers, are also consistent with the adolescent's search for individuation and identity. In the personal search for identity, young people may choose hair styles and make-up which reflect contemporary teenage standards, they may wear unconventional clothes which are fashionable for their peer group, engage in body piercing and have tattoos. All of these ways of presenting themselves are subject to fad and are directed towards both the achievement of individuation and peer group affiliation.

Many adults tend to interpret the way in which many contemporary teenagers present themselves as anti-establishment, destructive and as having negative connotations. However, the way they present themselves can be viewed as an indicator of their search for personal identity in ways which may be constructive for them. As Martin (1997) points out, what is seen by an adult as mutilative or destructive may, from the adolescent's point of view, be decorative.

Peer groups and gangs

During adolescence the formation of peer groups is normal developmentally. The tendency to form such groups starts in childhood. Playmates, school friends, boy and girl scout groups are examples of the natural inclination of young people to form group attachments which provide a social outlet.

Adolescent gangs are peer groups. However, they are groups whose behaviours are perceived negatively by the majority in society. Gangs are generally considered to be socially pathological and the result of infiltration of peer groups by individuals with violent and/or other anti-social tendencies (for example, drug dealers). Gangs tend to develop mostly in urban areas and may exert undesirable influences on impressionable young people (Sigler, 1995).

It is quite understandable how gangs can become a part of adolescent behaviour. Unfortunately, research indicates that for females as well as males involvement with gangs is associated with increased levels of delinquency, substance abuse and sexual activity. Further, female gang members have low expectations of completing school (Bjerregaard and Smith, 1993). Similarly, research results indicate that high school students who are members of gangs have significantly lower self-esteem than students who are not gang members (Wang, 1994).

Because of the negative concept which many adults have of gangs and the destructive impact which they can have on society, traditional school programmes generally consider gang membership anti-social. As a result, schools tend to outlaw gang presence by banning symbols of gang membership. Even so, it needs to be recognized that gangs do serve a purpose for many adolescents. In particular, where adolescents are members of minority groups, belonging to a gang can help them in retaining their own culture. The downside of this is that assimilation with the majority culture is then less likely to occur (Calabrese and Noboa, 1995).

A major problem for both female and male gang members is the possibility of abuse. Gang members generally, but especially females, can become victimized by other gang members and subjected to physical, sexual and psychological abuse (Molidor, 1996). Clearly, adolescents in peer groups or gangs will generally be subjected to strong social pressures to conform to group behaviours. Where these behaviours are self-destructive or anti-social there are likely to be negative consequences for the young person. In addition, young people in groups tend to compete for status and attention. Consequently there is likely to be strong pressure to participate in life-threatening risk-taking behaviours.

Smoking, sniffing, alcohol and other drugs

Many, if not most, adolescents in contemporary Western society are confronted with the dilemmas of deciding whether to use, and to what extent to use, available addictive substances. Some of these are legal for adults and others are not, although most are illegal for adolescents below certain ages in most states and/or countries. Addictive substances include cigarettes, volatile substances which can be inhaled, marijuana, a variety of chemical substances such as amphetamines, including ecstasy, psychotropic substances such as fantasy, 'magic' mushrooms, datura, LSD and hard drugs including cocaine and heroin.

Part of adolescent development is to explore, find out and experiment. Adolescents are curious; they want to know more about the world in which they are progressively having more freedom to make their own decisions. Consequently, they are likely to consider experimenting with the use of addictive substances. However, experimentation with addictive substances will depend on a number of factors including availability of the substance, family and peer influences.

A number of research studies on adolescents have investigated the effects of family and peer influences. These studies make it clear that both family and peer influences are important. Webster et al. (1994) found that whereas peer influences are exerted predominantly through modelling behaviour, parental influence is exerted predominantly through perceived normative standards. Frauenglass et al. (1997) found that deviant peer modelling was strongly associated with levels of adolescent use of tobacco, alcohol and marijuana, but family support of the adolescent reduced that influence with regard to tobacco and marijuana use. Robin and Johnson (1996) also identified the importance of peer pressure regarding adolescent use of alcohol, cigarettes and drugs. They found that both peer approval and disapproval were important. The greater the peer pressure against use the less frequent the use. Bauman and Ennett (1996) claim that the magnitude of peer influence in adolescent drug behaviour has been over-estimated by some authorities in the area, and correctly make the point that the individual is able to make a personal decision within the context of peer influence. However, the evidence demonstrating the importance of peer influence is strong.

Smoking

Exposure to smoking is a hazard which some children face in childhood. However, in adolescence, because of the developmental issues of adolescence, it presents a real challenge even though it is publicly acknowledged that smoking is a health hazard. Peer influences are particularly important with regard to smoking. Hu et al. (1995) found that even though there are differences in the reasons adolescents smoke, in general the influence of friends' smoking is more important than the influence of parents who smoke. Further, Wang et al. (1997) found that the smoking behaviour of best friends was the only consistent and significant social factor in predicting adolescent smoking.

Michell and West (1996) were interested in what causes an adolescent to start smoking. They noted that previous research had suggested that smokers persuaded others to smoke through coercion, teasing, bullying or rejection from a desired group. However, their own research suggested that the process was complex and included strong elements of self-determined behaviour by the adolescent. This suggests that individuals may play a more active role in starting to smoke than has previously been acknowledged and that social pressures other than peer pressure need to be taken into account. This fits with the theory of adolescent development where the adolescent, although wanting to be part of a peer group for acceptance, is also making strong moves towards individuation and the establishment of a personal identity.

It is interesting to note from a community health perspective that data on cigarette smoking show that smoking uptake usually occurs during adolescence through a gradual process of change from non-smoking to susceptibility, experimentation and then adoption of regular use. Consequently, from a public health point of view, it is important to address the cigarette-smoking issue during adolescence (Wills et al., 1996).

Sniffing volatile substances

Some adolescents seek to achieve an altered state of consciousness by sniffing volatile substances such as glue solvents, petrol, butane gas, and the fumes from aerosol cans. Substances used for sniffing are easy to obtain and are inexpensive. For example, in most countries a young person can walk into a craft shop and buy a tube of glue without raising suspicion. Unfortunately, sniffing is highly dangerous and can cause brain damage and/or death.

Ives (1994) examined the use of volatile substances in England, Scotland and the USA. He identified the importance of a number of factors which are helpful in reducing sniffing behaviour. These include parental involvement, the promotion of decision-making skills, peer involvement in treatment, and self-esteem. These factors are clearly important for consideration when counselling an adolescent sniffer.

Alcohol, marijuana and other drugs

A major factor in the use of drugs by adolescents is connected with sensation-seeking and risk-taking tendencies (Perry and Mandell, 1995). These tendencies are part of the normal developmental process for adolescents. Adolescents are in the stage of their lives where they experiment and look for new experiences. Adolescents want to try things out for themselves rather than relying on information provided by others. This sets them up to be vulnerable to the temptation to experiment with alcohol and other drugs.

Adolescents tend to justify their use of alcohol and other drugs by statements such as 'It's cool' or 'Everyone else drinks alcohol (or uses drugs).' As might be expected, peer use and peer pressure are major factors for introducing young people to the use of alcohol and other drugs, such as marijuana and ecstasy, or hard drugs such as heroin and cocaine. Several research studies support this. Dupre et al. (1995) found that 55 per cent of young people in their study were first given alcohol or drugs by a friend. Jenkins (1996) found that the strongest correlate with starting to use drugs was affiliation with drug-using friends. Similarly, Yarnold and Patterson (1995) found that adolescent crack users tend to have friends who use crack. The relationship between drug use and peers who use is not surprising, for two reasons. First, adolescents are seeking acceptance by their peers. Secondly, those who socialize with friends who are users are likely to have easier access to the substance concerned.

Not surprisingly, abstainers from alcohol, marijuana and other drugs tend to come from families that are less likely to use drugs. These adolescents are also less likely to have friends who use drugs, and are not as likely to have psychosocial or school problems as are users of alcohol, marijuana and other drugs (McBroom, 1994). With regard to school problems, Jenkins (1996) found, as might be expected, that level of academic performance is inversely related to drug use.

Sexual behaviour

It is natural and appropriate that in adolescence the young person will experiment with adult behaviours and this is almost certain to include some level of sexual behaviour. Unfortunately, because adolescents are inexperienced they are likely to engage in sexual activity without fully understanding the social, psychological and physical consequences of this behaviour.

Among adolescents there is a significantly high and disconcerting frequency of self-reported risk-taking sexual behaviour (Downey and Landry, 1997). Interestingly, once adolescents have experienced sexual intercourse, they tend to engage in it relatively persistently rather than sporadically (Tubman et al., 1996). This may be because they enjoy sex and see sexual behaviour as a sign of maturity and adulthood.

Clearly, there are significant risks in sexual behaviour. There are risks of pregnancy and disease, and there are likely to be risks to self-image if sexual activity is undertaken in the absence of a context of respect and caring. Because males do not run the risk of pregnancy, the consequences of risky sexual behaviour are less salient for males than for females (Word, 1996). Females naturally see teen parenthood as more of a problem than do males and are more likely to believe that sexual urges can be controlled (DeGaston et al., 1996). Clearly, there are gender differences with regard to sexual issues for adolescents. DeGaston et al. found that, in early adolescence, females, as compared with males, saw sexual activity as more detrimental to them with regard to their future goal attainment. Although female adolescents viewed parents as less approving of their sexual behaviour, they were more likely than male adolescents to discuss sex and their dating practices with them.

The discussion so far has related to heterosexual behaviour. However, we also need to take account of homosexual adolescent behaviour. Although a number of early adolescents engage in homosexual exploratory behaviour, as they grow older the majority engage exclusively in heterosexual behaviour. Unfortunately, gay and lesbian adolescents who recognize their homosexuality experience intense conflicts with their social environments, particularly at school. In addition, there may be deleterious effects on family life, peer relationships and the development of close relationships with others (Anderson, 1993). Consequently, gay adolescents may have diminished ability to achieve a sense of identity and self-esteem because of social stigmatization (Radkowski and Siegel, 1997), and are thus susceptible to loneliness, isolation and depression. Further, Sussman and Duffy (1996) suggest that there is a need for more research on the sexual practices of gay males (aged 13–19 years) so that fact-based preventative interventions can be devised to combat the growing number of AIDs cases among this group throughout the world.

We need to remember that sexuality is a major and positive dimension of human development. It is important that adolescents come to terms with their sexuality in ways which are positive. Unfortunately, the unintended consequences of a narrow focus on fear and disease may lead to increased rates of sexual inadequacy and interpersonal problems (Ehrhardt, 1996). Counsellors therefore need to achieve a sensible balance when providing information for adolescents about protective behaviours.

Risk-taking involving anti-social behaviour

Adolescent experimentation may involve a significant amount of risk-taking behaviour. Many adolescents like to have fun and excitement and to do things that their parents have not allowed them to do. This predisposes them to consider engaging in anti-social behaviours. They may be tempted to do things such as:

- shoplifting
- vandalism
- driving cars at high speed
- fire-lighting
- listening to loud and/or aggressive music.

All of these things may be done for fun and thrills and with the influence of peer modelling and/or pressure.

Shoplifting

It has been found that the tendency for teenagers to shoplift is not related to socio-economic variables, but is related to fun, thrills and peer pressure (Lo, 1994). Shoplifting is strongly influenced by friends' shoplifting behaviour, but may be moderated by adolescents' attachment to their parents and their own beliefs regarding this behaviour (Cox et al., 1993).

Vandalism

Many adolescents feel a sense of powerlessness and a lack of respect by society in general and consequently become frustrated and/or angry. These feelings may be acted out by vandalism. Similarly, some will express their feelings through the use of graffiti. Usually, graffiti has to be created clandestinely, and the risk factor is appealing to many young people. Graffiti can be artistically creative and satisfying, and can be used to convey messages and express ideas. Peters (1990) observed that for some adolescents graffiti could express a concern for belonging and identity, and for others it might emphasize popular values taken to the extreme.

Driving cars at high speed

Adolescents are tempted to drive cars recklessly. As previously mentioned, they often have the impression that they are indestructible. They are looking for an identity of which they can be proud. They therefore like to test their skills in difficult situations. High-speed driving raises their level of adrenaline, is risky, exciting, fun and gives them an opportunity to show off in front of their peers.

Fire-lighting

Although serious addiction to fire-lighting is an indication of psychiatric disorder, some adolescents like the thrill involved in lighting fires and enjoy watching things burn. Fires present risk, excitement and challenge, exactly what the adolescent may be seeking. It is also easy to light fires.

Listening to loud and/or aggressive music

Adolescents want to explore every facet of their existence and this includes exposure to sensation. Loud music, especially of the hard rock or heavy metal variety, provides a high level of auditory and somatic stimulation (Arnett, 1992). In discos, high noise levels seem to change the state of consciousness of the participants so that they become engulfed by the music and transported from the pressures of their daily lives. Additionally, the lyrics of popular teenage music often hook into the young person's current emotional frustrations and experiences.

Unfortunately, there are dangers in listening to loud music. Bronzaft and Dobrow (1988) raise concerns not only about adolescents listening to loud music at discos, but also playing electronic games in noisy arcades for long periods. Excessive noise can be intrusive to others and damage relationships and, more importantly – concerning the long-term well-being of the adolescent – it can and does result in deafness.

Weight control

There are clearly hazards for adolescents with regard to body-weight control. A study by Grigg et al. (1996), involving 14–to 16-year-old female students, showed that over one third of the subjects had used at least one extreme dieting method in the previous month, such as crash dieting, fasting, slimming tablets, diuretics, laxatives and/or cigarettes to lose weight.

Unfortunately, the problem for adolescents is in their search for identity which makes them particularly vulnerable to modelling by others. They are subjected to heavy modelling in the print media and on television where underweight female models are portrayed as beautiful and desirable and slightly overweight males and females are seen as unattractive and worthy of derision. Female adolescents tend to be more susceptible to pressure from friends regarding the importance of thinness and the desirability of engaging in weight-loss strategies. Peer pressure may involve modelling of dieting behaviour, and taunting and teasing. Taunting and teasing are also problems for males who are either under- or overweight.

Weight problems include not only the extreme cases of anorexia nervosa and bulimia but also obesity. Although the incidence of both anorexia nervosa and bulimia is low in males compared with females, there are males who suffer from those conditions. Obesity is a problem for some young people of both sexes. A number of research papers show that there are some cultural differences with regard to problems associated with teenage weight control (Raich et al., 1992; Wardle et al., 1993; Story et al., 1995).

In summary

In this chapter we have dealt with some of the hazards of adolescence. Confronting these hazards can be harmful for those who are unable to respond adaptively. However, confronting hazards is an essential part of the adolescent's journey towards adulthood. As an adult, the individual has to take responsibility for dealing with whatever situations and events present themselves. Learning how to do this is one of the adolescent's developmental tasks.

Adolescents often seek help from counsellors at times when they are unable to deal adaptively with particular hazards. It is the counsellor's task to enable young people to find satisfactory methods for overcoming hazards so that they can move forward along the required developmental path.

5   The development of mental health problems

In this chapter we will discuss the ability of adolescents to cope and the development of pathology in those who are unable to cope adaptively. We will also describe some of the more common mental health problems which affect adolescents. Although this book is not intended to be used as a treatment guide for those who manage adolescents with mental health problems, it is hoped that mental health workers will find the proactive counselling approach useful as part of an overall treatment plan for many troubled adolescents. Our assumption is that many counsellors who read this book will be working in settings where their role is to help troubled adolescents who have not developed serious mental health problems. However, it is important for all counsellors to be able to recognize the early signs of the development of mental health problems. By recognizing these early signs, appropriate referrals to specialist professionals or mental health services can be made.

Referral

Assisting those adolescents who have not been able to develop successful coping strategies and resources is quite obviously an important function for a counsellor. However, it is essential that counsellors recognize their personal and professional limitations with regard to treating adolescents who are demonstrating signs of developing pathology. It is important to recognize these limits and be open with clients regarding them.

We are firm in our belief that all counsellors need to have experienced and qualified supervisors with whom they can discuss both personal issues and client-related matters. Where there are indications that an adolescent is developzing pathology, counsellors need to consult with their supervisors and to make decisions with regard to continuing treatment or referral to specialists.

The correct diagnosis of the onset of pathology can be complicated, particularly when the client is an adolescent. Miller (1983) cautions counsellors not to over-interpret typical and perhaps seemingly bizarre behaviour, thoughts or feelings of adolescents as necessarily being indicative of severe psychopathology. They may be indicative of the adolescent's developmentally appropriate response to the environment. However, the flip-side is that the consequences of incorrectly disregarding symptoms as typical adolescent behaviour can be serious and may deprive adolescents of much-needed psychiatric help. We therefore believe that it is wise and ethically necessary to err on the side of caution by ensuring that specialist assessments are made where there are possible indications of developing psychopathology.

Certainly, when an adolescent is consistently using dysfunctional or maladaptive coping strategies and where counselling interventions have failed, there is a strong indication that referral may be necessary. Such adolescents need assessment by an experienced mental health worker who can devise an appropriate treatment plan which may include the use of medication in conjunction with psychotherapy.

Ability to cope with the challenges of adolescence

There are remarkable differences in the abilities of adolescents to cope with the challenges which confront them. Some adolescents have great difficulty in dealing with problems which for others would be minor. Because these young people are not able to cope with stresses in an adaptive manner they may develop problem behaviours and are at risk of developing mental health problems. Other adolescents with major problems seem to be able to emerge from stressful encounters not only successfully, but also with increased abilities and resources (Seiffge-Krenke, 1995). For them, dealing with stressful situations stimulates personal growth and helps them to move along the adolescent developmental path towards adulthood.

Differences in the ways in which adolescents cope and respond to the challenges which confront them raise the question of why these differences occur. In order to understand why they occur, we need first to understand what it is that adolescents find stressful.

What do adolescents find stressful?

Adolescents consider an event to be stressful when they make an appraisal that the event has negative implications for their own well-being. Sandler et al. (1997) suggest that adolescents ask themselves three questions:

1   Should I care?
2   Is this positive or negative?
3   In what way am I or my goals or commitments involved?

If the answers to these questions are 'Yes, I should care', 'This has negative implications for me' and 'My goals or commitments may be compromised', then the adolescent is likely to appraise the situation as stressful. In making this appraisal, the adolescent may also take into account whether the event has occurred previously, once or on a number of occasions, and the extent to which the event is perceived as controllable. Adolescents may also take into consideration their own perception of their ability to deal with the stressor. Once an event is appraised as stressful, the adolescent's coping resources will be called into play.

The adolescent's coping resources

The adolescent's personal coping resources are relatively stable characteristics of the individual. They influence how the young person copes in specific situations. Most importantly, coping resources include temperamental and personality characteristics. They also include beliefs about self and about the world. When an adolescent perceives him or herself as a competent person who copes, and believes that the environment is basically friendly or at least benign, the likelihood of successful coping strategies being used is increased. Clearly, the adolescent's coping resources will be related to the individual's self-esteem, locus of control, optimism and skills and knowledge of problem-solving techniques (Sandler et al., 1997).

Individuals who cope most successfully are those who make the best use of their own personal coping resources and also make use of other resources which may be available and of value. For example, an adolescent might use a friend, parents or a counsellor as a resource at times when the young person's own resources are being stretched. Similarly, they might use an environmental resource, such as a peaceful place in which to relax, think and make decisions.

The adolescent's coping style

The ability to make use of available resources, including personal coping resources, has little to do with the nature of specific problems or childhood history or the current environmental situation in which the adolescent lives; instead, it has more to do with the personal qualities of the individual concerned. Each individual will have a personal coping style. This may be influenced by cultural factors, gender, socio-economic status and current environmental factors. Frydenberg and Lewis (1993) suggest three styles of coping which can broadly be described as follows:

1 *Solving the problem*: behaviours such as seeking social support, focusing on finding a solution, seeking a relaxing diversion, investing in close friends, seeking to belong, working hard to achieve and being positive. In this style of coping the individual works on the problem while remaining optimistic, fit, relaxed and socially connected.
2 *Reference to others*: turning to others, such as peers or professionals, for social and spiritual support.
3 *Non-productive coping*: worrying, seeking to belong, wishful thinking, not coping, ignoring the problem, keeping things to oneself and self-blame.

Styles of coping (1 and 2 above) involve an active process, whereas style 3 is a passive process. In the active process, the individual takes action to deal with the stress and the stressor. In the passive process, no positive attempt is made to address these. It has been suggested that the use of active coping strategies tends to decrease with declining socio-economic status, and that the more passive coping of lower socio-economic groups is dysfunctional because it leads to problems for the individual (Jackson and Bosma, 1990). If this is correct, it is particularly unfortunate for people from these groups as it may tend to prevent them from attempting to change their current socio-economic status. Clearly, helping an adolescent to move from a passive coping style to an active one may be an important goal for a counsellor.

The use of cognition in coping

Cognitive functions can have an important role in coping with stressful events. By thinking things through, the coping process can be goal-directed and flexible while still allowing an appropriate level of emotional expression. It is therefore useful for counsellors to help adolescents to learn cognitive strategies for assessing stressful events and for working out ways of responding which might have positive outcomes.

The need to respond to stress promptly

The most adaptive way for individuals to deal with stress is for them to deal with the emotional and psychological outcomes as soon as possible after a stressful event has occurred. Where adolescents are unable to deal effectively with stressful events themselves, help from counsellors is most effective if it is offered at the earliest available time. The truth of this is supported by research regarding the short- and long-term consequences of stressful events which clearly indicates that counselling interventions should take place immediately after an event has occurred in order to promote positive coping behaviours (Seiffge-Krenke, 1995).

Development of psychological disorder as a response to stress

Simeonsson (1994) cites many studies which estimate that between 15 and 18 per cent of children and adolescents present with behavioural disorders which are psychological in origin. These disorders can broadly be divided into internalizing or externalizing disorders. Internalizing disorders are characterized by social withdrawal and feelings of loneliness, depression and anxiety. In contrast, externalizing disorders are characterized by behaviours such as disruptive acting-out, aggression, hyperactivity and other behaviours which are typical of conduct disorders.

Where adolescents are not able to deal adaptively with stressors, pathology is likely to develop. It is therefore important for counsellors to be able to distinguish between adolescents who are making use of adaptive coping processes and adolescents who are making inappropriate use of defence mechanisms to avoid facing stressors. It needs to be recognized that defence mechanisms do serve a purpose in enabling individuals to deal with the shock of the initial intense stage of trauma. For example, when someone first discovers that they are dying, they may hold on to a belief in a miracle cure until they are able to accept and deal with reality. The initial use of the defence mechanism of denial can cushion the person's response, enabling them to gather the emotional strength to move forward. However, using defence mechanisms clearly distorts the individual's perceptions of reality and if their use persists then the result will be inappropriate behaviour and inappropriate emotional responses.

In severe cases where adolescents are unable to cope adaptively with stressors, they may present with a wide variety of pathological reactions such as the development of somatic symptoms, panic attacks, obsessive-compulsive behaviour, or a process of fragmentation with behaviour becoming automatic, ritualized and irrational. Instead of responding adaptively, some adolescents subjected to stress switch into pathology (Haan, 1977).

While this is not a mental health textbook, we believe that it is important to consider a number of psychological disorders experienced by adolescents and will consider the following:

- depression
- anxiety disorders
- suicidal ideation and behaviours
- early signs of developing psychosis
- post-traumatic stress disorder.

We will discuss each of the above because they are conditions which all counsellors who work with adolescents need to recognize. First, depression and anxiety are the most common internalizing disorders which are recognized as psychiatric conditions. Secondly, it is essential for counsellors to be able to recognize and respond appropriately when young people are suicidal or are showing signs of possible early symptoms of psychosis. Thirdly, counsellors are frequently confronted by adolescents who have experienced trauma. Therefore, counsellors need to be able to recognize the symptoms of post-traumatic stress disorder so that the necessary management and treatment are offered.

Depression

Depression is characterized by significantly impaired mood with a loss of interest or pleasure in activities that are normally enjoyable. Depression may be mild, moderate or severe, as described below (World Health Organization, 1994):

Mild depression:	effort is required to do normal daily tasks.
Moderate depression:	involves occupational and social impairment. Depression prevents the individual from doing things that need to be done.
Severe depression:	involves marked social and occupational impairment and may include psychotic symptoms such as hallucinations or delusions.

Most people experience depression from time to time. However, psychiatric illness involving a major depressive episode can be distinguished from normal depression by its severity, persistence and duration (World Health Organization, 1997).

Dysthymia, a milder but more persistent form of depression, involves long periods, of at least two years, during which time the individual experiences depressed mood, loss of interest and energy, social withdrawal, poor concentration and memory, feelings of inadequacy, low self-esteem, guilt, anger, hopelessness, irritability and despair. Dysthymia does interfere with social and occupational functioning and some individuals with dysthymia experience major depressive episodes during the course of their dysthymic disorder.

Children demonstrate a relatively low incidence of depression. However, most adolescents experience depression, from time to time, as part of their normal life and they consequently have an increased risk of the development of depression at troubling levels. Often, loneliness and social withdrawal are antecedents to depressive disorders in adolescents (Simeonsson, 1994).

Depression in adolescence may result from a wide variety of situations or stimuli such as the following:

- a succession of loss experiences
- a history of parental separation and/or divorce
- a series of moves, perhaps including moving away from trusted friends
- death of a loved one, friend or pet
- receiving low levels of positive reinforcement
- being unable to escape from punishment.

Depression may also result from negative thoughts. These thoughts might include negative views of self, negative interpretations of one's experiences and negative views of the future.

Adolescents respond to depression in a variety of ways. Some adolescents run away from home. Some, particularly boys, express their feelings through externalizing behaviours and may act out aggressively. Girls more often express depression by internalizing it, worrying and/or becoming anxious.

Anxiety disorders

Everyone is anxious at times and being anxious can be useful. Relatively high levels of anxiety can be helpful when they are consistent with the demands of a situation. For example, during a game of football, an exam or a job interview anxiety may help to increase alertness and performance. Unfortunately, too high a level of anxiety may reduce performance.

Suffering from an anxiety disorder is not just a matter of being too anxious. Individuals with anxiety disorders suffer levels of anxiety which are more pervasive than the anxiety generally experienced in normal life. The disorder will usually have social consequences for the person, with relationships being impaired.

Four common types of anxiety disorder in adolescents, as described in *DSM–IV–TR* (American Psychiatric Association, 2001), are generalized anxiety disorder, social phobia, specific phobia, and obsessive-compulsive disorder. *Generalized anxiety disorder* is characterized by long periods of persistent and excessive anxiety and worry, the source of which is non-specific. Adolescents experiencing generalized anxiety disorder may present with symptoms of nervousness, restlessness, trouble falling or staying asleep, poor concentration, frequent urination, irritable mood, depressed mood, light-headedness, dizziness, muscular tension or becoming easily fatigued. Adolescents with generalized anxiety disorder often exhibit an additional anxiety disorder such as social or specific phobia.

Social phobia is characterized by significant anxiety when exposed to certain types of social or performance situations. This disorder often leads to avoidance behaviours. *Specific phobia* is characterized by a persistent and irrational fear of a particular object or situation, and can also lead to avoidance behaviours. With *obsessive-compulsive disorder* individuals may experience unpleasant and intrusive thoughts which are difficult to control. For example, they may be obsessively concerned about contaminating or harming themselves or their family. The obsessional thoughts often lead to uncontrollable compulsive rituals; for example, repetitively cleaning, checking or counting.

Counsellors working with adolescents need to recognize that adolescents exhibiting behavioural problems and symptoms of anxiety may also be experiencing depression, because the symptoms of anxiety and depression often overlap. Both anxiety and depression can sometimes be difficult to diagnose because they can be masked by observable behaviours which do not directly suggest these conditions.

Suicidal ideation and behaviours

Many individuals experience some level of suicidal ideation at some point during adolescence. Stress, anxiety and depression in young people are increasing in Western society, resulting in suicidal ideation, attempted suicide and completed suicide (Dacey and Kenny, 1997). Whether an adolescent thinks of suicide as an option, and/or chooses it, will depend on their personal coping resources and style. Particularly vulnerable to suicide are those adolescents who suffer from a depressive illness. They are more likely to commit suicide than adolescents with other psychiatric or medical illnesses (World Health Organization, 1997).

Adolescents who choose suicide as their option for coping are obviously seriously psychologically disturbed. For many, this may be a result of stress, anxiety and depression. For others, it may be related to psychotic illness or a result of substance abuse. Adolescents who attempt suicide often exhibit some of the following characteristics:

1   They tend to over-invest themselves in very few but very intense interpersonal relationships.
2   They tend to express troubled feelings through behaviour rather than verbal communication.
3   They perceive themselves as unable to control their environment and are more at risk of attempting suicide than adolescents who feel in control of their environment.
4   They express high levels of hopelessness and the belief that things will not get better. They tend to overreact to situations and may be hypersensitive.

Adolescents who attempt and complete suicide often have more stressful lives, fewer coping skills and are under-achieving, with poor school performance (Dacey and Kenny, 1997). Quite often suicide is related to problems such as:

- family problems, particularly those which threaten family stability
- serious impairment of communication between parents and the adolescent
- peer relationship problems
- not having any friends and not belonging to a group
- inability to live up to parents' or others' expectations.

The availability and accessibility of firearms has added to suicidal risks in adolescents. Recent research also suggests that well-publicized suicides bring out latent suicidal tendencies in adolescents (Dusek, 1996). Clearly, counsellors need to be able to recognize and appropriately deal with suicidal thinking and behaviour to prevent tragedies from occurring. They also need to recognize the limits of their competence: counsellors working with suicidal clients need to work under close supervision and refer to other specialist helpers.

Early signs of developing psychosis

Psychosis involves a loss of ego boundaries with gross impairment of reality testing. Symptoms include hallucinations and/or delusions. Where hallucinations are in evidence they occur in the absence of insight by the individual, according to *DSM–IV–TR* (American Psychiatric Association, 2001).

There is evidence that genetic factors play a role in the development of psychotic illnesses. However, psychosocial factors involving stress or substance abuse are likely to act as triggers that bring about the initial and subsequent episodes in vulnerable people. During an acute episode of psychosis adolescents are particularly at risk of self-harm. They may have hallucinations which command them to harm or kill themselves. The strength of these thoughts and the individual's ability to act on them need to be assessed by a mental health professional.

One of the most common psychotic illnesses is schizophrenia and this can develop during adolescence. Psychosis resulting from substance abuse, such as the use of cocaine, amphetamines, alcohol or marijuana, shares many of the symptoms of schizophrenia, including hallucinations, delusions and abnormal speech. *Schizophrenia* can be divided into three phases: the prodromal phase, the active phase and the residual phase. Clearly, it is in the best interests of clients if counsellors are able to recognize symptoms during the prodromal phase so that treatment can be provided at this early stage.

1   *The prodromal phase* This phase occurs in the weeks or months preceding the first onset of the typical symptoms of schizophrenia. During this phase, it is common for a number of non-specific symptoms to be in evidence, particularly in young people. These symptoms include a general loss of interest, avoidance of social interaction, avoidance of work or study (for example, dropping out of school or college), being irritable and oversensitive, having odd beliefs (for example, superstitious or magical beliefs), and engaging in strange behaviours (for example, talking to oneself in public). It needs to be recognized that many normal adolescents display some of the described symptoms of prodromal schizophrenia and this can make accurate assessment difficult. However, it is important that counsellors are alert to the possibility of schizophrenia in young people and when in doubt refer clients for mental health assessment.

2   *The active phase* During the active phase of schizophrenia, psychotic symptoms such as delusions, odd behaviours and hallucinations are prominent and are often accompanied by the expression of strong emotions such as distress, anxiety, depression and fear. If untreated, the active phase may resolve spontaneously or may continue indefinitely.

3   *The residual phase* The active phase of the illness is usually followed by a residual phase. The residual phase is similar to the prodromal phase where psychotic symptoms are less likely to be accompanied by the expression of strong emotions.

Another type of psychotic disorder which may present in adolescence is *acute and transient psychotic disorder*. The symptoms are usually associated with acute psychological stress and occur over a matter of days, resolving within two or three weeks (World Health Organization, 1997).

Post-traumatic stress disorder

The precursors and symptoms of post-traumatic stress disorder were discussed in Chapter 2. This psychological disorder occurs following acute or ongoing trauma. If post-traumatic stress disorder (PTSD) is left untreated it can develop into a severe incapacitating disorder which will impact on the adolescent's social and occupational functioning. Additionally, many of the symptoms of PTSD can be confused with some of the other major psychological disturbances previously mentioned; for example, depression, generalized anxiety disorder and psychosis. The latter is due to the possibility of symptoms of dissociative hallucinosis in PTSD.

In summary

Where adolescents are demonstrating symptoms of mental health problems they should be referred to mental health services or psychiatrists who can assess and treat their condition. Mental health disorders can usually be managed through the use of appropriate medication and psychotherapy. Without medication, many individuals suffering from these disorders will continue to feel over-whelmed, distressed and worried by intrusive thoughts and uncontrollable behaviours.

PART TWO

PROACTIVE COUNSELLING
FOR ADOLESCENTS

6 Making counselling relevant for adolescents

Although some counsellors specialize in working only with adolescents, many counsellors work with children, adolescents and adults. It has long been recognized that counselling children is very different from counselling adults. When working with children, counsellors not only need to use specific counselling skills, as they do with adults, but also need to involve the child in the counselling process through the use of media and activity. Just as there are differences between counselling children and counselling adults, there are also important differences between counselling adolescents and counselling both children and adults.

Differences involved in counselling adolescents

Counselling adolescents is different in the following ways:

1 If adolescents are to be encouraged to use counselling, we need to offer a special type of client–counsellor relationship which is appropriate for them (see Chapter 7).
2 The process of counselling adolescents needs to be different from the processes used when counselling children or adults (see Chapters 7 and 8).
3 Particular skills and strategies which enhance the adolescent counselling conversation are required (see Chapter 10).

Even though counselling adolescents involves the above differences, there are some features which are common to counselling children, adolescents and adults (for example, many of the micro-skills used and some of the counsellor attributes). For most counsellors, those common features make it easier to move from counselling one age group to counselling another. However, it is the differences which, when ignored, may result in disappointing outcomes.

Counselling children

Counsellors working with children need to be able to select and make use of relevant media and activities as described by Geldard and Geldard (2002). They need to pay particular attention to the child's developmental age and consequent ability to resolve issues. Additionally, they need to recognize that the child's capacity for self-reflection may be limited because it is a developmental skill which comes through maturation, social experiences and the development of communication skills.

Children cannot usually leave their families. They are dependent on them, and their families generally provide the main social system within which they grow and develop. It is from within the family that the child develops ideas about their own personal value, abilities and aspirations (Woolfe and Dryden, 1996). Unfortunately, many children have little power or influence on their families. As children's problems are often related to their family environment, counsellors working with children often need to work with the child's family in order to enable the family to make the necessary changes for the well-being of the child.

Differences between counselling adolescents and counselling children

There are three major differences which are relevant when counselling adolescents as compared with counselling children. These are:

1 Unlike children, adolescents have less dependence on their families. For most adolescents, their social system involves peer relationships, together with other relationships developed within the educational system and/or at work. Their relationship with their family is changing as they seek more independence. Counsellors therefore need to recognize and respect that some adolescents will not want to have their families involved in the counselling process in any way, because this might compromise their growing individuation. This may create difficulties for the counsellor, at times, because families who are experiencing problems in accepting the changes of adolescence may want to be involved in counselling. However, some adolescents are willing to have their families involved in the counselling process. For them, a combination of family therapy and individual counselling may be an option. Sometimes it can be useful for counsellors to act as advocates for young people in negotiations with their families or parents.
2 Adolescents have more complex cognitive processes and more advanced cognitive skills than children. This more mature level of functioning allows the counsellor to choose more advanced cognitive intervention strategies which usually cannot be used when counselling children. Also, although sometimes it is useful in adolescent counselling to make use of media and activity (see Chapters 13 and 14), care must be taken to respect the maturity and self-image of the client.
3 The counselling relationship needs to respect the developmental needs of the adolescent which include respect for the young person as an individual who is neither a child nor an adult. The counselling relationship must give the client the right to make decisions with regard to involvement in the counselling process and must allow the client to have a genuine sense of personal responsibility for counselling outcomes.

Differences between counselling adolescents and counselling adults

Counselling adolescents also differs significantly from counselling adults. The adult is generally relatively free to make decisions and choices without excessive influence from family or others. Consequently, counselling with adults is based on the assumption that adults have personal autonomy and have choice regarding their actions as individuals (Woolfe and Dryden, 1996). Although most adolescents achieve a level of cognitive independence, this does not usually free them from what may be considerable influences of their families and social environments. As a result, most adolescents do not have a full sense of personal autonomy and are not certain about the extent to which they can make choices for themselves because they are not yet adults. They are in a developmental process of identity formation and individuation and being in this process tends to inhibit them from believing that they can have considerably more control over their lives than they did when they were children. Consequently, counsellors have to respect the adolescent's developmental dilemma regarding the extent of their personal ability to choose for themselves and take responsibility for their own lives.

Another difference relates to the normal developmental tasks which are appropriate for adolescents and tasks which are appropriate for adults. For example, the adolescent is striving for personal identity, individuation, sexual identity and new relationships with peers, whereas most adults are striving for goals such as stability, continuity, raising a family and success at work. Clearly, the issues which need to be addressed when counselling adolescents will generally be different from those which are relevant when counselling adults.

Counselling adolescents needs a specific approach

It is clear from the above discussion, that adolescents are a special group because of their developmental stage and the special problems which this presents. If we try to counsel them using strategies and techniques which are suitable for either children or adults, it is unlikely that we will have a high level of success. As counsellors, we need to remember that adolescents are not children and they are not adults: they are in transition. We therefore need to tailor our counselling approaches to engage the adolescent directly and actively and to use strategies which will specifically address their needs in ways which are acceptable to them.

The whole of the counselling process must take account of the young person's developmental process. As counsellors of adolescents, we need to deliberately strive to ensure that each of the following fits with that developmental process:

- the adolescent – counsellor relationship
- the counselling skills needed for successful outcomes
- the strategies to be used to address particular problems.

The proactive approach described in this book is designed to achieve the required fit between the adolescent's developmental processes and the counselling process.

It is widely recognized that individual counselling with adolescents is not the only way to help adolescents manage emotional, psychological and behavioural problems. Family therapy, group therapy and self-help support groups, or a combination of these, may all be useful in helping adolescents deal with troubling issues.

Differences between individual counselling and family therapy

Family therapy primarily addresses interpersonal relationship issues within the family. It does not directly address an adolescent's internal emotional and psychological needs. These intrapersonal needs are best addressed through individual counselling in a private and confidential situation where the focus can be on the adolescent's unique personality, developmental process and personal distress. In the individual counselling setting, the therapeutic approach and strategies used can be formulated to address the young person's individual needs specifically (Vernon, 1993).

Combining individual counselling with family therapy

We have noticed that in the past there have been two differing traditions with regard to counselling young people. One tradition involves individual counselling of the young person, whereas the other involves family therapy.

Many counsellors who belong to the individual counselling tradition, believe that it is sufficient to work with the adolescent alone in helping them to address and resolve troubling issues. Similarly, many counsellors who are committed to the family therapy tradition believe that family therapy alone is sufficient.

Some family therapists argue that working individually with a young person is undesirable because they become scapegoated, stigmatized, and pathologized. On the other hand, some counsellors who work with adolescents individually believe that family therapy does not provide an opportunity for the young person to address intensely personal and sensitive troubling issues. We certainly agree with the latter position as we have noticed that when we work with an adolescent individually they will be likely to reveal personal information which would have been too difficult to disclose in the context of the whole family. However, we have found that once troubling information has been disclosed by a young person in an individual counselling session, subsequently they are often able to share this information with their family or parents. If family therapy alone is used this information is unlikely to surface, with the consequence that the adolescent's troubling issues are likely to persist. For this reason we believe that if we are to actively facilitate change quickly we are likely to be more successful if we integrate individual work with the young person, with family therapy.

Readers who are interested in combining individual counselling for adolescents with family therapy might like to read the chapter entitled 'Counselling children in the context of family therapy' in our book 'Counselling Children: A Practical Introduction' (Sage, 2002). In that chapter we describe a method for combining individual counselling with family therapy. The approach described applies to both adolescents and younger children.

The relationship between the adolescent's world and the counselling environment

Figure 6.1 illustrates systemically the position that the counselling environment occupies in the adolescent's world. In this figure the adolescent's journey from

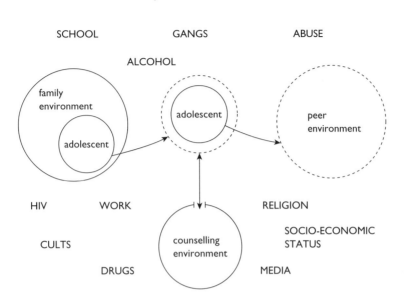

Figure 6.1   *The adolescent's world and the counselling environment*

child to adult is demonstrated as a move from the secure base of the family to the rather less secure base of the peer environment. The family is shown with a solid boundary to represent a place where containment, nurturing and healthy growth are fostered. Not all children have the opportunity to develop in environments like this. For many children the family boundary is fragmented so that they are deprived of some of the benefits which they might otherwise have. The environment into which the adolescent is moving (the peer environment) is depicted as having a broken boundary because it is open to outside influences and also allows movement into and out of the environment by the adolescent so that individuation can develop.

Peer groups do not meet all the needs of the adolescent. In Figure 6.1, the adolescent is depicted as having both an inner and an outer boundary. The inner boundary holds the adolescent's personality, past history and accumulated skills, while the outer boundary is broken and open to outside influences. The outer boundary represents the adolescent's newly emerging sense of self. This sense of self will consolidate as the adolescent moves through the journey to adulthood. As this boundary strengthens it will allow the adolescent to exist in the peer environment more comfortably and with more freedom to make individual decisions and choices. The consolidating boundary allows a sense of self-containment to develop within the open peer environment, with the consequence that adjustments to peer relationships will need to be negotiated. As adolescents move out from the family circle they develop a different relationship with their families and with individual family members. This is possible because of the newly developing sense of self.

Although the counselling environment is located in the adolescent's world, it is separate from the family and peer environments. The counselling boundary, as shown in Figure 6.1, is solid, to depict a place of safety, security, dependability and consistency. However, it has an opening for easy access and departure. Positive experiences within this environment will encourage adolescents to return when their own internal and external boundaries become fragile and/or overwhelming. In addition, the young person is subjected to a wide variety of external influences as illustrated in Figure 6.1.

Why do adolescents seek counselling?

In looking at why adolescents seek counselling, we need to recognize that the word 'counselling' when applied to young people has a wide range of meanings. Counselling for adolescents, as generally understood by the community and young people themselves, can involve any of the following:

1 Giving advice, where reaching the right decision is seen as very important.
2 Guidance, where the young person is experiencing difficulties because of immaturity and/or behaviours, and would like some directive help.
3 Psychotherapy, where the focus is on psychological and emotional distress. The expectation is that counselling will result in changes in attitudes and patterns of behaviour so that the adolescent feels more comfortable.

Counselling may involve a combination of all of these (Tyler, 1978), although we believe that generally, although not always, advice-giving is not helpful for adolescents who need to start taking responsibility for their own decisions. It is, however, appropriate for counsellors to provide useful and correct information which the young person may need in order to make sensible decisions. Naturally, many adolescents consult with counsellors in order to receive advice. This may be because they need to make difficult decisions and may recognize that they do not have the necessary experience which can provide them with the information which they need in order to reach a decision. Others seek counselling because they are emotionally distressed.

When adolescents do come for counselling help they generally have the belief that they will get help to solve problems or will receive directions or advice. They expect that the counsellor will be knowledgeable, that is experienced in life, and will have knowledge regarding their specific problem. They also expect that the counsellor will be a person who will have concern for others, be understanding, caring and supportive (Gibson-Cline, 1996). Counsellor characteristics will be discussed more fully in Chapter 7.

Adolescents seek professional help generally when life has become very difficult because of serious problems where previous attempts at resolution have failed. Unfortunately, though, many adolescents will not seek help for problems on their own. This is particularly the case for young adolescents who have more immature cognitive patterns than their older counterparts. These adolescents may have to rely on their parents to recognize when they might need help and to find out where they can get that help.

Parents are most likely to seek professional counselling for their adolescent children when the young person's behaviour is posing problems for the parents themselves or, alternatively, when the adolescent's problems have become serious (Raviv and Maddy-Weitzman, 1992). In the latter case, parental assistance will depend very much on the parents' own ability to recognize and identify problematic and dysfunctional behaviour in their children. Not all parents are able to do this. Consequently, adolescents are often referred for counselling by other community systems such as schools, statutory organizations, the juvenile justice system, self-help groups and community organizations.

Many young people go through adolescence without consulting with a counsellor. Research suggests that those adolescents who are better adjusted tend to use their own resources or to seek help and advice from others in their immediate social environment (Billings and Moos, 1981; Lazarus and Folkman, 1984; Compas et al., 1988; Ebata and Moos, 1991; Frydenberg, 1999). However, many adolescents feel unable to use the resources in their own environment, so will directly seek help from counsellors. Several authors have contributed to the growing literature on help-seeking behaviour in adolescents and have identified factors such as the age and gender of the adolescent, racial and ethnic differences, seriousness of the problem, low socio-economic status and locus of control as variables which influence the likelihood of a young person seeking counselling. A comprehensive summary of research in this area is provided by Schonert-Reichl and Muller (1996). Unfortunately, for some adolescents there is a stigma connected with the need to use counselling services. This is particularly so for those who may be suffering from the emerging symptoms of psychosis because they may additionally be concerned about negative stereotypes of mental illness, and may have negative ideas about the type of service which they may receive. As a consequence they may delay seeking help (Lincoln and McGorry, 1995).

Self-disclosure and confidentiality

Self-disclosure will usually only occur where there is a strong sense of privacy. Of particular interest to counsellors is the research finding that whether or not a young person seeks help depends on the perceived benefits of seeking help and also the perceived threat of negative consequences which might result from seeking help. For example, in substance-abusing adolescents, fear of police and statutory involvement has been found to be a deterrent with regard to seeking help (Darke et al., 1996). Clearly, seeking counselling help can be threatening for many adolescents because counselling requires self-disclosure about personal feelings, thoughts and problems. Counsellors therefore need to be aware of issues which might arise for the adolescent regarding confidentiality, privacy and the sharing of information with others (see Chapter 7).

7   Foundations of the proactive approach

From the discussion in Chapter 6 it is clear that for adolescents to be engaged in counselling with optimum success, the counselling process needs to be tailored specifically to meet adolescent needs. When counselling adolescents, we recommend what we will call a *proactive approach*. This is an approach to counselling which enables the counsellor to meet adolescent needs, as described in Part 1, by using a range of counselling skills and strategies in ways which will be described in this and subsequent chapters.

The proactive process for counselling adolescents will be described in the next chapter (Chapter 8), but first, in this chapter, we will describe the underlying philosophies, and counsellor and relationship characteristics which combine to create a foundation for the proactive approach. These are:

- an existentialist philosophy
- constructivist thinking
- personal qualities of the counsellor
- particular qualities of the adolescent–counsellor relationship.

Figure 7.1 illustrates the way in which the proactive approach is supported by the four elements listed above, with each new element sitting on a foundation created by the ones below. Thus, proactive counselling has as its primary foundation existentialism, upon which is seated constructivism. The other elements are then supported by this base to create a foundation for the proactive counselling approach for adolescents.

By utilizing the underlying philosophical orientations of existentialism and constructivism as a base to support the other elements of proactive counselling, it will be seen that we are able to tailor the counselling process so that it parallels and fits with the adolescent's own developmental processes.

Existentialism

Existentialism is concerned with the human search for the meaning of life. The existentialist view is that the only way human beings can make sense of their existence is through their personal experiences. The existentialist philosophy fits closely with the adolescent's own developmental processes because making sense of life through their own personal experiences is precisely what adolescents are trying to do.

The existentialist approach emphasizes that human beings are free to choose and are therefore responsible for their choices and actions. However, these choices are not limitless but lie within situational boundaries. We are not free to choose whatever we want; rather, we are free to choose how to respond to unavoidable and unpredictable 'stimuli' which our world presents to us (Spinelli, 1996).

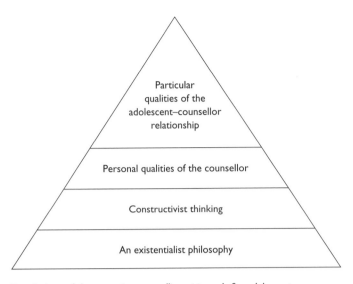

Figure 7.1   *Foundations of the proactive counselling approach for adolescents*

The assumption of freedom of choice in existential philosophy matches the adolescent's new-found sense of freedom. Adolescents generally have the opportunity to make choices and decisions about life but only within the limits of the boundaries inherent in their social environments. Emphasizing freedom to choose within the inevitable constraints of the real world helps the adolescent to focus on acceptance of personal responsibility.

Existential philosophy does not focus on psychopathology, which stresses deficits rather than strengths. The philosophy promotes a growth-oriented model which is focused on the future, on the goals that provide direction in life and on the ability of adolescents to create their own destiny. This approach respects the individual for exploring new aspects of behaviour.

Existential philosophy places emphasis on the search for meaning in life, on freedom and responsibility, on creating one's personal identity, and establishing meaningful relationships with others. Additionally, existentialism places emphasis on anxiety as a condition of living, with awareness of death as a major cause of that anxiety (Corey, 1996). All of these ideas fit very closely with the fundamental tasks and condition of adolescence. Consequently, an existential counselling philosophy is very appropriate when counselling young people as it parallels much adolescent thinking, encourages the client to accept anxiety as a reality and moves the client towards taking responsibility for making decisions within a realistic sense of freedom.

The existential approach stresses that the counsellor's techniques are far less important than the quality of the therapeutic client–counsellor relationship and emphasizes the relationship as the major factor that leads to constructive personal change (Corey, 1996). Existential therapists invite clients to grow by modelling authentic behaviour. The existentialist counsellor has the task of encouraging clients to examine their personal experiences to make sense of them and of life, and to explore their options so that they can create a meaningful existence. Thus, the counselling relationship can be likened to that of mentor and student. Mentors encourage young people to go in a direction determined by themselves and dictated by their conscience. This will inevitably bring a realization of responsibility towards one's self and towards others. Experiences of success and defeat will be seen as a normal part of life.

Constructivist thinking

The proactive counselling approach makes use of a constructivist philosophy which is superimposed on an existential foundation. It is important to understand that constructivism is not a theory of counselling. It is a theory which can be useful in helping explain how we set about trying to make sense of the world in which we live (Fransella and Dalton, 1990). As described in existentialism, in trying to make sense of the world in which they live, human beings use their personal experiences of the world to conceptualize and develop ideas or beliefs about the world. In other words, using constructivist terminology, they form *constructs* which encapsulate their concepts about the world in which they live. These constructs or personal interpretations of the world will not be fixed, but will be revised and replaced as new information becomes available to the individual concerned. Thus, personal construct theory is based upon the philosophical assumption that all of our present interpretations of the universe are subject to revision or replacement (Kelly, 1955). Each of us behaves like a scientist, formulating hypotheses, using our experiences to test them out and if necessary revising them (Winter, 1996). This is precisely what adolescents do.

The adolescent is in a stage of development which involves a high level of exploration, so that new, previously unmet experiences challenge the young person to revise and replace inappropriate and/or inadequate constructs with new ones. As Kelly (1955) pointed out, constructions can be reconstructed at any time and reconstruction usually occurs when constructs are invalidated by experience.

Constructivists believe that people actively and proactively construct their worlds so that personal identity and personal equilibrium are maintained. Individuals have some core constructs and these are particularly resistant to change because they are tied in to the person's own sense of personal identity. To change them may be threatening and may cause guilt or anxiety. Individuals adopt different strategies to avoid such anxiety or guilt. Some may tighten constructs so that the world becomes more predictable, whereas others loosen constructs to avoid the possibility of them being invalidated.

When counselling adolescents, we need to stay in touch with ways of thinking that are similar to theirs. As the principles of constructivism fit with adolescent development, so counsellors working with adolescents will find it useful to use constructivist ideas as a frame of reference.

Implications for counselling

Some counsellors use a construct counselling model as described by Fransella and Dalton (1990). Briefly, this involves determining the clients' constructs, using them to hypothesize about the reasons for their problems, and enabling them to revise their constructs. The proactive approach does not rely on this model. It merely uses the constructivist philosophy as a frame of reference.

By using constructivist philosophy, the counsellor can engage with the adolescent in an assessment procedure which encourages the client to express their view of the world and explore this view in the client's own terms, using the young person's own constructs, rather than those of the counsellor. The constructivist assessment process is consistent with the adolescent's need to be believed at a time of internal and external change. The counsellor's primary interest is in understanding and exploring the adolescent story and associated constructs. Clearly, constructivism demands that the counsellor actively listens to the young person's personal and individual narrative, and explores, understands and respects the constructs on which the narrative is based. Such an assessment process provides an opportunity for the counsellor to select therapeutic strategies and techniques which fit with the adolescent's personal constructs. Crespi and Generali (1995) highlight the significance and value of this process when working with young people.

Personal qualities of the counsellor

We have described the required foundations of a proactive counselling approach for adolescents as being constructivism grounded in existentialism. We believe that the next requirement for successful counselling of young people is that the counsellor be able to demonstrate particular personal qualities (see Figure 7.1). The personal qualities required include:

1 A sound understanding of adolescent developmental processes.
2 An ability to connect with the counsellor's own inner adolescent.
3 An ability to symbolize and model individuation.
4 Rogerian qualities of congruence and unconditional positive regard.
5 An ability to relate easily and with empathy to adolescents.

A sound understanding of adolescent developmental processes

When counselling adolescents it is essential that counsellors have a clear and in-depth understanding of adolescence, including adolescent development, developmental needs and tasks. An overview of adolescence is given in Part 1. However, counsellors who specialize in working with adolescents may wish to explore the underlying developmental theory of adolescence more fully by referring to the references cited in Part 1.

There is no doubt that counselling adolescents requires special skills and abilities. We believe that all counsellors working with young people require continuing supervision from suitable professionals who are themselves experienced in counselling adolescents. Clearly, this is particularly important for new counsellors.

An ability to connect with the counsellor's own inner adolescent

In the transactional analysis model of communication between adults, each individual is seen as having within them a 'parent', 'adult' and 'child' (Berne, 1964). We believe that the standard transactional analysis model omits a significant part of the human personality – the adolescent. We believe that each person has within them a capacity to get in touch with those parts of themself that are associated with parent, adult, adolescent and child cognitions and behaviours. We carry with us the adolescent part of our personalities and are capable of activating that part whenever we choose (and sometimes without realizing what we are doing). It is likely that most readers will be able to recognize a friend, acquaintance or client who makes considerable use of their inner adolescent by exhibiting adolescent thinking and behaviours. Interestingly, for some people the adolescent part of their personality emerges strongly in mid-life when some of the major responsibilities of adulthood, such as raising and providing for a family, are diminishing.

The adolescent is part of our person and does not just represent an in-between stage linking childhood and adulthood; it is a valid stage of lengthy duration which has its own characteristics as described in Part 1. Just as aspects of the child persist in our personalities, so, in the same way, aspects of the adolescent persist, providing us with an 'inner adolescent'. The inner adolescent is not a part of us which needs to be discarded, but is a part which can be useful. It is the part of our personalities which encourages risk-taking, exploring and experimenting with new behaviours, having fun and thinking creatively. The adolescent is freer and less constrained cognitively than the adult and is therefore more able to think and conceptualize with fewer boundaries.

Counsellors who wish to join with adolescents so that they are 'on the same wavelength' need to be able to get in touch with their own inner adolescent. We are not suggesting that a counsellor should behave exactly *like* an adolescent. To do that would be phoney and confusing for the client. We are suggesting that counsellors need to be able to get in touch with, and make use of, their own adolescent so that they can be freer to accept the client's constructs without being overly impeded by adult thinking, can be more readily able to perceive the world as the adolescent perceives it and can be better prepared to meet the client on their own ground.

Clearly, counsellors also need to be able to utilize the adult part of themselves much of the time during the counselling process. The counselling relationship can be defined by either Figure 7.2a or 7.2b, where the arrows indicate the communication paths. (Notice that in Figures 7.2a–f the adolescent is shown with an 'inner parent'. This is correct because children learn parental thinking and behaviours by modelling on their parents and are thus capable of behaving in a parental way.)

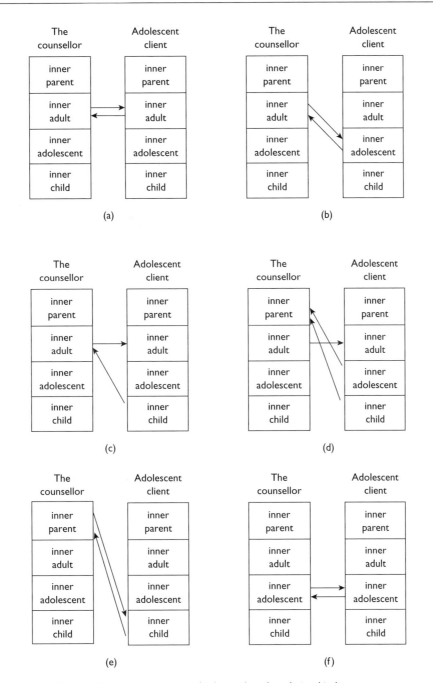

Figure 7.2 (a–f)   *Possible communication paths (arrows) in the relationship between counsellor and adolescent client*

At times, the counsellor may use their inner adult to communicate with the client's adult or adolescent, but the client may respond from their inner child as shown in Figure 7.2c. Worse still, the client may perceive the counsellor as a parent and respond either as a child or adolescent to the counsellor's inner parent, as in Figure 7.2d. Such crossed communication is described as very undesirable in transactional analysis, and is clearly not useful in counselling. It is similar to the transference relationship described by psychoanalysts, and there is a danger that the counsellor will assume the counter-transference position and respond from their inner parent, creating the communication pattern shown in Figure 7.2e. We believe that Figure 7.2a demonstrates the most useful way for an adolescent client and counsellor to relate. However, Figure 7.2b is also useful, as both Figures 7.2a and 7.2b allow for the mentor–student relationship described previously.

Sometimes it is both appropriate and necessary for the counsellor to communicate by using their own inner adolescent as shown in Figure 7.2f. At times, this is highly desirable to enable joining to occur. As stated previously, this does not mean that the counsellor behaves exactly like an adolescent, but it does suggest that the counsellor makes use of the adolescent part of their personality to think and communicate, at times, in a way which has some matching with the style of communication of the young person. Thus, the counsellor will not remain locked into using only their inner adult, but will also be able to make use of their inner adolescent. If the counsellor is able to switch from using adult to adolescent and vice versa with ease, a spontaneous and dynamic counselling interaction is possible. Adolescents are themselves very adept at changing their own styles of communication. As they are moving away from making use of their inner child, they naturally experiment with using both adolescent and adult ways of relating. If the counsellor is able authentically to match such behaviour, joining may be enhanced. However, the counsellor needs to be able to do this naturally and with ease, or it will not fit and will be seen to be phoney.

Interestingly, if a counsellor is able to use their inner adolescent to communicate with the young person's own inner adolescent, then the client is likely to start to model on the counsellor and to follow when they move into an adult communication mode. Switching in this way allows counselling sessions to be creative, lively and spontaneous.

An ability to symbolize and model individuation

Counsellors working with adolescents require the ability to communicate their own individuation symbolically by demonstrating their personal individuality and in the process joining with the client. When counselling adolescents, the counsellor needs to join their own 'self' with the young person in a dynamic process (Fitzgerald, 1995). We believe that the counsellor needs to be proactive in this process if the process is to be dynamic. The way the counsellor dresses, sits and speaks can indicate to the adolescent that individuality is encouraged and respected. If the counsellor is able to project qualities prized by adolescents, such as risk-taking, resilience, flexibility, vulnerability and creativity, combined with appropriate humour and gravity, the young person will be likely to have an experience of acceptance and one that values and honours uniqueness.

Joining is clearly critical when counselling adolescents. Joining at a more personal level than is appropriate when counselling adults can be useful provided that ethical boundaries are respected. The adolescent, although narcissistic, is, as has been discussed, inquisitive, and may seek to connect with the counsellor and to get to know who the counsellor is at a personal level rather than as someone hidden behind a professional façade. Adolescents are more likely to do this if they have some interests in common with the counsellor, and/or if they recognize some similarities between the counsellor's behaviours and ways of relating and their own. Clearly though, as stated, professional ethical boundaries must be maintained. These should not be difficult for the adolescent to respect if they are framed in terms of the counsellor's own individuation needs.

Rogerian qualities of congruence and unconditional positive regard

Two of the qualities identified by Rogers (1955, 1965) as desirable in counsellors are *congruence* and the ability to demonstrate *unconditional positive regard* towards the client. Many authors since then have accepted that these qualities are useful. We believe that they are not only useful but are necessary for successful counselling of adolescents.

Congruence   When counsellors fail to be congruent, young people are quick to recognize this. They will easily identify counsellor behaviours which are inconsistent and not genuine. Adolescents are inquisitive about other people because they are seeking models of adulthood, so they are likely to be critical in assessing the attributes and behaviour of the adults they meet.

Unconditional positive regard   This involves unconditional, non-judgemental and positive acceptance of the client regardless of their behaviour. It is difficult, and at times may be impossible, to achieve unconditional positive regard, but without this quality the counsellor will have difficulty in creating a useful working relationship with the young person.

Adolescent behaviours typically do not match up with the standards of adult behaviour. Not surprisingly, adolescents frequently feel judged and criticized by adults and also sometimes by peers. They tend to be very quick to recognize disapproval. Consequently, they are unlikely to talk freely with counsellors if they believe that negative judgements are being made about them. Moreover, making negative judgements does not fit with the constructivist approach which demands that the counsellor work from the client's frame of reference to explore the client's own constructs concerning their behaviour. Counsellors need to be able to accept the adolescent's story and constructs and it can be helpful in doing this if counsellors stay in touch with their own inner adolescent. To do this they may need to deal actively with their own personal feelings, at times, in order to stay within the constructivist paradigm. If a counsellor fails to do this, the adolescent will not feel able to talk freely about personal experiences and beliefs.

Being non-judgemental and offering unconditional positive regard to an adolescent whose behaviour is, by the counsellor's own standards, unacceptable, may not be easy. As stated, being non-judgemental will at times be impossible. However, being non-judgemental and treating clients with unconditional positive regard are goals which counsellors should strive to achieve if they are to work successfully with adolescents. Where this is difficult, the counsellor needs to explore in supervision any personal issues which may be interfering with their ability to be more accepting.

An ability to relate easily and with empathy to adolescents

Some counsellors have personalities which allow them to relate easily with adolescents so that the young people they meet feel comfortable when in their presence and are able to talk to them freely. These counsellors have a natural advantage which, when combined with counselling skills and strategies, can enable them to achieve success in their work with young people. Other counsellors may find working with adolescents more difficult but can still achieve success if they have a good understanding of the processes required for successful outcomes.

Rogers (1955, 1965) also identified *empathy* as important in counselling. Empathy is the ability to understand fully and share the client's feelings. In being empathic, the counsellor joins effectively with the client, understands their constructs, and is able, at some level, to share the feelings of the client in a way which the adolescent can recognize. Although we strongly believe that counsellors must be able to demonstrate appropriate levels of empathy when working with young people, we also believe that they need to be able to disengage from the adolescent's feelings at times. This disengagement is required so that they can protect themselves from being overwhelmed by the client's feelings, and so that they can observe the client and the counselling process and make decisions about that process.

It is essential for the counsellor to be able to convey warmth and caring. Although young people expect their counsellors to be warm and caring, they also tend to be tentative when building relationships and want to preserve their individuation. In order to enable satisfactory joining to occur, the counsellor needs to parallel the adolescent's cautious behaviour and to demonstrate warmth and caring in ways which are appropriate and not overwhelming, or the adolescent's individuation will be compromised and the counsellor may be perceived as shallow and lacking congruence.

Particular qualities of the adolescent–counsellor relationship

The qualities of the adolescent–counsellor relationship will clearly depend on the philosophical base for counselling (existential and constructivist), and on the personal qualities of the counsellor (see Figure 7.1). It is widely accepted that the outcome of any counselling intervention is determined by the quality of the relationship between the counsellor and client. This is certainly true for adolescents where the quality of the relationship is critical in influencing outcomes and client satisfaction (Eltz et al., 1995; Kendall and Southam-Gerow, 1996). For successful outcomes, it is desirable that the counselling relationship should have the following qualities:

1 An authentic person-to-person relationship.
2 The relationship should be accepting and understanding.
3 The relationship should have appropriate levels of warmth and empathy.
4 The relationship needs to have an element of balance.
5 The relationship should take account of cultural issues.

These relationship qualities are ones that counsellors of adolescents should strive to achieve. However, sometimes there are specific environmental and/or internal stimuli, including the counsellor's own prejudices and unresolved issues, which make it difficult for the desired relationship qualities to be achieved. It is here that counsellor supervision can be invaluable in helping a counsellor to identify reasons why particular client–counsellor relationships are impaired, and to enable the counsellor to resolve their own personal issues regarding the relationship.

An authentic person-to-person relationship

The adolescent world is an uncertain one in which all aspects of relationships are tested. As an adolescent, the young person's relationships with adults will be different from what they were during childhood. Consequently, the young person needs to try out new ways of relating with adults and may be unsure of their expectations. In order to help the adolescent client to feel relaxed and have a sense of trust, the counsellor will need, above all else, to be congruent (as explained above), open and honest, sincere and respectful. By demonstrating these characteristics, an authentic person-to-person relationship can be created.

The relationship should be accepting and understanding

Adolescents are striving for acceptance in the world outside their families. Generally, adolescents believe, and come to counselling believing, that no one has understood them, and doubting whether anyone will be able to understand them. In adolescent–counsellor relationships it is therefore of major importance that counsellors are able to convey the message that they have heard and do understand. Additionally, as discussed above, the relationship needs to be one where the client feels accepted and valued regardless of their behaviour.

The relationship should have appropriate levels of warmth and empathy

Warmth and empathy are essential, but they need to be appropriately demonstrated. The adolescent is striving for individuation and is unlikely to want to be enveloped in an overwhelming blanket of caring. The young person may also be wary of new relationships, particularly with adults, and may see high levels of warmth emanating from a stranger as incongruent and lacking in genuineness.

While recognizing the need for a warm, caring, empathic relationship, counsellors need to allow an appropriate relationship to develop at a pace and intensity comfortable for the client.

The relationship needs to have an element of balance

The adolescent–counsellor relationship does not need to be a predominantly heavy one. It should be balanced, so that although serious and distressing matters may be discussed, there can additionally be some pleasant times involving friendly conversation and/or the use of humour. It is interesting to note that humour has been found to be a useful treatment technique when working with adolescents (Mann, 1991; Bernet, 1993; Chapman and Chapman-Santana, 1995).

The relationship should take account of cultural issues

While most helping professionals work with limited information concerning their clients' environmental backgrounds, this may present difficulties where the adolescent and counsellor are from different ethnic and cultural groups (Ivey et al., 1993). Tharp (1991) found that clients prefer counsellors from their own ethnic group and concludes that, whenever possible, counselling for all adolescents should be in the context of their family's and community's belief systems, relationships and language.

8   The proactive process for counselling adolescents

In Part 1 we discussed the nature of adolescence, and in Chapters 6 and 7 we have explored the counselling needs of adolescents and the foundations of the proactive approach. The process used when counselling adolescents using the proactive approach needs to be understood in the context of all the information discussed previously.

When young people are progressing satisfactorily along their developmental path from childhood to adulthood, they feel good, and usually do not need counselling help. When problems arise in their lives, these interfere with, and block, the natural developmental process. Generally, adolescents will then successfully draw on strategies and resources within themselves to overcome

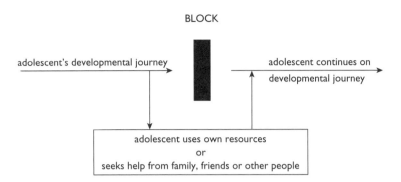

Figure 8.1   *Adolescent problem-solving behaviour*

challenges. Alternatively, they may be able to deal adaptively with these problems with the aid of peers, parents or significant others, as shown diagrammatically in Figure 8.1. Sometimes problems may be more serious, severe, accumulative or extremely private, and adolescents may be unable to manage them without counselling help. If an adolescent is unable to resolve or negotiate a block in the path of normal development, and is unable to receive the necessary counselling help, there are likely to be resulting maladaptive behaviours in response to stress. Typically, these behaviours might include withdrawal, aggression, truancy, substance abuse and/or suicide.

We will explain the proactive counselling process by describing:

1   Proactive counsellor behaviours.
2   Flexibility of the counselling process.
3   The primary counselling functions.
4   The use of single or multiple sessions.

Proactive counsellor behaviours

Proactive counsellor behaviours are supported by the foundations described in Chapter 7. Thus they are based on existentialism, constructivism, the personal qualities of the counsellor and particular qualities of the counselling relationship.

We believe that there are five essential characteristics of appropriate counsellor behaviour when working with adolescents. These are:

1   Being responsive to the adolescent's developmental needs.
2   Believing the adolescent.
3   Joining an adolescent style of communication.
4   Being proactive.
5   Respecting the adolescent's disclosure processes.

Most counsellors of young people are adults, although there are some young people who have been specially trained to counsel their peers. Many adult counsellors either have, or have parented, adolescent children of their own. Some counsellors from this group may find it hard to accept some of the suggestions in the following paragraphs. This is almost inevitable because it can be difficult for counsellors who are parents to avoid using the *parent* part of themselves. This can make it hard for them to join with young clients as counsellors by using the *adolescent* and *adult* parts of themselves, which is what is needed. However, we know that this can happen because although we are parents ourselves, we are able to enjoy the satisfaction of joining with and helping young people.

Many counsellors make strong statements about the need to meet adult clients with empathy and to join in their perceptions of their world. However, surprisingly, there is often resistance to the idea that counsellors of young people should, at times, use the adolescent part of their personality. Yet using this part of the personality enables close matching and joining with the adolescent client.

As stated before, using the inner adolescent does not mean behaving like an adolescent or pretending to be an adolescent. It does involve recognizing and getting in touch with the adolescent within ourselves so that we are able to think, conceptualize, perceive the world, examine constructs about the world and communicate in a way similar to that of our young clients. If we are not able to do this we will not join with them as counsellors but may be seen as parental. They may perceive us as telling them what we think they should do and how they should behave. This is certain to disempower and alienate the young people we are trying to help.

In exercising unconditional positive regard, we also need to accept adolescent behaviours such as changeability and unreliability uncritically. These are developmentally normal. At times, adolescents will present counsellors with challenging behaviours (Mabey and Sorensen, 1995) because some young people regard adults with suspicion and may act out their feelings within a counselling session. They may become withdrawn, unwilling to trust or may be openly hostile or surly. In response, the counsellor needs to be accepting, flexible and adaptable.

Being responsive to the adolescent's developmental needs

It is essential that counsellors working with young people understand adolescent developmental processes, as described in Part 1, so that they are able to make informed use of the counselling process described in this chapter. They also need to be actively responsive to young people's developmental needs during each counselling session. In attending to developmental needs, fundamental adolescent issues of power and autonomy need to be addressed.

Adolescents are generally moving from a situation where their lives are heavily controlled by others to a situation where they have more autonomy and responsibility. Counsellors therefore need to allow adolescents to express their autonomy and individuality within the counselling experience. This may, at times, be uncomfortable for the counsellor. If so, the underlying counsellor issues need to be addressed by the counsellor in supervision.

The adolescent needs to have choice about how to use each counselling session within mutually agreed limits regarding what is relevant and appropriate. They also need to have the right to decide whether to come to appointments or not. Where counselling is mandated, the adolescent still needs to feel able to choose to come or not, taking into account the consequences of that decision. Contracts need to be mutually negotiated and agreed so that the adolescent feels equally responsible for determining these. With regard to ongoing appointments, the adolescent needs to know that they have control of the decision to come back or not. As adolescents are seeking control in their lives they will be less likely to return if they believe that the counsellor is trying to make a decision for them.

Believing the adolescent

First, we need to define what we mean when we refer to 'believing the adolescent'. When, in the proactive counselling of adolescents, we say that we believe the client, we mean that we will listen to their story and will accept it at face value as the adolescent's truth even if the story stretches our credulity. We will be totally accepting of the story and will not challenge its veracity. However, if there are inconsistencies in the story we will draw attention to them and explore them, provided that the client is happy to engage in such exploration with us.

Adolescents will often tell counsellors stories which are difficult to believe. However, such stories fit with the constructs which the young person is currently using. If counsellors are to help adolescents to move ahead to the point of reviewing and challenging existing constructs, then it is essential that they first accept without question what the client is saying. However, where inconsistencies arise in the client's stories these can be discussed so that existing constructs can be revised where necessary (see Chapter 11).

It is well known that adolescents often feel that they are misunderstood and not believed by adults. If counsellors are seen to behave in a way which matches adolescents' stereotypical perceptions of adults, by not believing their stories, then the possibility of building a helpful counselling relationship where the client trusts the counsellor is diminished. Additionally, adolescents often have stories to tell which the young person may legitimately feel are difficult to believe. They may be true, but difficult to believe. It is therefore essential that we believe what we are being told. If we do not believe what we are told, then we will not be trusted and we are unlikely to be able to help the adolescent to move forward into telling stories which more accurately reflect adult perceptions.

We know that some counsellors will disagree with the suggestion that we should always believe the client. However, in our experience, by doing this, trust develops and the client is empowered to review and evaluate constructs, discarding those which do not fit with reality and replacing them by more adaptive constructs. In the process, more objective truth is revealed. However, the counsellor does need to be alert to the possibility of the symptoms of mental disorder, as described in Chapter 5, and to refer to appropriate helpers when necessary. Believing the client is an essential component of proactive counselling.

Joining an adolescent style of communication

As will be discussed more fully in Chapter 9, the conversational style of adolescents is generally not the same as that of most adults. Many adolescents are likely to move in and out of the conversational process, flit from one idea to another and desire to be in control of the conversation at all times. As counsellors, if we are to be able to join effectively with adolescents we need to deliberately parallel their conversational style rather than trying to contain it. Thus, digressions may be actively and deliberately encouraged. At times the counsellor can make use of such digressions to help in the joining process, and then later return to discussion of the young person's problems.

Parents often feel that adolescent children are intrusive in wanting to talk at inappropriate times. They also often find that their adolescent children will not talk about personal issues when invited but want to talk at length at times which are inconvenient. This is developmentally normal adolescent behaviour. Counsellors need to respect and take advantage of this.

Adolescents who have difficulty in talking about the things that trouble them most will want to do this in their own time. They therefore need to be allowed to digress and move towards and away from discussing matters of importance. Thus, rather than running away from important issues in the counselling conversation, the adolescent may well be diverting temporarily, waiting for a time when it is more comfortable to continue. The counsellor need not be dismayed by this process but merely needs to follow the adolescent and add energy to the conversation. This may involve being patient and actively deciding to enjoy listening to a conversation which, at times, may not seem to be directly relevant.

As noted above, counselling conversations do not need to be continually heavy and serious. It is more helpful in putting a young person at ease if friendly conversation and humour are encouraged, to balance the impact of the discussion of serious issues.

Being proactive

When working with adolescents the interactional style required differs markedly from the style of interaction which commonly occurs when working with adults. Adults seem to cope well with structured counselling sessions where the counsellor stays within the boundaries of a well-defined counselling contract. They are generally clearer than adolescents about why they are engaging in counselling and are generally more confident within the counselling process.

In contrast with adults, adolescents are often restless and uncertain when engaged in counselling. It is usually not sufficient for the counsellor to be a quiet listener. Adolescents are generally restless beings who need to be actively engaged. They quickly become impatient and bored, so the counselling relationship needs to be dynamic. This requires spontaneous behaviours combined with creativity, and the use of a more active counselling process than that used with adults.

The proactive counselling approach enables counsellors to meet adolescent needs, as described in Part 1, by proactively selecting counselling skills and strategies from commonly used, well-established and tested counselling theories and methods. The selection of counselling skills and strategies is carried out in response to the adolescent's immediate needs, as they are identified at any point in time, during the counselling session. Decisions regarding the timing of the introduction of particular skills and/or strategies are critical to the proactive process. Thus, sessions are dynamic, with the counsellor deliberately choosing particular skills and introducing specific strategies from a range of available skills and strategies, as these are required. This does not mean that counselling sessions are chaotic. They are not, but the process will continually shift and change in response to the adolescent's conversation, behaviour, mood, issues and needs.

It is essential to proactive counselling that the counsellor should be active, lively, spontaneous and creative. Most importantly, the counsellor needs to be quick, flexible and *opportunistic*. This means responding quickly and actively through the selection and use of appropriate skills and strategies, so that opportunities are not lost. Thus, the counselling process becomes energized. The use of the proactive counselling approach will be illustrated in Chapter 16 by case studies.

Respecting the adolescent's disclosure processes

Perhaps the most important factor in counselling success with adolescents is to enable them to self-disclose. By self-disclosing, they have an opportunity to express themselves openly, they receive validation about the content of their disclosure, gain a sense of control over issues discussed and, most importantly, are enabled to review and revise personal constructs. All of this assists in the adolescent development process (Rotenberg, 1995).

Self-disclosure in adolescents serves as a catharsis for both positive and negative emotions. It allows adolescents to experience strong emotions connected with their stories and to identify issues and constructs related to these emotions. If counsellors are able to join with young clients by expressing similar emotional responses to them when listening to their stories, the clients' experiences will be validated and they may be able to release their emotions more fully with cathartic effect. Having done this they can move on to reviewing and revising constructs which will determine future behaviours.

As discussed in Chapter 6, in their everyday lives adolescents initiate, build and maintain relationships with their peers, in part through the use of mutual self-disclosure. In particular, adolescents are attracted to others through the disclosure of similar experiences. This mutual sharing creates a sense of safety and intimacy. Just as self-disclosure promotes closeness and intimacy in peer relationships, a level of mutual story-telling during counselling can be useful in establishing trust because it parallels the young person's experience with peers.

Many counsellors, particularly those who are used to working with adults, have concerns regarding counsellor self-disclosure. Counsellor self-disclosure should not be used to satisfy the counsellor's needs. It must be limited to preserve boundaries which are appropriate for the counsellor's own personal individuation and most importantly to respect professional and ethical boundaries. However, when counselling adolescents, a limited level of counsellor self-disclosure is required in initiating, building and developing the counselling relationship. The use of counsellor self-disclosure will be discussed more fully in the next chapter.

Adolescents are continually exploring new constructs and comparing them with their own. Often they will make strong statements about their own beliefs while at the same time being open to, and interested in, other people's ideas. They may either directly or indirectly invite peers, parents, teachers and counsellors to share their ideas with them so that they can test their own constructs against those of others. It is important for counsellors to recognize this typical adolescent behaviour and to make use of it in the counselling process.

The issue of *confidentiality* is crucial to the willingness of young people to disclose. They expect confidentiality and loyalty in the counselling relationship in the same way that they expect it from peer friendships (although they do not always get these things from their peers).

Unfortunately, the issue of confidentiality is complicated because of the rights of others to have information. Many young people are living at home and may be brought for counselling by their parents. Those who are in care may similarly be brought for counselling by carers. Parents and legal guardians have a right to receive information concerning adolescents in their care. However, many parents and carers will respect the young person's right to have confidential counselling, provided that they know that they will be told if there are matters of major concern.

Initially, when adolescents are brought for counselling by parents or other carers, it can be useful to discuss the issue of confidentiality in the presence of the adolescent and the adults concerned so that agreement can be reached regarding confidentiality and its limits. Where an adolescent has taken the initiative to set up a counselling interview for themselves, it may be possible for the counsellor to respect confidentiality fully. However, this will be subject to legal, ethical and professional obligations. Where there is disclosure of abuse, or of suicide plans, or of plans to harm others, counsellors have a duty of care to the client and others, and need to take appropriate action. At times like this, it is important to talk with the young person about the necessity of informing others. Whenever possible, after taking account of legal, ethical and professional requirements, the client should be given the right to decide *how* and *when* disclosure will take place. This enables them to have some control of the disclosure process and, it is hoped, a sense of some control over the consequences of disclosure. To do otherwise disempowers the client, and is likely to result in disillusionment with the counselling process. If this occurs, the client may never seek counselling again.

When adolescents are brought to counselling by parents or carers, once confidentiality issues have been negotiated and agreed, it is usually best to talk with the adolescent first in order to be able to obtain their trust. Adolescents who are under pressure to attend are usually reluctant to engage in the counselling process. If their parents or other adults are consulted first, they may conclude that unfavourable reports about them have been made before they have a chance to state their own points of view.

A good way to respect the rights of the parents and retain the confidence of the adolescent is to meet with parents or carers only at times when the adolescent is present, or to meet with the whole family with the adolescent present. By doing this, the adolescent can hear what parents (or other family members) are saying, and what the counsellor is saying, and is free to offer alternative points of view or versions of reality (Barker, 1990). When a third party is involved in setting up a counselling contract for a young person, it is vital that the issues of confidentiality, and of further communication between the counsellor and the referral source, are clarified before counselling starts.

Confidentiality is a way of providing the adolescent with privacy in which to discuss issues which are too difficult to disclose to others. However, as discussed above, there are limits to the extent to which the confidentiality can be offered, and counsellors have a responsibility to be open with young people about these limits. Different countries, and states within countries, have varying policies on the rights of adolescents, and concerning the responsibilities of counsellors and other professionals. It is essential that counsellors are familiar with the ethical, professional and legal issues relating to confidentiality when working with young people.

Flexibility of the counselling process

When compared with counselling children or adults, counselling adolescents needs to be more flexible and freer in structure. The counselling process will generally not be as well defined and predictable. Adolescents are less likely to stay engaged in a counselling process which follows sequentially through stages of therapy over time. They are often unable to see the big picture of the world in which they live because they are struggling with changing constructs. They may also have difficulty in articulating their difficulties and may only be able to focus on, and describe, fairly discrete parts of their world which tend to be disconnected from the broader picture. Their discovery process is one which involves trying to connect and make sense of differing parts of their picture. The counselling process therefore needs to take account of this, with counsellors using strategies which will enable adolescents to draw their ideas and beliefs together to form constructs which will help them to make sense of their world.

The counselling process needs to allow adolescents to explore in ways which are similar to those which they use generally. Thus, they may jump from subject to subject and wish to explore seemingly disconnected parts of their world and experiences. The proactive approach allows for this as it requires the counsellor to be spontaneous, creative, flexible and opportunistic, while attending to the primary functions of the counselling process.

The primary counselling functions

Figure 8.2 illustrates diagrammatically the process for counselling adolescents using the proactive approach. The counselling process depends on a central core of *primary counselling functions*. The three primary counselling functions are:

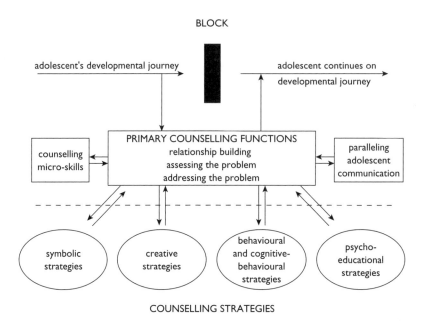

Figure 8.2   *The proactive counselling process*

- relationship building
- assessing the problem
- addressing the problem.

Details of these primary functions will be discussed below. The three functions do not necessarily occur in sequence, but may overlap or be performed concurrently. Each function may happen continuously or be repeated several times during a counselling session. At all times, during a counselling session, the proactive counsellor is involved in attending to one or more of the primary functions. To do this, whenever necessary, the counsellor draws on counselling micro-skills, as illustrated by the arrows in Figure 8.2 (micro-skills are discussed in Chapter 10), or may allow diversions by paralleling the adolescent's conversational style, as indicated in Figure 8.2. These diversions should not be viewed as lost counselling time because they serve a useful purpose by contributing to the primary counselling functions. Engaging in the adolescent's general conversation can be useful for relationship building and also in helping the counsellor to learn about and understand the young person's constructs about his world.

Counselling strategies used to operationalize the primary counselling functions

The ellipses in Figure 8.2 describe four different groups of counselling strategies which can be useful when counselling adolescents. It is the proactive counsellor's task to select from these groups of strategies and to use those strategies which are appropriate at particular points within the counselling session.

During one counselling session, one or more strategies may be utilized. The strategies are an available resource. The counsellor needs to be opportunistic and skilled in selecting and using relevant strategies at particular times. *The proactive counsellor takes full responsibility for orchestrating the counselling process to fulfil the primary functions, while allowing the adolescent freedom within the process to explore and resolve issues.* This is central to proactive counselling of adolescents. Counselling strategies are selected in response to the adolescent's cognitive, emotional, somatic, verbal and non-verbal behaviours and the issues being discussed. The strategies selected are the ones which the counsellor believes will have the most successful outcomes.

The timing of the introduction of strategies selected is particularly important because this will influence the young person's level of interest and engagement in the counselling process. If the timing is inappropriate the young person will not be engaged in the use of the strategy. In addition, if the strategy selected does not fit the immediate needs, personality and mood of the young person, then it is likely to fail. The strategies within each group are discussed in Chapters 12–15, together with information about the selection and suitability of each strategy.

Each session is complete in itself

In the proactive counselling approach each of the three primary counselling functions is used in every counselling session. Thus, if an adolescent comes to several counselling sessions, all three functions will be involved in all sessions. However, the balance between the use of the three functions may change as required. Thus each session is complete in itself so that if the client does not return for further counselling useful work has been achieved.

Making each counselling session complete in itself is particularly important for young people. This is because many adolescents will come to see a counsellor at a time of crisis but will stop coming as soon as the crisis is over. They may then come back later when a new crisis occurs. It is clearly advantageous if counsellors can not only help young people to deal with current crises but also enable them to make changes so that when new crises occur they have the skills to deal with the new crises themselves without the need for counselling. When we are counselling adolescents it is useful to remember that because of their developmental stage in life they may be unreliable with regard to keeping appointments. Consequently, it can be useful for us to assume that each appointment with a young person may be the final appointment. We can then endeavour to achieve a level of completion in the counselling work undertaken in the session.

Relationship building

This primary counselling function involves:

- joining with the adolescent
- developing a relationship with the adolescent
- contracting with the adolescent.

Joining with the adolescent

Joining with adolescent clients is the most critical part of counselling young people. It can sometimes be difficult, but without joining counselling cannot take place. Adolescents have a natural tendency to want to move away from the influence and control of parents and other adults, so they are likely to regard adult counsellors with suspicion and mistrust. They may ask questions such as 'How is this person different from my parents or teachers?' and 'Why should I expect them to treat me as a person or individual of value rather than as a child who needs to be told what to do?' Proactive counsellors join by understanding and paralleling some specific adolescent behaviours. They make use of important components inherent in adolescent friendship formation and particular communication and disclosure processes of adolescents as will be described in the next chapter. Thus, proactive counsellors model some of their own behaviours on those typical adolescent behaviours which adolescents use to connect and talk, at a personal level, with peers. This does not mean that they behave like adolescents but it does mean that they make sensible use of some typical adolescent communication processes. The joining process can be enhanced by selectively making use of particular counselling micro-skills, as discussed in Chapter 10.

Clearly, joining is most critical at the start of, and during, the first session of counselling. However, joining does not just happen at the start of a session, but is a continuing process. Adolescents tend to be changeable and sometimes fickle in their evaluation of friends. They are quick to take offence or to disengage through restlessness or lack of interest. Consequently, the counsellor should continually attend to the need to maintain and develop a positive connection with the client.

Developing a relationship with the adolescent

The development of a relationship with the adolescent involves a deeper level of joining than the initial connection which occurs on first meeting. Initial joining needs to occur at the beginning of each counselling session, not just the first session. Such joining engages the adolescent in the counselling process, and enables the development of a more complete and trusting relationship so that work which may be intensely personal can occur. The development of such a relationship needs to be ongoing and to occur throughout the counselling process. Counsellors need to be constantly attending to relationship development and maintenance because adolescents continually re-evaluate their relationships. They are most likely to be vigilant in re-examining their relationships with counsellors because counsellors are generally adults, and adolescents are particularly sensitive to relationship issues with adults.

As rapport develops between a counsellor and adolescent, a relationship which involves the qualities described in Chapter 7 can develop, enabling the client to feel safe in talking about troubling personal issues. The counselling relationship creates a climate in which useful counselling work can take place. Additionally, it is helpful in itself because it may provide a useful setting in which the adolescent can examine and revise constructs about relationships, can experiment with the relationship itself and can discover new relationship skills.

There is safety in doing this in an environment where there can be some level of confidence that judgement and/or disapproval are unlikely to occur. Thus, the counselling relationship can provide an opportunity for the development of social competence and can be used as a model for future relationships.

Contracting with the adolescent

During the initial joining process, the counsellor needs to make an agreement, even if loose, with regard to the purpose and possible duration of counselling. This agreement may need to be updated and amended from time to time.

Adolescents who are not used to the counselling process need to be familiarized with the opportunities and limitations of counselling. They will need to know:

- that it is OK to take time to talk things through;
- that the counsellor will not provide solutions but will try to help them to find their own solutions;
- that what they say will be in confidence but that there may be limits to that confidentiality;
- that coming to counselling is their choice (although for some there may be consequences if they decide not to attend);
- that they will have choice about what they do, and do not do, within the counselling process;
- that one session may be all they need or want, but that if they wish to continue coming for further sessions that can be discussed so that mutual agreement can be reached.

Assessing the problem

This primary counselling function involves the following:

- listening to the client's story and believing it
- identifying themes, issues and problems
- evaluating the client's emotional state.

It needs to be remembered that this function does not occur at a particular point in the overall counselling process. It may happen continuously and/or at various times during a counselling session.

Listening to the client's story and believing it

As discussed in Chapter 7, listening to the client's story without judgement and believing it are essential to the constructivist basis of the proactive approach. By believing the client's story, we mean that we accept it totally as the adolescent's truth so that the adolescent's experience is one of being believed. As the young person tells us their story, being empathic, we match emotional responses, and we verbally affirm the client's experience. Thus the client feels validated. At times, the young person may experience a sense of relief at being believed by an adult. This is particularly so if the story stretches credulity.

By believing the story, the counsellor is entering the adolescent's world and has a sense of what it is like to be in that world. Where there are inconsistencies, the counsellor may be puzzled, and may share this with the adolescent. Thus, the counsellor will be seen to be congruent and, most importantly, to be keenly interested in trying to fully understand the young person's world and its inconsistencies.

Identifying themes, issues and problems

As the adolescent tells their story, the counsellor will progressively piece together a picture relating to that story. Further, as the story is expounded, the counsellor can identify themes, issues and problems, and may feed these back to the client, seeking clarification if necessary. The counsellor may select particular strategies and/or techniques to make it easier for the client to clearly identify and clarify themes, issues, and problems. Suitable strategies and techniques are described in Part 3.

Evaluating the client's emotional state

Evaluation of the client's emotional and mental state, including mood, feelings, thoughts and perceptions, is necessary to provide a complete picture for the counsellor of how the adolescent is coping. This is needed so that the counsellor can make decisions regarding strategies to be used during counselling, and also to enable the counsellor to determine whether mental health problems which need specialist treatment are in evidence or are developing.

In making an assessment, counsellors need to draw on their knowledge of adolescent development, and understand the impact that past and current experiences have had on the adolescent's life (see Part 1). This evaluation needs to be seen as an ongoing process throughout the course of a counselling session or series of sessions.

Specific counselling skills to evaluate the adolescent's emotional and mental state will be discussed in Chapter 10. Adolescents generally tend to like assessment techniques which they believe might help them discover and understand who they are, or what they might be feeling. This explains why many of them show an interest in philosophies such as astrology or numerology. Consequently, some young people find it interesting to do self-report inventories. Recognizing this, some counsellors find it helpful to use formal assessment tools such as depression inventories or self-esteem assessments. These may be particularly useful in identifying mental health problems. However, many experienced counsellors who work with adolescents are able to make assessments using clinical judgement alone. This is satisfactory for the purpose of counselling those who are not experiencing mental health problems, and fits with our own practice.

Addressing the problem

This primary counselling function involves the following:

- working through the problem
- exploring solutions
- planning to experiment.

Working through the problem

Adolescents generally come to counselling seeking solutions to problems, so during the counselling process there is likely to be commitment to the resolution of specific issues. The counsellor therefore needs to select and use strategies which will be appropriate for the task.

Some young people may only wish to explore their issues in counselling and come to a clearer understanding of their problems without seeking solutions. These clients may wish to seek solutions later without counselling help. This fits with the adolescent need for individuation. Such clients should be encouraged to do as they wish and be complimented because they are accepting responsibility for finding their own solutions. They can be commended for their confidence in their own ability. Additionally, they can be invited to seek counselling, in the future, if they think that it might be useful.

Exploring solutions

Working through the problem will often lead naturally to the discovery of possible solutions which will need to be evaluated. The evaluation should take into account positive and negative consequences associated with solutions and the extent to which the young person seems comfortable with each possible solution. Some solutions may not fit with the client's fundamental beliefs or constructs. When this occurs, there is an opportunity for re-examination of beliefs with possible revision of constructs. Solutions which are more inviting need to be considered in terms of the young person's ability and commitment to using them. The only solutions which will work are ones which appeal to the adolescent, fit with their personal constructs, or revised constructs, and are ones which the young person has the will and capacity to put into practice.

Planning to experiment

Young people are inexperienced and sometimes devise solutions which seem to be attractive but which may be impractical or have undesired consequences. As counsellors, we need to remember that most human beings learn best through personal experience. Having found a possible solution to a problem does not necessarily mean that the problem is solved. The solution needs to be tested.

Adolescents are vulnerable and may feel a deep sense of failure when solutions do not work out in practice. Counsellors should therefore discuss the need to test solutions by putting them into practice. This can be framed in terms of doing an experiment to test a solution. Where an experiment demonstrates problems with a particular solution, the experiment can be seen, not as a failure, but as having been useful in providing new information. That new information can be used to revise constructs and formulate other solutions.

The use of single or multiple sessions

Many adolescents will benefit from a single session of counselling, finding resolution of their problems and thus resuming their developmental journey with relative ease. However, for others, this will not be the case and they may require further counselling help. Unfortunately, making appointments and maintaining a commitment to counselling is difficult for many young people. In particular, open-ended counselling contracts may be daunting for some. Even when contracts are made for ongoing counselling, many young people will not turn up regularly but will be inconsistent in their attendance.

Several research studies have compared the effectiveness of short-term or brief counselling with longer-term counselling of adolescents (for example, Slavin, 1996; Warner, 1996), and other studies have examined the issue of adolescents attending counselling where they have been sent by others and not self-referred (DiGiuseppe et al., 1996). These studies do not make definitive recommendations regarding the most desirable and effective duration of the counselling relationship. However, it is clear that, generally, adolescents can benefit from single-session or short-term brief interventions (Fitzgerald, 1995; Mabey and Sorensen, 1995; Mortlock, 1995). Short interventions are more in keeping with the way in which adolescents run their lives.

Proactive counsellors encourage adolescents to be in control of the decision about whether to return for further counselling. This is achieved by encouraging them to examine their needs and readiness for either short- or longer-term counselling without introducing options prematurely, so that their own decision-making processes are not unduly contaminated by the counsellor. However, it is appropriate for a counsellor to provide feedback and information regarding their own perceptions of the adolescent's suitability for brief or long-term counselling. Where clients have high ego strength, single-session counselling is likely to be effective, but this is unlikely to be so for clients with low ego strength who may require a longer and more supportive process (Alexander, 1965).

When an adolescent decides that further counselling sessions would be helpful and expresses a wish to have these, a contract regarding continuing counselling needs to be negotiated collaboratively by the counsellor and adolescent. This may result in a specific contract for counselling sessions with firm dates and times. However, some adolescents prefer an open-door arrangement which will allow them to come to counselling when they feel that they need it. If this is suitable for the counsellor, an open-door policy can be used. Where an agreement is reached and further appointments are made, it is desirable that the adolescent be invited to cancel appointments if they become unnecessary or are no longer desired. This is to encourage the young person to be in control of the process.

Clients who drop out

Adolescents drop out of counselling for a number of reasons:

1   They may find the joining and engaging process too threatening.
2   The counselling experience may have been unsatisfactory for them and may have failed to meet their expectations.
3   They may have hoped for magical solutions and be disappointed when they realize that, ultimately, they themselves are responsible for finding solutions and putting them into practice.
4   They may believe that the counsellor does not see their problems as sufficiently important.

Adolescents who have been sent to counselling by parents or other referral sources are most likely to want to withdraw when painful issues are confronted or awareness of issues is heightened.

It is often assumed that the main reason why clients drop out of counselling is because they are dissatisfied with the treatment received or because facing their problems is too overwhelming. However, research on people who drop out of all forms of therapy reveals that most clients who drop out do so because they have accomplished what they intended.

Many clients who drop out of counselling report as much improvement as those who stay on for the longer term (Talmon, 1990; Budman and Gurman, 1992; Rosenbaum, 1994; Kaffman, 1995). Counsellors of young people are well advised to recognize this, because coming to counselling regularly does not fit very comfortably with an adolescent lifestyle. Additionally, adolescents tend to be impatient and want quick results. Often, for young people, a single counselling session may be enough to help them to overcome their block and continue on their developmental journey. It is therefore wise for counsellors who work with adolescents to realize that the first session may also be the last, although it may also have been a useful and complete counselling experience which will predispose the young person to seek counselling again in the future, if the need arises.

Counsellors need to take account of the adolescent's developmental needs for power and autonomy. It is essential that the adolescent is given free choice about whether to continue with counselling or not. If this choice is not offered, then the client may become extremely resistant to the counselling process and avoid offers of counselling in the future. Paradoxically, if the client is offered a free and open choice about whether to continue, resistance and hostility are likely to be minimized. It is important for counsellors to be clear with their clients that they are committed to providing continuing counselling, if it is required. They need to let their young clients know of their willingness to work with them for as long as is needed, provided that useful goals are recognized.

9   Making use of adolescent communication processes

We have noticed that many counsellors find it difficult to join with adolescents and engage them in a way that enables them to talk freely. This can be a serious problem because it is impossible for a helpful counselling process to develop unless the counsellor is able to gain the trust of the adolescent so that the young person feels comfortable enough to talk about intimate personal issues. In our opinion this is the biggest problem that counsellors face when trying to help young people. When we think about this problem we shouldn't be surprised by the difficulty counsellors have in trying to engage young people in a counselling process because there is abundant evidence in the literature to support the notion that young people are generally reluctant to talk to adults about sensitive issues (Boldero and Fallon, 1995).

As we have explained previously, adolescents are in a process of individuation. They need to become individuals in their own right with a level of separation from their parents and other adults so that they can make decisions for themselves. It is appropriate for them to make friends with their peers. As noted by Readdick (1997) and Santrock (1993) they tend to associate more frequently with their peers than with adults.

We know that parents commonly complain that their adolescent children won't talk to them openly. This is not surprising, as avoiding talking about particular topics is the way that individuals create boundaries in their relationships, as a number of authors including Guerrero and Afifi (1995) and Ryder and Bartle (1991) point out. Thus by avoiding talking about sensitive personal issues with parents and other adults, young people establish their boundaries so that they can satisfactorily perform their task of individuation.

We also need to recognize that young people are going to be reluctant to talk to adults about sensitive or personal issues, as doing so might be embarrassing or lead to them becoming emotionally overwhelmed. If they refrain from sharing such information they retain their privacy and avoid the possibility of becoming closer to an adult at a time when they are trying to individuate. In particular, by withholding disclosure from their parents about their daily activities, adolescents create arenas of privacy and protect themselves from parental interference and unwanted supervision (Buhrmester and Prager, 1995).

If we take account of the reasons why young people tend to avoid confiding in adults, we shouldn't be surprised by the fact that many adolescents are reluctant to talk to counsellors. However, if we are to be effective in helping young people, we need to discover useful ways to engage them in conversation and this is made easier by understanding the ways in which they themselves communicate comfortably. As described in the literature, and from observation, it is clear that commonly used adolescent communication processes are in some ways different from commonly used adult communication processes.

If we want to have a fuller understanding of normal adolescent communication processes, it can be useful to observe young people as they talk to each other. Because young people may object to being observed and may behave differently when they are being observed, such observations can often best be done in public places. For example, if you are travelling on a train or bus or are sitting in a restaurant with young people nearby, you may find it easy to listen into their conversation without being intrusive. If you notice the processes that they use, you will probably discover that many young people use several distinct processes when talking with peers.

When adolescents meet with and join with peers at a personal level they usually engage in some of the following behaviours (Rotenberg, 1995; Seiffge-Krenke, 1995):

- They positively connote aspects of the other person's presentation, including appearance, behaviours and adornments or possessions.
- They use direct closed questions to get information.
- They disclose information about themselves and assume that the other person will similarly self-disclose.
- They validate the other person's views, if possible.
- They use praise when relevant.
- They are very direct about what they like and do not like.
- They match and exaggerate the other person's emotional expressions in response to story-telling.

Additionally we have noticed that many young people tend to:

- Frequently digress, move away from a topic of interest, and then return to it
- Take the lead in a conversation and feel as though they are in control of it
- Give and receive advice.

If, as counsellors, we are to engage young people in conversation, we can learn from their communication processes so that we ourselves can make use of these processes when appropriate. We believe that it can be helpful if counsellors working with adolescents are able to proactively engage in behaviours such as those listed above. However, as counsellors, we do need to behave naturally so that what we do fits with our own personalities and is not fake. Thus, counsellors helping young people need to be able to get in touch with, and use, their own inner adolescent, while remaining true to themselves as adults.

Because of the importance of paralleling at some level normal adolescent communication processes we will discuss those processes in more detail and consider their relevance when counselling.

The use of direct closed questions to get information

When adolescents make use of direct closed questions in their typical peer conversations they demonstrate the way in which young people tend to be more direct and inquisitive in their conversations than older people. Consequently, in the counselling situation, many young people like to have a direct approach from the counsellor, whereas older people probably prefer counsellors to be more circumspect in the questions they ask. As counsellors, we don't think that it is useful to be limited to direct closed questions. Moreover, we doubt whether it is useful to use many direct closed questions at all. However, we can learn from the way in which young people like to have direct and open communication. Such communication can be achieved by using a wide range of questions that come from a variety of therapeutic approaches. These useful questions will be described in the next chapter.

Mutual self-disclosure

It is interesting for us to note that many parents are troubled because their adolescent children are not prepared to talk with them about sensitive personal issues. However, we have also noticed that not many parents are willing to talk openly with their adolescent children about their own personal issues. Consequently, in many families there is little or no mutual self-disclosure between adolescents and their parents. Although it is easy to understand why most parents are unwilling to disclose personal information of a sensitive nature to their adolescent children, their reluctance to do this increases the likelihood that their children will similarly be reluctant to disclose to them. Many adolescents would be uncomfortable with an unequal and uni-directional self-disclosure process in which they self-disclosed to their parents but their parents did not self-disclose to them. The self-disclosure situation between peers is usually quite different. Good peer relationships are equal relationships where mutual self-disclosure is appropriate. Moreover, there is considerable evidence to support the notion that self-disclosure is important when developing friendships and establishing intimacy (Monsour, 1992; Derlega et al., 1993; Berndt, 1995 and Parks and Floyd, 1996).

The value of self-disclosure to young people is described by Buhrmester and Prager (1995). They point out that by self-disclosing young people are able to evaluate for themselves the appropriateness and correctness of their opinions, attitudes, beliefs, values, and standards, as they share their thoughts with someone else. This is clearly very important in adolescence, as during this stage in life the young person has to re-evaluate for themselves the beliefs, values, and standards, which they have inevitably learnt from their parents and others. By doing this re-evaluation they are able to reject what doesn't fit for them, accept what does, so that they can develop their own personal moral belief systems. By mutual sharing with a peer they are able to compare their own ideas with those of another person who is in the same life stage as themselves.

Mutual self-disclosure can provide an opportunity for a young person to share pent-up feelings, express them, and also to release them. Additionally, while self-disclosing the young person implicitly invites the listener to offer emotional support and advice (Cutrona et al., 1990). Self-disclosure is therefore a useful way for young people to deal with stressful issues that are troubling them.

Mutual self-disclosure when counselling adolescents

Most counsellors who work with adults believe that counsellor self-disclosure should either be strictly limited or not occur at all. However, there are exceptions to this view. For example, feminist counselling theory suggests that self-disclosure in counselling by both the client and counsellor is essential in order to be respectful, achieve equality, and minimize the power imbalance occurring between the client and counsellor. However, we ourselves generally limit the amount of self-disclosure we use when counselling adults because we believe that it is more important for us to value the client by focusing on them and their lives rather than introducing material of our own. We believe that the situation is quite different when working with adolescents, and that there are good reasons for deliberately making use of counsellor self-disclosure.

When working with young people we like to parallel normal adolescent communication processes. We believe that appropriate counsellor self-disclosure enables adolescents to feel more comfortable when self-disclosing to us. When a counsellor shares personal information with an adolescent the young person is implicitly invited to relate to the counsellor as an equal. They are likely to see the counsellor as a real person who has feelings and experiences which may have some similarity with their own. There do need to be some clear limits to counsellor self-disclosure, however. It is not appropriate or ethical for the counselling process to lead to undesirable closeness with the client and over-involvement by the counsellor.

Generally, counsellor self-disclosure should not involve talking about the counsellor's own past or present problems, unless these are both minor and resolved, and are useful for joining or are directly related to demonstrating a depth of understanding of the adolescent's situation. For example, if an adolescent is discussing their response to a recent parental separation and the pain involved in that experience, and if the counsellor has suffered a similar experience, then disclosure might be appropriate. Through such self-disclosure by the counsellor the grief experience will be normalized and the young person may be encouraged to disclose more information. Such disclosure should only occur if the counsellor's own issues relating to the relevant events have been fully resolved by the counsellor, in counselling for themselves, or in supervision. Otherwise, the counselling session might be inappropriately used to enable the counsellor to work through their own problems. The focus must always be on the client's problems.

Self-disclosure by a counsellor may help an adolescent to gain a sense of confidence, believing that it should be possible for them to come to terms with, work through and continue on their developmental journey to achieve success, just as the counsellor has done. Generally, when self-disclosing, counsellors should not describe the complete process of their experience around any significant event. It is helpful to provide only a summary which is sufficient to enable the client to recognize some similarities. Additionally, counsellors need to own, and let their young clients know, that there will inevitably be differences between the client's experiences and responses and their own. If the differences are not acknowledged, then the adolescent may believe that the counsellor is pretending to understand fully, whereas full understanding is impossible because two people's experiences will never be identical. This needs to be acknowledged. In addition, adolescents may be tempted to match their own responses inappropriately to those of the counsellor in an attempt to normalize their experience.

Validating the young person's views

Generally, but not always, young people will validate each other's points of view. By doing this their conversations become collaborative explorations rather than one-sided and argumentative. Together, they will share their beliefs, attitudes and constructs, examine these together, and quite possibly revise them. Even if we do not agree with a young person's point of view, if we can validate what they are telling us by letting them know that we understand their beliefs, attitudes and constructs, and accept them for who they are, then collaboratively we have the opportunity to help them explore, review, and revise their constructs. By letting them know that we understand their point of view, even though we may also let them know that we have a different point of view, we show them that they are valued as a person. Thus we join with them and create a genuine, open, and honest relationship, where they can feel safe in exploring their own ideas with us.

Use praise when relevant

Because of their developmental stage most young people are continually questioning themselves and their achievements. They generally use praise in a natural way when communicating with each other. Similarly, counsellors can usefully give praise and other positive feedback when appropriate. Clearly, when we do this we need to be careful to ensure that we are seen to be genuine and not patronizing.

Being direct about what we like and do not like

Most young people are very direct about what they like and what they don't like. If we are to build a useful counselling relationship with them, they need to see us as real people who are open in our communication with them about who we are. Whereas, when working with adults, most counsellors are cautious about disclosing information about their likes and dislikes, when working with young people it can be very useful to be direct in this regard. In doing this, we need to be respectful of the young person by letting them know that we accept them fully with their own likes and dislikes, even though they may be different from us.

Matching and exaggerating the other person's emotional expressions in response to story-telling

As discussed previously, young people typically match and exaggerate each other's emotional expressions when they are talking to each other about things that have happened to them or other people. As counsellors, we can learn from the lively and dynamic ways in which young people communicate. Young people generally put a great deal of energy into their conversations with their peers. We can learn from this, and ourselves be energized when we communicate with them rather than being measured in our speech and flat in our tone of conversation.

Digression

A very common feature of adolescents' conversation is that they tend to frequently digress from a topic of interest, talk about something else, and then return to the topic. Of course, some adults do the same. However, we believe that, especially for adolescents, this tendency to digress and then return to the topic of conversation serves some useful purposes. Because adolescents are continually revising their constructs, they are often trying to grapple with many differing thoughts and ideas at the same time. While a friend is talking to them, a new idea will come into their consciousness and they will want to move away from what they were listening to, or talking about, and discuss something else. Realizing that they have moved away from something which might have been of interest or importance, they may later return to that topic. By digressing they are able to deal with new thoughts without putting them on hold. A more mature person might stay on track and talk about new ideas later. However, for young people, there is an impatience to be heard and often an impulsive need to talk about their latest thought without waiting.

Digression also has a very useful function in allowing a young person to move away from something that is very troubling for them. By changing the topic they can stop talking about issues which are emotionally disturbing and instead talk about less troubling things. They may then return to talking about the emotionally troubling issues after having a period of time during which the conversation has been less intense. If they were not allowed to digress, then it is likely that they would shut down the conversation altogether to avoid talking about issues which were distressing for them.

We have noticed that when young people are talking with peers, digression is often a mutually employed process. It is usually accepted as normal behaviour rather than as inappropriate.

Using digression when counselling adolescents

Adolescents are often troubled by extremely powerful emotions as they confront new and challenging experiences. As a consequence, in a counselling situation they may at times worry about getting in touch with strong emotions, or feel overwhelmed by their emotions. At these times they can find it very helpful to be allowed to move away from talking about their troubling issues by digressing. If they know that they have the opportunity to digress when they want, they are more likely to feel safe in the counselling environment rather than finding it threatening or worrying. Additionally, they will experience something more like a peer conversation than a conversation between an adult and an adolescent. Clearly, this is likely to be more comfortable for them.

When talking about a serious issue, sometimes an adolescent will become distracted and temporarily withdraw from the counselling process. They may play with their shoes or jewellery, or look out the window at something that is happening outside. This distraction may serve the same purpose as a digression. It may allow the young person to escape from continuing to talk about an important but very troubling issue. However we also need to recognize that they may have just lost the energy and desire to continue talking, and consequently have become distracted.

When a young person becomes distracted the counsellor has an opportunity to introduce a digression and by doing so to join more closely with the young person. For example, if the young person starts to play with their shoes, the counsellor might comment on their shoes and ask about them, saying something such as, 'They're colourful; where did you get them?', or, 'I had some shoes rather like those, but mine weren't very comfortable. What are yours like?' Notice, that if the counsellor digresses in this way, the conversation will no longer involve addressing issues, but instead a low key conversation will develop which will be likely to help the young person relax. Also, the young person is likely to experience a closer connection with the counsellor through this mutual sharing and self-disclosure about something of common interest. Consequently, the climate in the counselling room will change. A friendly and relaxing conversation will take place which will enable the young person to re-gain energy, and join more effectively with the counsellor. After having such a conversation, it is easy for the counsellor to help the young person return to addressing an important issue. This can be done by using a transitional question as described in Chapter 10.

As discussed, we believe that it can be useful for a counsellor to join with an adolescent when the adolescent digresses and also useful for the counsellor to deliberately introduce digressions at appropriate times. Digressing and self-disclosing about everyday matters can considerably enhance the relationship between the counsellor and an adolescent. Don't be worried if at times a counselling session becomes an enjoyable chat about irrelevancies. When working with adolescents this is the key to establishing a good relationship.

Controlling the conversation

Many children grow up in families where they have to do as they are told much of the time. As young children they are usually not allowed to control their conversations with adults. As they grow older and enter adolescence they want to be more in control of their world. They don't want to be told when they can speak and when they can be quiet. When they talk with their friends, they expect that there will be a mutual sharing with control of the conversation moving from one person to the other and back again. In particular, they do not like being told what to talk about or when to talk about it.

Adults, particularly when talking with a professional such as a medical practitioner, often have an expectation that the professional will have a considerable amount of control over the process of the conversation. It is usually quite different when adolescents talk among themselves. They expect to be in control of the conversation rather than to be influenced either directly or indirectly into talking about specific issues.

Control of the conversation when counselling adolescents

When counselling adults, some counsellors, particularly person-centred counsellors, try to give the client control of the direction of the conversation. Even though they do this, they do adhere to a particular process in giving their responses, and in our view this process has a big influence in controlling the quality and direction of the conversation. Other counsellors, while respecting the client needs as much as they can, deliberately direct and control the counselling conversation.

We believe that when we are working with adolescents we do need to be proactive. As described in later chapters, this means that we have to take responsibility for responding to the adolescent's current emotional state by proactively introducing new direction and strategies into the counselling process as described in Chapter 8. However, while doing this we need to try to ensure that the young person is empowered to control the conversation when and as they wish.

Just as with adolescent peer conversations, a good counselling conversation with a young person involves handing control of the conversation backwards and forwards between the two participants. However, at all times, it is essential to try to ensure that the young person understands that they have *choice* about what they say and do, so that they do not feel inappropriately controlled during those times when the counsellor takes the initiative by deliberately influencing the process.

Seeking advice

Typically, when adolescents are uncertain about what to do, or what decision to make, they will talk to a peer or a number of peers, and will ask for advice. This is something that they would be less likely to do with a parent, because they want to make their own decisions without parental direction. When they ask for advice from a friend of their own age, it is unlikely that either they, or their friend, will expect that they will necessarily take the advice. This is different from parent or adult advice-giving. When adults are asked for advice and give it, they usually have an expectation the advice will be taken and feel aggrieved if it is not. In contrast, when peers seek advice they are usually just trying to get another point of view, and to draw on another person's experience. Advice-giving then, for adolescents, involves the sharing of ideas about possible solutions rather than an injunction that these solutions should be adopted. This is consistent with the notion that adolescents strive to explore constructs, discard those that don't fit and discover those that do.

Giving advice when counselling adolescents

Most counsellors who work with adults try to avoid giving advice and instead try to empower their clients to find their own solutions. It is obvious that this is also a good policy with young people, as they don't want to be told what they should do. However, it is well documented that young people generally have expectations that counsellors will give advice (Gibson-Cline, 1996). Additionally, they have expectations that counsellors have experience and knowledge which they do not have themselves.

Counsellors working with young people have an obligation to share information with them which has been gained through either education or life experience. When a young person asks for advice, we believe that, rather than declining to give it, it is better to join with the young person and offer them an invitation to explore their situation with us, so that together we might come up with a possible solution. By doing this, the young person is invited to join in a collaborative process in which there is a mutual sharing of ideas and information. Solutions can be explored, together with their consequences.

Where possible it can be useful for a counsellor to confirm that they believe that the young person's choice of a particular option seems to be a sensible one. Of course, the counsellor can only do this if they believe that the solution chosen *is* the sensible one. Additionally, the counsellor needs to be careful to make it clear that they think that it is possible that the young person might change their mind and do something different; that it is up to them to do what they believe feels right for them at the time rather than stick to a predetermined option. Giving this message is very important, as young people are continually changing their points of view. If they do not follow through on a decision made in a counselling session, they need to believe that they will not invoke the counsellor's disapproval.

10   Useful counselling micro-skills

In the previous chapter we discussed the way counsellors can make use of typical adolescent communication processes such as mutual self-disclosure and digression. We also discussed issues of control and advice-giving. In this chapter, we will discuss a variety of counselling micro-skills which, when counselling adolescents, can be used to promote change. We strongly believe that these micro-skills need to be used in a context which at some level parallels the normal adolescent communication processes as described in the previous chapter.

Counselling micro-skills commonly used with adults are also useful when counselling adolescents, but there are some important differences in the way in which they are selected and used when working with adolescents.

Many counsellors who work with adults typically make extensive use of those particular counselling micro-skills which fit with their primary theoretical frame of reference. This is sensible, even for counsellors who claim to be eclectic, because it enables them to bring some consistency and structure into the counselling process.

Counselling adolescents has different demands. By making use of a very wide range of counselling micro-skills, the counsellor can more easily engage the curiosity and interest of the young person in a changing and dynamic process. These skills can be used in a process which parallels the relatively low level of structure which is common in adolescent developmental processes. Counsellors who work with adolescents will therefore have an advantage if they have the knowledge and ability to enable them to use the widest possible range of counselling micro-skills. These need to be proactively selected at appropriate points in time to take advantage of presented opportunities in the counselling process, so that the young client becomes engaged and energized in seeking to discuss and resolve problems.

In this chapter we will describe a wide range of counselling micro-skills and, wherever relevant, will indicate how these can be of particular use when working with adolescents. The counselling micro-skills we will describe need to be used within the overall counselling process, as shown in Figure 8.2. It needs to be recognized that the micro-skills are used in the context of the primary counselling functions of relationship building, assessing the problem and addressing the problem.

Counselling micro-skills can be used either in direct response to the needs of the counselling process, or can be used in conjunction with any of the counselling strategies described in Chapters 12 to 15. Counselling micro-skills can be broadly grouped under the following headings, although there will be some overlap:

- observation
- active listening
- giving feedback
- use of questions
- challenging
- instructions
- the use of humour.

Observation

Observation can be extremely useful in contributing to the overall assessment of an adolescent's presentation. It needs to occur continually, as an ongoing activity, during each counselling session. However, when counselling adolescents, we have to be careful how we interpret our observations because they may sometimes be misleading. What a counsellor observes, when counselling an adolescent, is an external presentation which may disguise what is happening internally. This is because adolescents are uncertain about themselves and are uncertain about how open they can be if they are to continue receiving acceptance.

Because they are in a state of change, their cognitive processes are complex, and they tend to make use of their defences more quickly than most adults.

While recognizing that our observations of an adolescent may be observations of a façade hiding the real person, we need to respond to that façade as though it were the real person. By accepting and responding to the façade we demonstrate to the young person that we are accepting of what they are presenting to us. In effect, we are doing as described in Chapter 8: we are believing the adolescent. By accepting the façade we can create trust, and through that trust the adolescent is more likely to feel safe in showing us what is behind the façade. In addition, by accepting the façade, we validate the individual presentation which the adolescent wishes to show to us.

If we wanted to join with someone who only spoke a foreign language, we would need to learn that language in order to communicate effectively with them and join with them. Similarly, when counselling an adolescent, we need to learn from the young person's behavioural and verbal language. We can do this by observing their behavioural, speech and language patterns. We can then, at an appropriate level, parallel their communication processes so that, in effect, we speak the same language. By doing this we can gain the young person's trust, join with them and enter their world. When paralleling an adolescent's communication processes we need to be careful not to behave as though we ourselves were adolescents, but to use similar processes to theirs while remaining congruent and true to ourselves.

Observation can provide information about the adolescent with regard to mood, culture, self-esteem, creativity and social influences. Important attributes of the adolescent which need to be observed include:

- general appearance
- behaviour
- mood and affect
- speech and language.

General appearance

A young person's general appearance is a reflection of the way in which they wish to be seen and gives an indication of how they would like to be. It is an outward expression of the internal attempt to form a personal identity. Counsellors need to be careful about the way in which they interpret a young person's general appearance. Unfortunately, as counsellors, we all have our own personal prejudices and personal stereotypes. Consequently, a young person's appearance can seriously influence the way we feel towards and relate with them. We need to be careful that we do not over-interpret and we need to take time to get to know them so that we understand who they are and what is happening internally for them.

Imagine a young person who has tattoos and body piercing. Such a person might be aggressive and anti-social, or might be a person who is gentle, caring and vulnerable but wishes to appear to be tough and individualistic. We can't know which is true just by observing appearance.

An adolescent's appearance can tell us the extent to which they feel free to express themselves, and the extent to which they are constricted and constrained and unable to express themselves freely. Where an adolescent has put a lot of effort into presenting themselves in a particular way, they may be wanting to give the message 'Hey, take notice of me.' If this is the case, it may be extremely helpful in joining, for the counsellor to respond to the implied request, 'Take notice of me', by letting the young person know that they have noticed. This can be done by commenting on, and positively connoting, aspects of the adolescent's appearance.

Behaviour

An adolescent's behaviour can give a counsellor useful information about ways in which to match and join. For example, consider the case of a young client who is really talkative and has poor boundaries. In this case, it would be inappropriate for a counsellor to respond by being quiet and withdrawn; instead, the counsellor would need to match the conversational style of the adolescent and in this way to allow joining to occur with ease. If the counsellor were to do otherwise, the young person might receive an implied message which said 'The way you are behaving is not OK.' Similarly, consider the case of an adolescent who has poorly defined boundaries: it might be tempting for a counsellor to respond by modelling and displaying well-defined boundaries to try to get the adolescent to modify their behaviour. Unfortunately, this would be likely to undermine the joining process and alienate the client. To join, the counsellor needs to match the adolescent's behaviour while being congruent and appropriate. By doing so the behaviour is validated and the young person receives a message that this behaviour is acceptable for the counsellor. To do otherwise gives the adolescent the message that they are being judged and are not OK and are not accepted by the counsellor. Consequently, the chance of joining will be diminished.

When young people behave in ways which seem to be socially inappropriate it needs to be recognized that they may not have the skills to enable them to behave more acceptably. Although, at times during the counselling relationship, counsellors may be able to model desirable behaviours, the processes of joining and engaging demand that counsellors should to some extent modify their own behaviour, within the limits of their own personal identity, to match and satisfy the needs of the young people they seek to help. If they are unable to do this, their young clients are unlikely to be able to relate comfortably with them because they may not know how to relate differently.

Adolescents are in a process of learning how to relate in new ways as they move from childhood into adulthood. Thus it is not surprising that often their ability to use socially mature behaviour is limited. Modelling is certainly useful in helping young people to learn new behaviours but can only be effective within the context of an effective relationship.

Adolescent behaviours such as restlessness, agitation and lethargy can give a counsellor an indication of a young person's current emotional state. However, as will be discussed, some caution needs to be exercised in assessing mood from the observation of behaviour because many adolescents are skilled at hiding their true feelings.

Mood and affect

When observing adolescents we need to be clear about the difference between mood and affect. *Mood* is the internal feeling or emotion which often influences behaviour and the individual's perception of the world. *Affect* is the external emotional response (World Health Organization, 1997). The underlying mood of an adolescent may be disguised by the presenting affect. For example, it is not uncommon for young people who are suffering from an underlying emotional state of depression to present, not as depressed, but as anxious and agitated.

Consider the case of an adolescent boy whose parent has died. He may be inwardly experiencing a high level of depression and sadness, but may outwardly demonstrate hostility and anger. In such a situation, the counsellor needs to be able to go beneath the presenting affect so that the young person is able to identify, own, and experience the underlying mood. In order to do this, the counsellor needs to observe the presenting affect and deal with that fully so that, as a consequence, the client can move into a deeper level of experiencing with recognition, acceptance and ownership of the underlying mood of depression and sadness.

Often, the presenting affect will be appropriate for the young person's situation. It is, for example, understandable that a young person whose parent has died might respond angrily, even though the underlying mood is depression and sadness. By recognizing the presenting affect, the counsellor can reflect it back and also normalize it as being appropriate and normal at that stage in the adolescent's grieving process. Observation of the absence of affect is particularly important, especially where adolescents have suffered traumatic or stressful experiences. In these cases, an absence of affect might indicate that a young person is dissociating or is out of touch with reality and may be developing serious mental health problems.

Clearly, a major goal in counselling is to help the client to feel better. This means that in the long term both affect and mood need to be influenced by the counselling process. The first step in achieving this is for accurate observation to occur.

Speech and language

When observing the speech and language of adolescents, counsellors need to attend to:

- what is said
- how it is said
- the language used.

What is said   The content of what the adolescent says tells the counsellor what the young person is thinking and gives an indication of their beliefs, ideas and general constructs about their world. While listening to the client, the counsellor can gain information about the young person's intellectual functioning and thought processes. This will include information about the adolescent's ability to remember things accurately, to think logically, to use abstract thinking and to concentrate. This information is required to enable the counsellor to select suitable counselling strategies. For example, it is clearly not going to be helpful for a counsellor to use a counselling strategy which requires a high level of intellectual ability with a client who does not have that level of functioning.

How it is said   How the young person talks is also important. We need to remember that many adolescents do typically flit from subject to subject as a normal part of their communication. However, the counsellor needs to note whether the conversation has some logical sequence or is totally disjointed, with the continual introduction of unrelated ideas.

Sometimes an adolescent's conversation may be disjointed as a consequence of the young person being overwhelmed by current circumstances. In this case, the counsellor may need to help the adolescent to structure the conversation so that information is presented more clearly. Where adolescents are flitting from subject to subject between clauses, in other words where derailment is occurring with no meaningful relationship between the ideas being expressed, then the presence of severe mental health problems may be indicated.

The language used   The language used by the client gives an indication of the client's ability to be articulate and to be able to express ideas clearly. This information can be helpful in enabling the counsellor to select counselling strategies to match the client's intellectual ability. Some adolescents will use 'street language' when talking with a counsellor. This language involves the use of a vocabulary of jargon words which are commonly used by the young person's peer group. The use of these words may be meaningless or confusing for many adults, particularly as such vocabularies are subject to change with the inclusion of new words and new meanings from time to time. Counsellors working with young people need to learn the meaning of these jargon words, so that they can understand and join with the language of the client. Where a counsellor is unsure of the meaning of a particular word it is best to be honest about this and to ask the adolescent directly: 'What does that word mean – it's new to me?' It might also be useful to seek clarification of words which can have a variety of meanings in contemporary situations.

Active listening

As when counselling adults, active listening is designed to help the client to recognize that the counsellor is attending carefully to what is being said, to help the counsellor join empathically with the client and to encourage the client to continue talking. Active listening includes the following:

- non-verbal responses
- encouragers
- accenting and amplifying

- reflection of content and feelings
- matching the adolescent's language
- summarizing
- noticing what is missing.

Non-verbal responses

The counsellor's non-verbal responses are likely to give a young person an indication that the counsellor is listening, an indication of the counsellor's level of interest in what is being said, and information about the counsellor's attitude to them. Non-verbal responses include making appropriate eye contact, acknowledging what has been said by nodding or by using appropriate facial expressions, and matching the adolescent's body posture and movements.

Encouragers

To signify that the counsellor is listening and to encourage the client to continue talking, counsellors can use a range of minimal responses or encouragers such as 'ah-hm', 'mm-hm', 'yes', 'right', 'really' and 'OK'. It needs to be recognized that these responses not only indicate that the counsellor is listening attentively, but also carry meaning. They may convey indications of a counsellor's attitudes, including approval and disapproval. There are also a number of short responses such as, 'Tell me more', 'I see', 'I understand', 'Is that so?', 'I hear', and 'Go on', which can be used non-intrusively and similarly to the single-word minimal encouragers. When responding to the client, the counsellor's tone of voice and speed and volume of talking need to match the client's style and energy.

Generally, counsellors working with adults need to be careful to ensure that minimal encouragers convey a non-judgemental attitude. Many counsellors who work with adults will listen quietly and with a level of seriousness during the initial stages of counselling, and will demonstrate a fairly low level of emotional affect because they do not want to intrude on the adult's thought processes and conversation. Although, generally, counsellors working with adolescents also need to convey a non-judgemental attitude, joining with adolescents requires an emotional responsiveness which parallels adolescent communication. Adolescents tend to be more direct and open with each other about their feelings and attitudes. Counsellors therefore need to deliver minimal encouragers proactively so that the emotional energy and tone of the young person are appropriately matched. Additionally, counsellors working with adolescents may give an indication of their own attitudes, when responding minimally, where this is appropriate, and is not likely to make the client feel judged or criticized.

Accenting and amplifying

Accenting and amplifying involve a combination of verbal and non-verbal messages to feed back and emphasize what the client has said. The counsellor can do this verbally and also by using gesture, facial expression and voice intensity so that what the client has said is intensified and made newsworthy. By doing this the counsellor demonstrates positive support for what the adolescent is saying and encourages the adolescent to continue.

Accenting and amplifying are particularly important skills to use when counselling adolescents and should be used more than when counselling adults. This is because these skills enable the counsellor to validate what the adolescent is saying and also to join proactively with enthusiasm in the conversation, paralleling typical adolescent communication.

Reflection of content and feelings

Reflection of content and feelings were skills identified by Rogers (1955, 1965) as being important in counselling. Reflection of content involves reflecting back the content of what the client has just said. For example, if a young person has been talking about the way in which they have been in conflict with their brother recently, a reflection of content might be 'Your brother and you have been fighting recently', or 'You've told me that your brother and you have been fighting recently' or, 'So, your brother and you have been fighting a lot recently.' When reflecting, counsellors do not repeat what the client has said, but pick up the most important content information and, using their own words, feed this back to the client.

Reflection of feelings involves reflection of the perceived emotional affect of the client. The reflection may be as a result of things which the client has directly told the counsellor or may be the result of non-verbal behaviour by the client. For example, the counsellor may have noticed tears or a change in tone of voice. Examples of reflection of feeling are 'You're feeling sad' or 'You feel sad' or 'You're sad.' Sometimes, reflection of content and feelings are combined, as in the statement: 'You're sad because you've lost your best friend.'

When we are counselling adolescents we generally need to be careful not to over-use reflection. Instead, we need to use reflection in a limited way just to help the young person know that they are being heard and understood. The reason that we caution against the over-use of reflection when working with young people, is that they do not as a general rule use reflection in their peer conversations. If as counsellors we want to join effectively with adolescents we need to use a conversational style that is comfortable for them. Adolescents who are very verbal may be comfortable with a higher level of reflection than others. Unfortunately, many adolescents respond to reflection by sitting silently and not continuing to talk. If we are to encourage them to continue talking we need to use more proactive micro skills. As we will discuss later, there is a wide range of different types of questions which are extremely useful in raising the energy of a conversation with a young person and encouraging them to talk.

Matching the adolescent's language

There are three ways in which counsellors need to match adolescent use of language:

- the use of vocabulary
- representational style
- metaphor.

Use of adolescent vocabulary   Some adolescents make use of words from culture-specific adolescent vocabularies. They may also attribute meanings to words which are different from commonly accepted meanings. Use of such vocabularies commonly occurs with adolescents who belong to peer groups or gangs associated with particular activities. If counsellors wish to join effectively with these young people and to communicate effectively with them, they need to understand, and perhaps use, language which is familiar, natural and comfortable for them. Counsellors may therefore need to learn from their clients so that they are able to understand and communicate with them using words which have meaning for them, rather than being restricted to using words which are in general use in adult conversation.

Matching representational style   Counsellors need to match the representational style which each individual adolescent client uses to think and communicate. As described in neuro-linguistic programming, people typically think by using one of three different representational modes (Grinder and Bandler, 1976). Some people tend to think visually and conceptualize pictorially, others think verbally and frame their thoughts in terms of things which they hear, and a third group think mainly in a sensory, kinaesthetic or feeling mode. Someone who thinks in a visual mode might say 'I have difficulty seeing myself apologizing to Fred', whereas a person who thinks in an auditory mode might say 'I really can't hear myself saying sorry to Fred.' Another person might use a kinaesthetic or feeling mode, and might say 'I'd feel uncomfortable apologizing to Fred.' It is helpful if counsellors can join with their adolescent clients by using the modes of expression which they use.

Use of metaphor   Adolescents will often talk metaphorically. For example, a young person might say 'A black cloud seems to be over my head wherever I go.' In this case the metaphor of a black cloud might be being used to describe feelings of despair and depression. Where the client uses a metaphor, it is useful if the counsellor continues to use the client's metaphor. In the example quoted, the counsellor might explore the young person's feelings towards the cloud or might explore what the client believes would need to happen for them to be able to move from under the cloud into the sun. The counsellor might also refer back to the cloud at a later stage of the counselling process, thereby continuing the use of the metaphor (see Chapter 12 for a fuller discussion of the use of metaphor).

Summarizing

As with reflection of content and feelings, summarizing was identified as useful by Rogers (1955, 1965). Summarizing is very similar to reflection. When summarizing, counsellors feed back, in their own words, a brief and concise summary of what the client has said. This summary does not cover all the details of those things the client has discussed, but picks out only the most salient features.

Summarizing lets the client know that the counsellor has heard and understood, and also enables the client to clarify thoughts, identifying what is most important.

Noticing what is missing

It is not sufficient just to notice what the client has said; it is also important to notice what is missing. The counsellor needs to look for gaps and unfilled spaces in the client's story, and for evidence of conflicting information and hidden meanings. By sensitively, and without intrusion, inviting the client to explore these gaps or unfilled spaces, useful information may emerge. Through this process the adolescent may find alternatives and opportunities which are being missed. Noticing what is being missed is a concept which comes from narrative therapy (White and Epston, 1990).

We have discussed a range of skills which come under the heading 'active listening'. If the counsellor proactively introduces these skills wherever appropriate, the counselling conversation will be enhanced and the young person will be effectively engaged.

Giving feedback

As discussed, we can make use of reflection to feed back information which a young person has provided. This is one form of feedback. There are a number of other ways in which feedback can be given to adolescents.

Giving compliments

Adolescents often find themselves in situations where they are told that they have done things which they should not have done. This is inevitable, considering their lack of adult experience and their developmental need to experiment with new behaviours. Consequently, many young people expect that adults will be critical of them.

The counselling situation can provide an opportunity to give young people positive feedback to help them to feel OK about themselves. It is appropriate for counsellors to compliment adolescents on their behaviour during the counselling process where such feedback is likely to be useful. They can also be complimented for decisions which they have made or actions they have taken which demonstrate their personal growth.

Compliments need to be used sensibly or they may be seen as patronizing. Appropriately given compliments enable the adolescent to feel OK and to continue developing with confidence. Compliments given as feedback may also indicate that the counsellor has heard and understood the adolescent's story. For example, an adolescent may have been unduly provoked but may have responded with uncharacteristic control. After hearing the story, a counsellor might say 'Well done, that must have been very difficult to do.' Thus the behaviour is positively connoted and the adolescent is able to feel good about what they did.

Giving affirmations

Affirmations acknowledge and reinforce a personal truth which has been discovered by the client and shared with the counsellor. For example, an adolescent may have, in conversation, recognized that they are managing to achieve good results in a situation which is difficult for them. The counsellor might offer the affirmation, 'You are obviously coping extremely well under difficult circumstances.' Notice that in this affirmation the counsellor did not say, 'You believe that you are coping very well in difficult circumstances', but said, 'You, *are* coping very well.' This is the difference between affirmation and reflection. If the counsellor had used reflection, he would have said something like 'You *believe* that you are coping very well', which would have been a true reflection of what the adolescent had said. However, this is not very affirming and does not convey the message that the counsellor believes the client has done well.

Cheer-leading

Cheer-leading is a skill which comes from solution-focused therapy (Walter and Peller, 1992). Counsellors engage in cheer-leading when they show enthusiastic reactions of emotional support when clients relate that they have used new behaviours which are positive and different from behaviours which they have used before. Cheer-leading is based on the assumption that the adolescent has taken control and is responsible for the changes that have occurred.

Cheer-leading uses both questions and statements to encourage the adolescent to continue to describe the changing process. For example, the counsellor might ask, or say, with enthusiastic interest:

'How did you do that?'
'How did you manage to make that decision?'
'Well done. That must have been really difficult to do. How did you do it?'
'That sounds good!'
'That's amazing!'

Such counsellor responses help the young person to take responsibility for, and feel proud of, their success in achieving some change. Additionally, the client is encouraged to continue exploring the change and the process of change. This reinforces the idea that they can take responsibility for, and control, their behaviour. Such positive reinforcement is likely to help the adolescent to continue to take responsibility and control in their life, thus promoting the possibility of further change and a move towards adulthood.

Normalizing

Adolescents are in a changing world. As a consequence, they frequently become troubled by their emotions, responses and behaviours. Often these troubling emotions, responses and behaviours will be normal for the situation. Even so, at times, young people may believe that they are starting to 'go crazy', because they are experiencing high levels of emotional feelings which they have not previously experienced. In situations such as these it can be helpful for counsellors to tell adolescents that what they are experiencing is normal for the situation, if that is genuinely the case.

Sometimes adolescents may react in ways which are disappointing for them, and they may have expectations of themselves which are unrealistic. Once again, it can be useful to normalize such responses and behaviours. Clearly, normalizing needs to be done in cases where unacceptable responses and behaviours are not already minimized.

We know that when adolescents are disclosing personal information with peers, a major goal for them is to validate their own experiences by checking out whether their peers have had similar experiences (Rotenberg, 1995). Adolescents are very concerned with what they appear to be in the eyes of others, as compared with what they feel they are (Erikson, 1987). Normalizing is therefore one of the most important counselling skills when working with adolescents.

Reframing

Reframing is an idea which is particularly useful when working with adolescents. It was developed as part of neuro-linguistic programming (Bandler and Grinder, 1979). Adolescents often have a very compartmentalized view of their world and are unable to see the broader picture. This can lead to unrealistically negative perceptions at times. Reframing encourages the adolescent to consider not just the part of the picture which they have been considering, but to see their part of the picture as part of a larger picture. It is as though the young person had a frame around a small part of the whole picture and was looking at what was within the frame. By choosing a larger frame, what was in the original frame is seen in a wider context.

To illustrate reframing, consider the example of an adolescent girl who is complaining that she frequently has to look after her young nephew, whereas her twin sister never has to do this. In exploring the wider picture, it might emerge that she is allowed much more freedom than her twin sister and that she gets satisfaction out of being able to parent her young nephew more competently than his mother (an older sister). A suitable reframe might be: 'My impression is that you may be more mature than both your sisters. Even though it must be tiresome for you looking after your nephew, you seem to be proud of your ability to parent him more capably than his mother, and your parents seem to trust you by giving you more responsibility and freedom than your twin sister.' This reframe might then enable the counsellor to help the young person explore her attitude and feelings related to wider issues of freedom and responsibility inherent in moving towards adulthood.

It is essential that reframes do not discount or deny the part of the picture which was initially in focus, but incorporate this part into the wider picture. Failure to do this would invalidate the perceptions of the adolescent. The reframe must embrace the adolescent's perception, but build on that and enlarge it. The adolescent will then be able to recognize that what they have said has been believed and they may be able to accept the reframe. Reframing needs to be done tentatively so that the young person does have the opportunity to reject the reframe if it does not fit for them. Reframing can enable clients to accept negative, destructive or oppressive situations or processes by viewing them within a wider, more positive context.

Use of statements

Counsellor statements are extremely useful when counselling adolescents and can be used in a number of ways:

- Statements can be used to provide feedback when the adolescent client is carrying out an activity associated with a counselling strategy (as described in Chapters 12–15). For example, if an adolescent is having difficulty in carrying out a particular task, the counsellor might make a statement like 'You seem to be finding it difficult to choose a symbol.'
- Statements can be used to enable counsellors to feed back to adolescents observations of the counselling process. For example, a counsellor might say 'I've noticed that we seem to be going round in circles without finding a solution.'
- Statements can be used to feed back to the adolescent things that they are doing. For example, the counsellor might feed back to the adolescent: 'I noticed that your hands are clasped together really tightly.' This type of statement would be used when a Gestalt therapy strategy was being used.
- Statements can be used paradoxically and with humour to feed back and exaggerate what the young person has said so that they will then challenge the exaggeration and recognize personal strengths. For example, the counsellor might say 'So, you are absolutely hopeless and nothing you do ever succeeds. You are a total failure.' This paradoxical approach should only be used with those adolescents who have the ego strength to deal with the implied challenge and needs to involve humour or it could be damaging.

Statements are also useful for purposes which are not related to feedback such as the following:

- Statements can be used to help the counsellor clarify what might be happening to the adolescent at a particular moment. For example, a counsellor might suspect that an adolescent is really pleased with themselves as a result of something that they have done and might say 'If I were you, I would feel really pleased with myself.'
- 'I' statements can be used to model taking responsibility for feelings, thoughts and behaviours. For example, the counsellor might, instead of saying, 'People don't bother about that these days', say, 'I don't worry about that nowadays.'
- The counsellor can also use statements to structure the counselling process. For example, statements can be made about levels of confidentiality which are available.

You may have noticed that, as with active listening, there are a number of different skills that can be used when giving feedback. If these skills are proactively selected the counselling conversation can be enlivened so that the young person's interest is maintained.

Use of questions

When we are working as counsellors with adults we are careful not to over-use questions. To do so might make the counselling conversation more like an interrogation. Similarly, when working with young children we are careful not to use too many questions. This is because when young children are asked questions by adults they will more often than not respond by saying what they think the adults want to hear. We believe that counselling adolescents is very different from counselling adults or children. In a counselling setting adolescents need to be engaged so that their interest is maintained. A good way of promoting such engagement is to make use of suitable questions at appropriate times. There is a wide range of questions taken from a number of counselling therapeutic approaches which are particularly useful in helping to engage in the interest of young people. We will describe each of these, but before we do we need to consider the two important types of question.

Questions can be divided into two types: closed questions and open questions. Closed questions demand a specific response which may be very limited. An example of a closed question is 'Do you use drugs?' This question is likely to lead to the answer 'yes' or 'no' and little else. When dealing with an adolescent before joining has occurred, the answer to this question is most likely to be 'no', regardless of whether the adolescent uses drugs or not.

An open question is one which elicits a wide range of descriptive answers. For example, instead of asking the closed question 'Do you take drugs?', the counsellor might ask the question 'What do you think about taking drugs?' This requires the person being questioned to think about possible answers and to describe an attitude or belief. It is more likely to result in an open discussion than a single-word answer.

Both types of question are useful, although generally the open question is more helpful in counselling because it encourages a conversational response and makes self-disclosure more likely.

At times, closed questions can be useful, particularly when specific information is required. For example, when enquiring about an adolescent's possible intention to commit suicide, answers to closed questions might enable a counsellor to make decisions about the ongoing safety and protection of the young person. We don't see a problem in asking young people closed questions at times. Indeed, we need to remember that adolescents are often very direct in seeking information from other adolescents. It can therefore be helpful for us to model their behaviour in this regard when appropriate. However, it can be risky to ask too many closed questions at a time because, if we do, the counselling session will be almost certain to degenerate into a question-and-answer session.

There are several different types of open question which are especially useful when counselling adolescents and these will now be described.

General information-seeking questions

We commonly use general information-seeking questions in everyday conversation in order to get information. Adolescents do the same with their peers. Often, when these questions are prefaced with words that indicate the counsellor's genuine curiosity and interest, the adolescent is likely to feel important as a source of information. For example, the counsellor might say 'I'm curious about your interest in collecting comics. What kind do you enjoy the most?' or 'I don't know much about the skateboard scene. Can you fill me in?'

Questions to heighten the client's awareness

These questions are commonly used in Gestalt therapy (Clarkson, 1989). The aim of these questions is to help the client to become more fully aware of what is happening within them, either somatically or emotionally, so that they can intensify those bodily or emotional feelings, deal with them, and move on to discussing associated thoughts. Typical questions in this category are:

What are you feeling emotionally right now?

Where in your body do you experience that emotional feeling?

Can you tell me what's happening inside you right now?

What's happening inside you right now?

If an adolescent is starting to cry, the counsellor might ask 'Can you put words to your tears?' This may enable the young person to verbalize thoughts related to the internal experience. By doing this, these thoughts can be processed, the counsellor is aware of them, and can achieve empathic joining and help the client move ahead. Similarly, if a young person seems to be stuck and unable to speak, the counsellor might ask 'Can you tell me what is happening inside you right now? What are you experiencing internally?'

Circular questions

Circular questions come from the Milan Systemic Model of Family Therapy (Palazzoli et al., 1980). A circular question is a non-threatening way of getting information from an adolescent. Instead of asking the young person directly about how they feel or what that they think, or what their attitude is, the counsellor asks the adolescent how someone else feels or thinks or asks what the other person's attitude might be. For example, a counsellor might ask, 'I wonder what your brother thinks when your mother starts yelling and screaming at you?' By asking circular questions such as these, the counsellor effectively invites the adolescent to talk about someone else's feelings, thoughts, attitudes, or beliefs. This is less threatening than asking the adolescent to talk about themself. Often, having answered a circular question, the client will continue by talking about their own feelings, thoughts, attitudes or beliefs to make it clear whether they agree or disagree with the person who was mentioned in the circular question.

Transitional questions

Transitional questions are particularly useful when counselling adolescents because such questions typically occur in the everyday conversations young people have with their peers. Examples of transitional questions are:

> You talked a great deal about how your mother feels and how your stepfather feels. I'm wondering where your sister fits in?

> Earlier you talked about the option of leaving school. I'm wondering about how you're feeling about that option now?

Transitional questions can be used for the following purposes:

1   To encourage the young person to move from talking about one aspect or topic to another.
2   To encourage the young person to return to discussion of an important topic or issue.
3   To make it clear that the counsellor is an active participant in the conversation.
4   To enliven the conversation.

When using transitional questions the counsellor is proactive, having made a clear decision to be an active participant in the conversation, to introduce change and/or to enliven the interaction. It needs to be remembered that the emphasis, when working with young people, is different from that commonly used by counsellors who work with adults. With adults, greater emphasis is often placed on the need to stay with the adult's processes rather than for the counsellor to be proactively engaged as a participant. By comparison, with adolescents we need to parallel their conversation, and transitional questions are extremely useful for this purpose.

Transitional questions do need to be used with some caution. They should only be introduced at points where the young person is not likely to be deflected away from discussion of important and/or painful material.

Choice questions

Choice questions have their origin in Reality Therapy (Glasser and Wubbolding, 1995). These questions imply that the adolescent has choice about the way they think and behave. Examples of choice questions are:

What would have been a better choice for you to have made at that time?

What would you like to do now? Would you like to continue talking about this issue or would you like to leave it there for now?

What alternative ways could you respond to that?

If the same situation arises during the coming weeks what do you think you will do? (Will you do this, or will you do that?)

Such questions about the past, present or future enable the adolescent to look at the likely consequences of different behaviours. By exploring choices and consequences, the adolescent is likely to be better prepared for future situations.

The guru question

Guru questions have their origin in Gestalt Therapy (Clarkson, 1989). When using this type of question, counsellors first invite adolescents to stand aside and look at themselves from a distance, and to give themselves some advice. For example, the counsellor might say 'Imagine for a minute that you were a very wise guru and that you could give advice to someone just like you. What advice would you give them?' Guru questions are particularly useful with young people because they commonly give advice to their friends. When they are invited to take up the guru position they can often give themselves useful advice. Having heard the 'guru's' advice they can then evaluate whether or not they want to follow that advice.

Career questions

Career questions are questions which exaggerate and extrapolate beyond the young person's present behaviour. They help the adolescent to recognize that they have choice about the direction in which they are heading and that this choice might lead to extremes of lifestyle. An example of a career question is: 'What would it be like for you to make a career out of being an extremely high achiever who set an example for everybody else by giving up everything except study?' This question raises the adolescent's awareness of a path or journey along which they can progress, if they wish. It enhances the young person's ability to make choices to bring about change, at the current point in time, which might have long-term consequences.

Career questions have a level of paradoxical intent, in that, it is hoped, ensuing discussion will result in satisfying behaviours which are not extreme. We need to be careful to use these questions with discretion or they may become self-fulfilling prophecies. Consider the question: 'Would you like to continue your shop-lifting behaviour, take more risks, and move on to becoming a career criminal?' This question would be useful for some adolescents, but for others might encourage them to follow the 'suggested' career.

Externalizing questions

These questions have their origins in Narrative Therapy (White and Epston, 1990). Externalizing questions separate the problem, or central issue, from the person. By doing this, the client is able to feel that they can control their problem, or central issue, if they wish, because it is something external to them which can be controlled, rather than something inherent in them which cannot be controlled.

A good example of the use of an externalizing question relates to anger control where a counsellor might externalize the anger from the young person by saying: 'My impression is that your anger has control of you rather than you having control of it. How does your anger manage to trick you into letting it control you?'

Externalizing questions often lead to discussion about issues of control. Control issues are important for adolescents who are struggling with the desire to have more control of their lives but may be reluctant to accept responsibility for controlling their own behaviour. Externalizing questions are often followed up with exception-oriented questions to help promote change.

Exception-oriented questions

A number of useful types of question have their origin in Brief Solution Focused Therapy. These include exception-oriented questions, questions which exaggerate consequences, miracle questions, goal-oriented questions, scaling questions and questions which presuppose change (Walter and Peller, 1992).

Exception-oriented questions aim to promote change by drawing attention to times or situations where an undesirable behaviour does not occur. Examples of exception-oriented questions are:

When do you not get angry?

When do you not get into arguments with your father?

In what situations do you have control of your impatience?

Exception-oriented questions aim to help the adolescent discover that there are times and/or situations where they behave differently, and to recognize what it is that enables them to behave differently. Gaining understanding in this way allows the young person to recognize that they can take more control of their behaviour and/or their environment. By recognizing this, they may be able to make choices to bring about positive change.

Questions which exaggerate consequences

Examples of this kind of question are:

How come things aren't worse?

What stopped total disaster from occurring?

How did you avoid falling apart?

These questions can be used to help a young person recognize that they have coped extremely well under adverse situations. They are aimed at encouraging the client to view their behaviour in a positive light and discover unrecognized strengths. Such questions can be extremely useful for adolescents who are unsure about how well they are coping with life.

Miracle questions

Miracle questions are used to help the client begin to find hypothetical solutions to the problems they are experiencing. Typical miracle questions are:

If a miracle happened and the problem was solved what would you be doing differently?

If things changed miraculously, what would life be like?

This sort of question appeals to adolescents because it lets them use their imagination to explore what would be different if their situation changed for the better. As a result of thinking about ways in which things might change, they are likely to explore new ideas which might be useful in helping them to make changes.

Goal-oriented questions

Goal-oriented questions are direct questions and are similar in some ways to exception-oriented questions because they invite exploration of ways in which things could be different. They help adolescents to identify broad changes which they might like to make. In exploring how things could be different, goal-oriented questions invite the client to look ahead to the future. Examples of goal-oriented questions are:

What do you think your life would be like if you didn't get angry?

How would you know that you had resolved this problem?

Can you tell me what your life would be like, and what sort of thing you would be doing, if you were no longer feeling miserable?

If you had a particular goal which you wanted to achieve with regard to … what would it be?

How would you like things to be?

When you think about … can you identify any particular goals?

Other goal-oriented questions identify perceived restraints, which in the young person's mind interfere with their ability to achieve particular goals. They help the client to identify ways to overcome these restraints. Examples are:

What stops you from achieving your goal?

What would you need to do to achieve your goal?

Scaling questions

Scaling questions have their origin in Brief Solution Focused Therapy. Scaling questions often lead into goal-oriented questions as they are related to goals. They help the adolescent to be specific when identifying and discussing goals. Examples of scaling questions are:

On a scale of 1–10, 1 being hopelessly incompetent and 10 being really competent, where do you think you fit right now?

On the scale of 1–10, 1 being very depressed and 10 being ecstatically happy, where would you like to be in the future?

If 1 corresponded to being an honest and upright citizen, and 10 corresponded to being a hardened criminal, where would you like to be?

Scaling questions lead into goal-oriented questions. For example, the counsellor might ask: 'What will you need to do to reach this point on the scale?'

Questions which presuppose change

An example of a question which presupposes change is: 'What has been different or better since you last saw me?' This question presupposes that some change has occurred and may help adolescents to identify things which have improved, so that they can feel good. Quite often, positive change goes unnoticed. For example, although there may have been fewer arguments during the week, the adolescent might not have recognized this. By using a question which presupposes change, the counsellor can bring the change which has occurred into focus and make small changes newsworthy, so that there is a recognition that improvement has begun. Once improvement has been identified, there is an incentive to make further improvement so that significant change can occur.

Challenging

There are a number of situations where counsellors need to challenge adolescent clients. Challenging needs to be done in a way which does not offend them but invites them to question what they have said, what they believe or what they are doing. Adolescents, in their peer relationships, are usually direct in challenging each other. Similarly, counsellors need to be direct, but in a way which is not threatening to the adolescent's ego. Situations in which challenging might need to occur are as follows:

- Where the adolescent has been talking about things in a way that is confusing because what they are saying is inconsistent or contradictory.
- Where the adolescent is engaging in behaviour which is inevitably self-destructive, but they are not recognizing this.
- When the adolescent is avoiding a basic issue which appears to be troubling them.
- Where an adolescent is excessively and inappropriately locked into talking about the past or the future and is unable to focus on the present.
- When an adolescent is going around in circles by repeating the same story over and over again.
- When the young person's non-verbal behaviour does not match their verbal behaviour.
- Where undesirable processes are occurring in the relationship between the client and counsellor; for example, where dependency or transference is occurring or where a client withdraws or shows hostility, anger or some other emotion towards the counsellor.
- Where the adolescent is failing to recognize possible serious consequences of their behaviour.
- When the client is out of touch with reality with regard to a specific situation, but is not exhibiting a mental health problem.

In situations such as these counsellors may challenge their clients by sharing what they feel or are observing. A good way to challenge is to:

1 Reflect or give a brief summary of what the client has said so that the client feels heard and understood.
2 Possibly include a statement of the counsellor's own feelings at the time.
3 Make a concrete statement of what the counsellor has noticed or observed. This needs to be given without interpretation.

Examples of challenging responses are:

You have just told me that … but I'm puzzled because I've noticed that several times you have briefly talked about your relationship with your sister and then have started to talk about something quite different.

You have talked about your relationship with your mother. However I'm confused; you've told me that you care very much about your mother, but you have also said that you are deliberately planning to try to hurt her.

Instructions

When counselling adolescents, there are a number of types of instruction which can be useful. When instructions are given, they need to be given in a way which is neither patronizing nor parentified or the adolescent is likely to be alienated. During a proactive counselling process counsellors select counselling strategies, as explained in Chapter 8, to facilitate the exploration of the adolescent's issues. When using these strategies counsellors need to give instructions to implement the selected strategies and help structure the process. This means that when counselling adolescents, counsellors do at times need to be directive.

Being directive

Before starting to give direct instructions related to the use of a particular strategy, the counsellor needs to give the adolescent a choice about whether or not to engage in the strategy concerned. In addition, the young person needs to be told that they have a choice about whether or not to do as directed. If these conditions are not met the young client will be disempowered, and, if the session continues, the client–counsellor relationship will be likely to deteriorate into a parental type of relationship. Negotiation about involvement in a particular process is essential to enable the adolescent to join co-operatively with the counsellor in accepting, or choosing not to accept, particular directions.

In being directive, the counsellor needs to give clear, concise instructions such as:

Tell me how you feel now.

Tell me more.

Tell your football coach how you really feel. (in role play)

I would like you to stand over here and imagine that you are your teacher. (in role play)

Change places and be your grandmother. (in two-chair work)

Choose a symbol to represent your disappointment. (when choosing symbols)

It is important for counsellors to monitor the outcomes of their directions. If a strategy is not working, the instructions and directions being used need to be modified. This might mean that a counsellor may need to abandon a strategy at a particular point.

The use of humour

Humour can be used to lighten the conversation when working with adolescents. It is important for counsellors to be able to get in touch with their own internal adolescent and to use humour which would be appropriate for a young person. Humour can be used directly to influence change as well as to create an easier climate.

In using humour to promote change, we can make use of paradoxical interventions. Paradoxical interventions have their origins in Strategic Family Therapy (Madanes, 1981, 1984). Frankl (1973) described paradoxical intervention as a technique to enable the client to develop a sense of detachment from their neurosis by laughing at it. By suggesting what is ridiculous, an adolescent may be encouraged to think creatively about new or alternative solutions to problems. For example, if an adolescent has been expressing anxiety about needing to achieve a very high standard in assignments, the counsellor might say in a deliberately humorous way: 'Well, maybe you should read your assignments through twenty times to make sure they are OK and then show them to half a dozen friends to get them to check and make suggestions, and then revise them before you hand them in.' Clearly, this approach should only be used with students where the counsellor has confidence that a positive outcome will be achieved.

Humour in counselling should never be hostile or derogatory. Adolescents themselves use humour by teasing, mimicking or acting out. These are clearly not suitable counsellor behaviours. The successful use of humour in counselling depends on sensible choice of content, and timing, with the counsellor being sensitive to the vulnerability of the young client. What may be amusing for one individual may not be for another.

11   Promoting change in adolescents

In previous chapters we have discussed the proactive counselling approach when counselling young people. We have described the way that this approach makes use of adolescent communication processes together with counselling skills and deliberately attempts to make the counselling process relevant for young people. We have described the foundations of the proactive approach and the process used to address the primary counselling functions.

Because facilitating change in a person is central to any counselling process we think that it is important for a counsellor to understand the various mechanisms for change that may come into play when using the proactive approach with young people.

Research has shown that positive change in counselling can occur regardless of the model of counselling used (Prochaska, 1999). Further, it has been shown that the relationship between a client and counsellor is a more important factor in facilitating change than the model of counselling used. Even so, we believe that change is likely to occur more quickly and effectively if the counselling process used is one that fits for the client. In our view, the advantage of the proactive approach is that it does generally suit adolescent clients because it is compatible with their developmental stage.

What kinds of change are useful?

Human beings are often troubled by unhelpful or intrusive thoughts, by uncomfortable emotions, and by behaviours that have negative consequences for them. Central goals in counselling young people are to help them to feel better and function more adaptively so that they can lead more satisfying lives. Thus, when counselling adolescents the aim is to facilitate change in the way they think, feel, and behave.

It is obvious that there is a definite connection between a person's thoughts, emotions and behaviours. For many years counsellors, psychologists and others have had various opinions about the precise nature of the relationship between thoughts, emotions and behaviours.

Some people believe that change in cognitions (thoughts) is sufficient to produce emotional and behavioural change. Others think that changing emotional feelings will inevitably produce changes in thinking and behaving. Not surprisingly there are other people who believe that changing behaviours will produce changes in a person's thoughts and emotional feelings. Trying to determine which comes first in promoting change is rather like asking the question, 'which comes first, the chicken or the egg?'. We don't think that we need to find a definitive answer to the question, 'Should we target emotions, or thoughts or behaviours in order to produce positive change?' It seems to us that emotions, thoughts and behaviours are interdependent, so if we are able to facilitate change in any one of these attributes, the others may also change.

Consider an example

Imagine a teenage girl who starts to find her schoolwork too challenging for her. As a consequence she feels overwhelmed and starts to misbehave in class in a subconscious effort to draw her attention away from worrying about her inability to focus on her set work. Her self-esteem is affected by her lack of achievement and the negative feedback she receives about her behaviour. As a consequence, she starts to think negatively about herself, saying to herself, 'I am not good at anything.'

Changing her emotions: imagine that a counsellor was able to help her change her emotional feelings so that she did not feel overwhelmed, but instead felt as though she could cope. If this happened, what do you think the effect would be on her thoughts and behaviour? Although we can't be sure, it is possible that if she was not feeling overwhelmed she would be able to focus on her schoolwork so that her performance improved. If she could do this, her behaviour might also change as she would no longer want to misbehave in class. Additionally, because she was able to attend to her schoolwork and not get into trouble in class she might start to think more positively about herself.

Changing her thoughts: imagine that a counsellor was able to help the young girl to change her thoughts so that instead of saying, 'I am not good at anything', she could say to herself, 'I can do reasonably well at most things if I put some effort in.' Once again, we can't be sure of the outcome, but it is possible that she might also feel better and behave differently. For example, once she realized that she was capable of doing reasonably well if she tried, she might begin to put more effort into her work. Thus her behaviour would have changed. Additionally, the positive message she would now be giving herself together with the changed behaviour might help her to feel better emotionally.

Changing her behaviour: imagine that a counsellor was able to help the teenager change her behaviour so that she stopped misbehaving in class. This might have an effect on both her emotions and thoughts. Because her behaviour had changed she might start to feel better about herself and think about herself more positively.

Can you see from this example how it is sometimes possible to bring about change in emotions, thoughts and behaviours just by targeting one of these? Sometimes it may be possible to simultaneously target all three attributes, although often counsellors will begin by addressing either thoughts, or emotions or behaviours, with the goal of eventually promoting change in all three.

Facilitating emotional change

As we know, most young people come for counselling help when they are experiencing a level of emotional distress. For some, their emotions are clearly expressed, either verbally or non-verbally. For others, although they may exhibit levels of anxiety or confusion, their emotional expression is more contained. Many young people are unable to identify with clarity the emotions they are experiencing. Sometimes their emotions are so repressed that in the early stages of counselling it may be impossible for them to get in touch with them at all.

Have you noticed that when you release your emotions you tend to feel better and enter into a calmer state? Let us consider an example. Have you ever felt very sad, maybe after someone you cared about died, or as a result of a broken relationship? If you have, did you cry? If you did cry, did you feel less distraught after crying? Our experience is that when we let our emotions out we usually feel better. Thus, when we are sad, crying helps. Although we may not feel happy after crying, we are likely to feel more comfortable and be less emotionally disturbed. Similarly, if we are very angry, we may need to release our anger in some way. This may be by shouting, punching a pillow or engaging in a symbolic ritual. It is the same for young people. They are likely to feel better if they have some way of releasing their emotions. Thus, one way in which a counsellor may help a young person feel better is to help them achieve catharsis through emotional release.

A good way to help young people get in touch with their emotions is to use Rogerian reflective skills and feedback of non-verbal behaviour (see Chapter 10). If you watch a young person's non-verbal behaviour, including facial expression and tone of voice, you may be able to identify the way they are feeling emotionally and reflect that back to them. As a consequence, they may get in touch with strong emotions. It can be helpful to allow the young person to fully experience any emotions which emerge (subject to safety when dealing with clients who are very angry).

Generally, if a young person starts to cry, it is useful to allow the crying to continue until it stops naturally. Consequently emotions are released and catharsis occurs. With regard to other emotions, such as frustration, anger and despair, encourage the young person, through reflection of content and feelings, to get in touch with and talk about their emotions rather than avoid dealing with them.

Some counsellors worry when a young person cries because they are afraid that they won't stop. Generally, this is not the case. Normal human beings self-regulate and after a while will stop crying naturally. After many years working with young people, we, the authors, have never been confronted by a situation where an adolescent has not stopped crying after they have adequately expressed their emotions. Clearly, if this were to happen, a psychiatric assessment would be needed.

You might ask, 'Is emotional release sufficient in itself?' Pierce, Nichols and Du Brin (1983) in their book, *Emotional Expression in Psychotherapy*, are clear in their belief that when feelings are fully expressed they lead to new ways for clients to view themselves and their world. In other words their perception of their situation changes and they think about things differently. The authors go on to say that the new ways of thinking and viewing the world then lead to more satisfying behaviours. However, they recognize that this process does not necessarily happen automatically.

Limitations of emotional release

We ourselves believe that emotional release is an important component of the healing process, but we do not believe that it is sufficient in itself. In our experience many young people who release emotions in counselling are unable to make significant changes to their thinking and behaviour without also being invited to deal directly with their thoughts and behaviours. Unfortunately, adolescents who are unable to make changes in their thinking and behaviours are quite likely to experience problems in the future. This may be because they continue to use self-destructive thought patterns or continue to engage in unhelpful behaviours. Additionally, when new troubling situations arise, they may not have learnt how to respond cognitively and behaviourally in adaptive ways.

Another problem with relying on emotional release to help adolescents feel better is that a significant proportion of adolescents have trouble getting in touch with strong emotions in a counselling setting. As a consequence they may not be able to use the emotional release process effectively.

Counsellors need to be careful when working with young people who have a tendency to become violent. First, if they are invited to let their anger out in a counselling session they may well act out in a way which is damaging to themselves, the counsellor, or the counselling room. Second, and more importantly, encouraging them to let their anger out may be unhelpful to them as they may learn to do this inappropriately in the wider social system. It is often better to help such young people learn how to manage their anger so that they can express it in adaptive rather than maladaptive ways. Hence, for them, facilitating change in thinking and/or behaviour may be more helpful than emotional release.

Facilitating changes in thinking

If we want to help a young person change the way they think we have several options. For example we could use:

- a psycho-educational strategy (see Chapter 15)
- a symbolic or creative strategy (see Chapters 12 and 13)
- a cognitive behavioural strategy (see Chapter 14)

We will discuss the use of each of these in promoting changes in thinking, but first we need to understand the normal processes adolescents generally use to change their constructs or perceptions of the world in which they live. These processes have been described by Young et al. (1999).

Normal peer conversations are generally egalitarian and reciprocal. This is appropriate in adolescence as such relationships are consistent with young people seeking to develop their own individual selves as they strive to become autonomous. In such egalitarian relationships young people have the opportunity to review their constructs, beliefs, attitudes and opinions in a climate where they are accepted and respected. As they talk with each other they define their individual positions and, in the process of conversation, re-examine and refine their constructs, adjusting them as they share information with each other. Together with one another they can co-operatively and collaboratively challenge their own and others' constructs, review them, accept those that fit and replace those that do not. It is not surprising then that adolescents report that they rely on friends and peers as their primary referents (Boldero and Fallon, 1995). It is through interaction with each other, in the safety of mutually respectful relationships where they can discuss and explore their constructs, that young people are often able to change the way they view the world.

As counsellors who want to be effective in helping young people to change, we need to recognize the way that young people challenge and review each others' constructs. Then we can use a similar interactional style when trying to help young people change. As explained earlier, we need to establish a respectful and as far as possible egalitarian relationship. We are then in the best helping environment to facilitate change by co-operatively and collaboratively working with the young person in the process of challenging, reviewing and revising constructs. By doing this we facilitate change.

Using a psycho-educational strategy to change thinking

In Chapter 15 we discuss a number of psycho-educational strategies which can be useful in helping young people to change the way they think.

As explained previously, young people are in a stage in life where they are exploring new ideas, beliefs and constructs. Although they may resent being told what to do by adults, they do have an expectation that counsellors will be able to provide them with information and ideas which they don't have themselves. When they come to see a counsellor they legitimately expect that the counsellor will have some expertise and will be willing to share it with them. Even though generally they don't like being told what to do, they are often receptive to new information and enjoy receiving it, provided it doesn't come from parents or significant others whom they perceive as being in a power situation relative to themselves. Consequently, young people are often receptive to new ideas when they are suggested by counsellors, and these ideas may promote change.

Using a symbolic or creative strategy to change thinking

Another way to produce change in a young person's thinking is to raise their awareness sufficiently for them to gain additional insight into their situation. It is interesting to note that psychoanalytic therapists believe that raising insight produces change, and similarly Gestalt therapists believe that raising awareness produces change. There is a clear parallel between the two styles of therapy (this is not surprising because Gestalt therapy grew out of psychoanalytic therapy). We have found that the best way to help young people raise their awareness and gain insight is often by making use either of a symbolic strategy (see Chapter 12) or of a creative strategy (see Chapter 13).

Symbolic strategies can be particularly useful in cases where the issues troubling a young person are so distressing or personal that they are unable to talk about them directly. By using symbols the adolescent may be able to share their thoughts about issues which are difficult for them to discuss without talking about the issues directly. As they share their thoughts in this way changes to their thinking may occur.

Many authors draw attention to the usefulness of creative strategies in bringing about changes in thinking and perceptions. For example, Clarkson (1989) identifies the way creative processes can bring dormant insights into awareness and provide the opportunity for this awareness to be shared so that change occurs.

Using symbolic or creative strategies is often more effective than just encouraging a young person to talk about their thoughts. This is especially true for those young people who do not have a high level of verbal skills. Creative and symbolic strategies enable them to make discoveries about themselves and others, and help raise their awareness and gain insight without a heavy reliance on language. Equally, creative and symbolic strategies can be very useful for those young people who have a high level of verbal competence. This is because such strategies tend to move the young person away from talking 'about' things in a way which is personally detached, and instead help them to get more fully in touch with their inner experiences and thought processes.

Using a cognitive behavioural strategy to change thinking

As discussed previously, young people are continually revising their constructs and beliefs. Because of this, they often have beliefs which are at best unhelpful and at worst self-destructive. Often self-destructive beliefs will relate to unrealistic expectations of themselves or of others. A young person who has self-destructive beliefs can be helped if these beliefs are challenged. They can then be encouraged to find alternative beliefs which are more helpful (see Chapter 14). Usually, replacing self-destructive beliefs by more constructive beliefs will result in the person feeling better and behaving differently.

Facilitating changes in behaviour

Up to now, we have discussed ways of bringing about change by using methods which involve emotional release and changes in thinking. For some young people releasing emotions and/or changing ways of thinking is sufficient to produce behavioural change, but for others the counselling process needs to be more strongly directed towards behaviours.

When directly targeting behaviours, counsellors can make use of choice questions which are described in the next chapter. If the young person is encouraged to look at their choices with regard to different behaviours, and the consequences of these behaviours, they will often recognize that it is in their own interests to change their behaviour so that they get better outcomes for themselves.

Sometimes adolescents will be clear in expressing a desire to change their behaviour but will be experiencing difficulty in putting the desired change into practice. In such cases it may be useful to try to check out what is driving the behaviour and what rewards, either practical or psychological, are associated with the behaviour.

Consider an example. A young person might be genuinely concerned about their continuing use of illegal drugs and be clear in their own mind that they want to stop. When exploring the situation more fully, the counsellor might discover that the adolescent's best friends are drug-users and are active in trying to undermine the young person's resolve. Consequently, there is a clear reward for the young person when they continue to use drugs. By using drugs, they join more fully with their close friends. On the other hand if they stop using drugs their friendships are likely to be compromised, so there is a cost involved in changing their behaviour. Once the problem is seen in its context, it is obvious that it may not be an easy matter for the young person to make the desired change. If they are to give up their drug habit they will first have to think through the process of how to do this, and decide whether they are prepared to put this process into action or not. In order to stop using drugs they may have to confront their friends directly, or relinquish some friendships. To do this they may have to make significant changes to their social life. In such a case the client and counsellor need to work collaboratively in drawing up a plan of action. Then role plays may be needed to help the young person learn suitable communication skills which may be necessary if the plan is to succeed.

As an action plan is being put into practice there needs to be an opportunity for the client in collaboration with the counsellor to review whether or not the plan is working. When doing this, the counsellor must continue to be non-judgemental and supportive, particularly if setbacks occur. Setbacks need to be explored to determine how the plan needs to be modified to suit the needs and desires of the young person if the goal is to be achieved. When engaged in the review process it can be helpful for the counsellor to remember that the young person is doing the best they can, and may feel uncomfortable when admitting to failure.

When a young person succeeds in achieving progress they can be encouraged to give themselves a reward so that they feel good not only as a result of achieving progress but also because they can enjoy the reward.

PART THREE

COUNSELLING STRATEGIES

12   Symbolic strategies

In this chapter we will consider five symbolic strategies, using:

- metaphor
- ritual
- symbols
- sand tray
- miniature animals.

Although these strategies are all symbolic, they are not interchangeable and need to be selected having regard to the relevant primary counselling function required at the time. (Readers may wish to refer back to Figure 8.2 regarding primary counselling functions.) Figure 12.1 indicates the suitability of the symbolic strategies for achieving primary counselling functions.

The use of metaphor

A metaphor is a figure of speech containing an implied comparison: it expresses one thing in terms of something else (Meier, 1989). Rather than making a direct description of some specific aspects, situations or processes within the client's life, the metaphor provides an alternative description. It uses an alternative picture and its contents to represent the real-life picture symbolically. If an adolescent says 'I'm trapped in a maze. Every time I turn a new corner it leads to a dead end' to describe feelings of frustration and inability to find resolution of problems, the maze is a metaphor for the real-life situation. In using metaphor, there is an underlying assumption that if some aspects of the metaphor agree with reality, that other aspects will also agree. This assumption can be useful in enabling a counsellor to make use of the client's metaphor to explore the client's perceptions of their actual situation more fully.

The value of using metaphor

Many authors have discussed the usefulness of metaphor in counselling and have suggested that it can be used to achieve the following:

1   Metaphor can be used to heighten the client's *interest* and thus improve co-operation with the counselling process (Sommers-Flanagan and Sommers-Flanagan, 1996). Because adolescents are searching, exploring and looking for new ideas, many of them enjoy the use of metaphor, and become interested and excited by the creation, discussion and expansion of particular metaphors. By becoming interested in a particular metaphor they are likely to become more fully engaged in the counselling process and become joined with the counsellor in the exploration of that metaphor. Joining can be

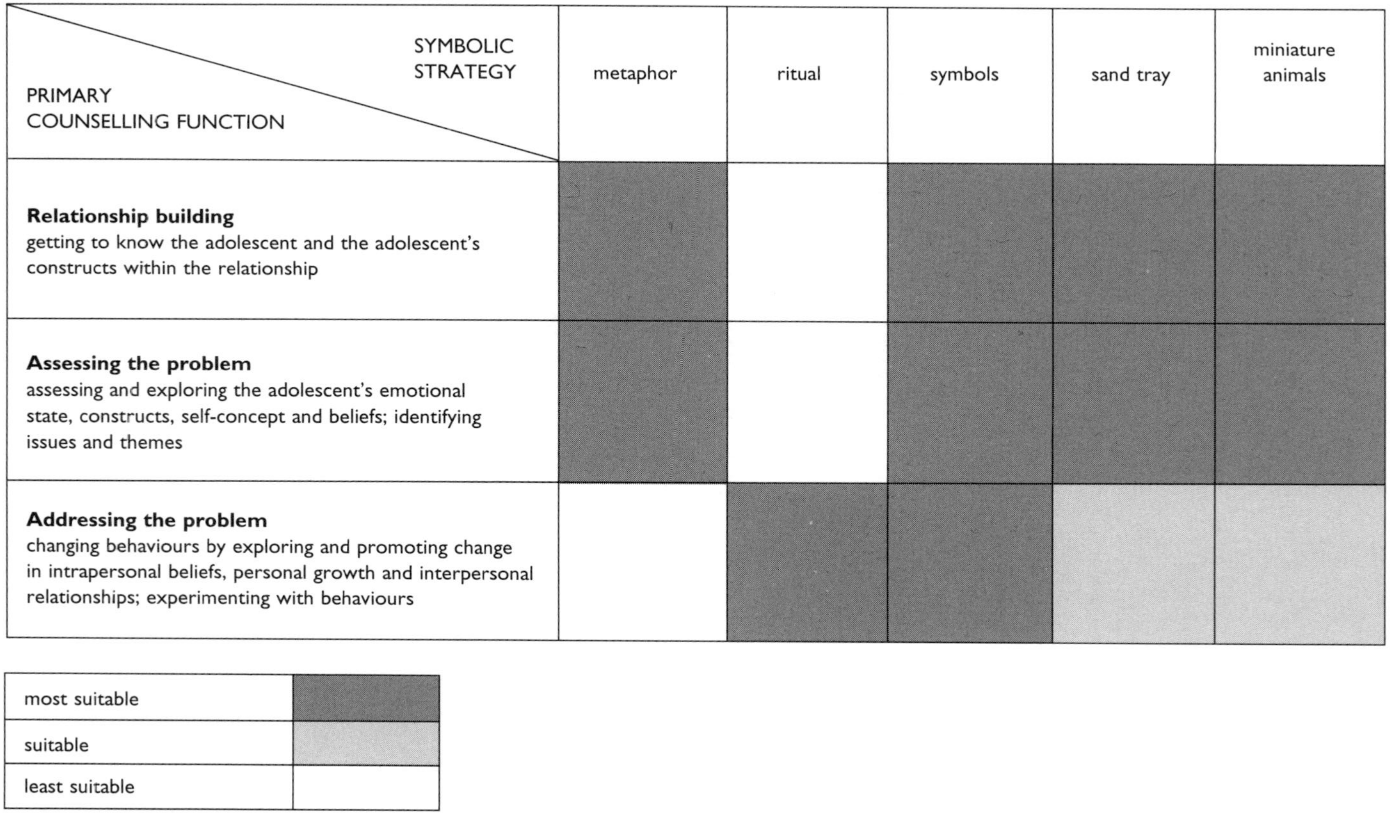

PRIMARY COUNSELLING FUNCTION \ SYMBOLIC STRATEGY	metaphor	ritual	symbols	sand tray	miniature animals
Relationship building getting to know the adolescent and the adolescent's constructs within the relationship	most suitable	least suitable	most suitable	most suitable	most suitable
Assessing the problem assessing and exploring the adolescent's emotional state, constructs, self-concept and beliefs; identifying issues and themes	most suitable	least suitable	most suitable	most suitable	most suitable
Addressing the problem changing behaviours by exploring and promoting change in intrapersonal beliefs, personal growth and interpersonal relationships; experimenting with behaviours	least suitable	most suitable	most suitable	suitable	suitable

Legend:
- most suitable
- suitable
- least suitable

Figure 12.1 *Suitability of symbolic strategies for achieving primary counselling functions*

enhanced if the counsellor matches and uses the adolescent's own metaphors and language.

2 Metaphor can be used to stimulate insight and present new constructs and paradigms for adaptive behaviour (Divinyi, 1995). By exploring a metaphor, the adolescent may more fully explore her life situation and its associated issues, beliefs and feelings, and discover aspects of her situation which had previously not been brought into awareness. Sometimes this will happen when the young person is surprised to discover unexpected similarities between the metaphor and her own situation. Thus, the use of metaphor may enhance insight and enable the young person to discover parts of herself and her own issues which were hidden in the subconscious.

3 Metaphor may be useful in providing solutions to problems. Often, young people are unable to identify solutions to their problems because their problems overwhelm them. Metaphor can be used to create an externalizing frame so that the person is separated from the problem and can exercise control over it (Peterson, 1994). By using an externalizing frame, adolescents are able to put some distance between their own selves and the painfulness and/or vulnerability associated with reality. Sometimes, a solution is then discovered within the metaphor, and this may trigger off ideas about how to provide a real-life solution.

4 Metaphor can be useful in producing behavioural change because, as discussed, solutions may be self-generated through exploration of the metaphor (Brown et al., 1996).

5 Metaphor can be used to promote significant life changes involving not only behaviour but also roles. Consider the example of a young person who describes herself as rowing a boat-load of friends down a river, while at the same time taking responsibility for steering the boat so that it does not crash into rocks. That person may discover other options, such as becoming a passenger in the boat, or taking a risk by leaving the boat and swimming to safety. As a consequence, she may see herself in a new role, as a person responsible for herself, rather than as someone who is responsible for the safety of others.

6 Sometimes, when using metaphor, the client will gain therapeutically by staying with the metaphor, without the need to make the transition consciously to discussion of real life. At other times, it will be useful if the counsellor helps the young person to relate the metaphor back to real life. For example, a counsellor might say 'I notice that you have talked about the possibility of jumping out of the boat on to dry land. What is it, in your life, that stops you from doing that?'

7 Metaphor can be used to help in the exploration of conflicts and increase empathy (Leavitt and Pill, 1995), to help in the exploration of feelings (Holland and Kipnis, 1994) and to give permission for the expression and acting out of thoughts, feelings and behaviours (Madonna and Caswell, 1991).

8 Metaphor can be used to set the scene for safe, non-threatening conversation and self-disclosure (Kingsbury, 1994). Because of this, metaphor is particularly suitable for use with adolescent clients. It provides a very non-threatening way of enabling them to talk about troubling situations and issues. Through the use of metaphor, the client is able to talk freely because, if they wish,

they are able to disown those similarities between their own life and the metaphor which may be too troubling. This makes it safer for them to commence disclosure of those things which may be difficult to discuss with someone else.

9   Metaphor can enable a person to tell her life story (Mazurova and Rozin, 1991). This is particularly relevant for counsellors. Sometimes it may be too hard initially for a young person to share her life story with a counsellor. However, they may be able to do this indirectly through the use of metaphor.

10 Metaphor can be used to help in the avoidance of resistance (Briggs, 1992). As describing life situations metaphorically is less threatening than direct disclosure, resistance is less likely to be encountered.

11 Metaphor may provide a link to other elements of the client situation (Angus, 1990). Sometimes the use of metaphor will enable the young person to recognize other aspects of their situation which initially did not seem to be important or relevant.

Ways to use metaphor

Counsellors working with adolescents can make use of metaphor in the following ways:

1   By exploring the adolescent's own metaphor.
2   By extending the adolescent's own metaphor.
3   By inventing a metaphor to describe a particular event or situation.
4   By using metaphor to tell a story.

Metaphor may also be used in conjunction with expressive arts, such as drawing, story-telling and guided imagery.

Exploring the adolescent's own metaphor   Adolescent clients often spontaneously use metaphors in their conversation. For example, a young person might say 'I've got a rocky road ahead.' Having introduced the metaphor of a rocky road to represent their expectations of future events, the counsellor now has an opportunity to take up that metaphor and use it. The counsellor can use the adolescent's own metaphor to invite the young person to describe the metaphor itself or parts of the metaphor in more detail. For example, the counsellor might ask 'Can you tell me more about that rocky road?' 'What is it like?' 'Describe it to me.' Alternatively, the counsellor might invite the young person to talk about how it would feel to be travelling down the metaphorical road. This enables the young person to get in touch with feelings which might be similar to those which will be confronted in the real-life situation, which the metaphor parallels.

Extending the adolescent's own metaphor   Using the example in the previous paragraph, a counsellor might use the metaphor by asking 'Do you think you will be able to ride your bike over this road or will you have to walk?' By asking this question, the adolescent's own metaphor can be explored further. There could be a number of outcomes from this. It may be that the adolescent will start to talk about different ways to reach her destination and this may lead to the discovery of new ways to reach real-life goals.

Inventing a metaphor to describe a particular event or situation   Sometimes it can be useful for a counsellor to invent a metaphor to describe a particular event or situation. For example, a counsellor might say 'It sounds to me as though you are walking along the edge of a cliff and are a bit worried about falling off.' The young person may then accept or reject the counsellor's metaphor. If the metaphor is rejected, the young person may replace the counsellor's metaphor by an alternative one, by saying, for example, 'Oh no, it's not like being on the edge of a cliff, it's more like trying to cross a rickety bridge over a pond.' In this case, the counsellor can explore the differences between the two metaphors, then focus on the client's metaphor.

Alternatively, the young person may agree with the counsellor's metaphor. In this case the young person is likely to develop that metaphor, and may, for example, say 'What's worse, my best friend looks as though she is going to push me over the edge of the cliff.' In this instance, the metaphor immediately connects with the adolescent's real life. Of course, the adolescent might have responded by saying 'I'm pretty good at walking around the edges of cliffs.' This would give the counsellor an opportunity to help the young person to explore strengths and the ability to cope with a difficult situation.

Using a metaphor to tell a story   This particular technique is used by narrative therapists (Hoffman, 1993). Sometimes adolescents will recount stories of their lives which suggest that they have behaviours or roles which have become pervasive. For example, an adolescent might incorporate all of the following in a description of self:

- I am the member of the family who stops my mother and father from fighting when they are intoxicated.
- I have been, and continue to be, responsible for preventing my young nephew from being abused by his mother.
- I act as peacemaker in situations when my friends and peers are in conflict.

This information suggests that the adolescent's self-perception is of a person who rescues others from unpleasant situations. The counsellor can describe the adolescent metaphorically as 'a rescuer', and can then encourage the young person to explore the possibility of using alternative metaphors (for example, 'observer', 'ostrich' or 'adviser') so that outcomes will be different.

Some narrative therapists encourage their clients to change their story or their metaphor by externalizing their problem (White, 1989). This approach encourages clients to see their problem as a separate entity, external to themselves. By externalizing the problem, clients often find it easier to loosen the restraints which stop them from changing.

The use of ritual

Rituals form a part of the lives of everyone. They are used to mark occasions, events and transitions. For example, many people help celebrate their friends' and relatives' birthdays by using rituals. Some people mark the event by buying a birthday cake, singing a song and blowing out candles. Others give presents.

Rituals have been used in ancient and contemporary cultures to mark transitions from one state to another, such as from childhood to adulthood. Examples of culture-specific rituals are the bar mitzvah in Jewish culture and initiation ceremonies in Aboriginal culture. Rites of passage involving initiation are often characterized by external 'ordeals', such as body-piercing, tattooing and recitation of passages from holy books. The externally observable ritual associated with rites of passage is paralleled by inner changes within the person which, it is hoped, enable him to get in touch with inner resources in response to the external ordeals. In such situations, young people draw on their ideas about their new roles, and get in touch with those parts of themselves which they will need when preparing for these roles. The transition involves a movement from being *what is* to becoming *something different*, and this is symbolized in the ritual.

Rituals are especially important for adolescents because they are continually in a state of transition. They mark their transitions by using rituals to demonstrate to themselves and to others that changes are taking place. For example, a young person who has had his hair shaved off may be saying to peers and adults 'I now have the choice to present myself as I wish. I am moving from being a child controlled by my parents into becoming an adult who can control his own life.' The head-shaving is therefore a ritual which demonstrates the rite of passage from childhood to adulthood.

Adolescents need to engage in rituals or they may feel constrained and unable to develop. In ancient cultures, initiates were able to get in touch with many different roles, parts of self and images, which came from their society's beliefs and cultural myths. Initiates were able to draw on these to enable the shift from one state of being to another. Unfortunately, contemporary Western society is somewhat impoverished in this regard as a consequence of the move from a multidimensional culture to an emphasis on individuality and separateness. It can therefore be useful to help adolescents get in touch with the various parts of their inner selves and to create and enact rituals to mark significant points in their journey to adulthood.

The use of ritual in counselling

Counsellors, in conjunction with their young clients, can proactively and imaginatively devise rituals for specific purposes. Such rituals can be devised to achieve catharsis and enable adolescents to move along their developmental path. For example, if a young client has been victimized and abused, they might be invited to draw a sketch of their oppressor and then burn it. The burning would enable them to act out their anger towards the person who abused them. This would allow for cathartic release and completion, and could be followed by cognitive resolution of issues.

Letter-writing can be used as a ritual. The process of putting down on paper thoughts and feelings which have not been openly expressed can often be cathartic and bring completion to troubling events. The letter does not have to be sent. Often, the ritual will be completed just in the writing of the letter.

Rituals can often be used in conjunction with symbols (see below). For example, where an adolescent needs to let go of an idea, thought, feeling or relationship, the young person might be encouraged to choose a symbol to represent the thing to be discarded. The symbol can then be ritualistically buried, disposed of in another way, or destroyed. During the ritual, the counsellor can help the young person explore their feelings and thoughts as they let go of their connection with whatever it is that the symbol represents. The main purpose of ritual is so that the young person can move on into a future which is less troubled by thoughts and feelings related to past events.

The use of symbols

Symbols for use in counselling adolescents are specific physical objects which can be used to represent feelings, thoughts, beliefs, people, relationships and a range of other things. It is useful for counsellors to have a collection of symbols available on a shelf or in a particular place in their room. Sometimes, counselling work with adolescents occurs in their own environment, and in this case anything that happens to be available can be used as a symbol.

A counsellor's own set of symbols should preferably include items which might be of interest to adolescents. These might include a rock, a piece of wood, a feather, an ornament, a toy, a miniature animal, a crystal ball, a pencil, a ball, a cushion, a candle, figurines, a box with lid, other containers and many other small articles (see p. 139 for a fuller list of symbols).

The importance of symbols

Jung (1968) believed that symbols can be helpful in uncovering unconscious material. Accessing unconscious material can be particularly useful when working with adolescents because the process of adolescent individuation involves an interaction between the unconscious and conscious self. By using symbols, a counsellor may enable an adolescent to bring unconscious material into conscious thinking, with the adolescent gaining in self-knowledge. With increased self-knowledge, the adolescent is likely to have more choice and control about how to behave and change.

Using symbols

When counselling adolescents, symbols can be used for the following purposes:

1   To help the adolescent access and disclose information consciously.
2   To enable the adolescent to get in touch with, and explore, feelings, beliefs and thoughts.
3   To represent particular alternatives so that these alternatives can be anchored for comparison.
4   To represent polarities within self so that these can be explored.
5   To represent particular people so that role-played dialogue between these people can be created.
6   To represent something of positive or negative value which may need to be discarded or dealt with in some way.

For each of the above purposes, the adolescent is first invited to select a symbol or symbols to represent whatever is relevant. Sometimes an adolescent will choose a symbol and be sure that it is the symbol they want for a particular purpose. At other times, an adolescent may find it hard to choose a symbol and may spend a considerable amount of time picking up and putting down symbols, or looking at them and thinking about them. In this case, the counsellor may choose to give feedback about the process which is occurring. For example, the counsellor might say 'You seem to be having trouble picking a symbol.' It is then likely that discussion will follow concerning the adolescent's difficulty in choosing a symbol, and this may yield useful information. It may be that the young person will say that no single symbol can satisfactorily represent the item in question. In this case, the counsellor might invite the young person to select more than one symbol to represent whatever it is that they are wanting to symbolize.

Once a symbol has been selected, the adolescent can be invited to describe the symbol and its qualities. The counsellor might say 'Tell me about this symbol', or ask 'What can you tell me about this symbol?' or 'What is this symbol like?' Notice that the questions do not ask the young person to interpret the symbol, but encourage her to describe the symbol itself. By inviting the person to describe the symbol, it is possible that qualities of the symbol may be identified which relate to whatever the symbol represents, but which surprise the young person because they had not previously been recognized. These qualities and related ideas may have been previously suppressed in the subconscious. Thus, previously inaccessible subconscious ideas may be drawn out through discussion of the symbol and made accessible.

As well as discussing the symbol as described, the counsellor can focus on the 'here and now' experience involved in choosing and describing the symbol. For example, the counsellor might ask 'What are you feeling emotionally as you pick up that symbol?', 'What thoughts do you have as you experience that emotion?' and 'Can you tell me what's happening inside you (or what you are experiencing emotionally) as you describe the symbol?' Thus, the experience of choosing a symbol and describing the symbol provides an opportunity for the adolescent to examine and explore their current feelings and responses related to the tasks of choosing and describing the symbol. This Gestalt 'here-and-now' approach may enable the adolescent to get in touch with important unconscious and conscious feelings and thoughts. In addition, the counsellor might provide feedback statements about the adolescent's behaviour. For example, the counsellor might say, 'I notice that as you are talking about your symbol, you are becoming more excited.' Throughout the process, the symbol remains important because of what it represents and the increased awareness that it engenders. When a symbol is an externalized part of the adolescent it needs to be treated sensitively and with respect for the young person's vulnerability.

Using symbols to access and disclose information   When a counsellor notices that an adolescent is having difficulty talking about a situation, event or experience, then it may be appropriate for the counsellor to invite the adolescent to choose a symbol to represent whatever is under discussion. For example, imagine a client who is having difficulty talking about what it is like at meal times at home. A counsellor might say 'Choose a symbol to represent what it is like in your house at meal times.' When the adolescent begins to describe features and characteristics of the symbol it is possible that they will also be able to get in touch with, and disclose, information that had been blocked from consciousness.

Using symbols to get in touch with and explore feelings, beliefs and thoughts
Sometimes it can be useful to ask an adolescent to choose a symbol to represent a particular feeling, belief or thought. By selecting the symbol, the counsellor is then able to invite the young person to describe the symbol fully. In this discussion it is likely that additional information will emerge about the adolescent's internal responses to whatever it is that the symbol represents. The adolescent can also be invited to talk to the symbol, and to tell the symbol anything they might wish to say.

Imagine, as an example, that an adolescent picks a symbol to represent resentment which they have towards a particular person. That resentment might be annoying the adolescent by troubling them continuously. After representing the resentment by a symbol, the adolescent might be able to express anger towards the resentment and to tell it to go away. The adolescent could then be invited to reply as the resentment. The counsellor might say 'I want you to imagine that you are the resentment represented by that symbol and to reply to what has just been said to it.' Thus a dialogue is created between the young person and their resentment which might enable them to deal with the troubling feeling. Externalizing a feeling in this way can empower an adolescent to take control of a feeling and its troubling intrusions.

Using symbols to anchor alternatives for comparison   Often adolescents are confused about various alternatives or choices available to them. In such a case, the adolescent can be invited to choose symbols to represent each of the available choices. The selected symbols can be processed by inviting the client to describe each symbol. Then the counsellor can give the instruction, 'Arrange the symbols you have chosen in this space here [counsellor indicates a space] to indicate the way in which they relate to each other.' By inviting the adolescent to do this, it may be that two alternatives which are similar are placed together and a third option which is quite different is placed a long way away. Discussion of the arrangement of symbols can thus be useful in raising the young person's awareness with regard to available choices.

The adolescent can next be invited to touch one of the symbols and to continue touching it while talking about it and describing the advantages and disadvantages associated with the alternative which it represents. By touching the symbol while talking about it, the young person anchors ideas related to that symbol on to the symbol. By moving from touching one symbol and talking about it to doing the same with another, the adolescent is able to get in touch with the positives and negatives associated with each alternative.

Sometimes it can be useful for the adolescent to create a dialogue between alternatives. To do this the adolescent needs to be instructed to touch one symbol while arguing for the alternative it represents. The young person can then touch another symbol, representing a different alternative, and argue for that. As this process continues, the adolescent may decide to move the symbols so that their relative positions change as levels of preference emerge. The visual image the adolescent gets from observing the placement of symbols is helpful as it externalizes the conscious and unconscious ideas that the adolescent has, representing them symbolically in concrete form. The method described above, using symbols, should be compared with the selection of choices by using cushions, as described in Chapter 13.

Using symbols to represent polarities within self   Symbols can also be used to represent polarities within the self. While adolescents strive for personal identity and individuation, it can be liberating for them to realize that within themselves there exist opposites. For example, adolescents, like adults, have the potential to be kind or cruel, to love and to hate, to be generous and mean. We all have these characteristics within us. To accept that these polarities exist can be a relief to a young person and may allow them greater freedom to choose, and take control of, how they behave.

Where a client is troubled by uncertainty about such polarities, it can be useful for a counsellor to invite the client to select symbols to represent each of the polarities in question, and then engage in a similar process to that used when exploring alternatives. Through this exploration the adolescent may be able to integrate the two polarities and recognize that it is possible to move along the continuum joining them, and to take up a specific position on that continuum at any particular point in time. For example, on the generous–mean continuum, an adolescent may decide to be fairly, but not overly, generous in a specific situation, and to be mean in another situation. Thus, the young person is empowered and able decisively to take control of her behaviour, rather than being constrained by rigid thinking introjected from external sources. As with using symbols to select alternatives, this technique, and the technique described below, need to be compared with the psychodramatic technique where dialogue is created between cushions (see Chapter 13).

Using symbols to represent people so that role-played dialogue can be created   Symbols can similarly be used to create dialogue between a symbol representing the adolescent client and symbols representing other people. When doing this, it is important for the young person to anchor what is being said in the dialogue by touching the relevant symbol while talking on behalf of the person it represents. This technique is particularly useful when a young person is troubled by relationship problems with others. In this situation it may provide insight into the adolescent's own issues as well as some understanding of other people's responses to them.

Using symbols to represent something which may need to be discarded   This has been discussed in the section on the use of ritual.

The use of a sand tray

Sand-tray work has traditionally been used with children, but can be extremely useful when working with adolescents (and even when working with some adults). When using the sand tray, we need to remember that adolescents are moving out of childhood, so it is important to reassure them that sand-tray work is not childish but is a technique which is used by some counsellors with adults. With some young people it may be useful to describe the history of sand-tray work briefly. Sand-tray work was initially developed by Margaret Lowenfeld (1967). She worked with children by using symbols in a sand tray to encourage non-verbal expression which was less influenced by rational thinking. She collected small objects, coloured sticks and shapes of paper, metal and clay and kept them in what her young patients called her 'Wonder box' (Ryce-Menuhin, 1992). This approach grew out of Lowenfeld's desire to find a way to help children to talk without the use of language.

Dora Kalff moved on from Lowenfeld's work to create a framework within which to work with adolescents and adults. She discovered that more could be gained through the use of symbolic representation in the sand tray than through talking directly. Kalff believed that sand-tray work gave the counsellor and client a non-verbal image which could represent meanings which were not yet known or fully grasped by either the client or the counsellor (Ryce-Menuhin, 1992). Thus, when counselling adolescents, these non-verbal images can be explored as the adolescent places symbols in the sand tray. The adolescent can be invited to discuss the arrangement of the symbols and their relationship to each other. This differs from work with children because, when working with adolescents, the counsellor does not usually intend to help them talk without language. Instead, the counsellor uses the sand tray to help adolescents to think by visually observing concrete symbolic representations of their ideas in the tray, so that these can be put into language.

Equipment and materials

You will need a sand tray which is an open box. A large tray is preferable so that there is space for different environments within the tray. The tray must be rectangular so that there are corners to symbolize places of safety or entrapment. A square tray with sides measuring about 0.75 m and about 150 mm high would be suitable. The depth of sand in the tray should be about 75 mm, giving a 75-mm space between the surface of the sand and the top edge of the tray when the sand is spread evenly.

Symbols to be used in the sand tray consist of a variety of small objects which are chosen because they have properties which enable them easily to assume symbolic meaning. Items such as the following are useful:

- rocks, shells, stones and pieces of wood
- small boxes and containers with lids
- ornaments
- beads
- padlocks and keys
- toy fences, vehicles, animals, trees
- small figurines.

There are really no restrictions on the types of article which can be used as symbols. Some symbols may be better for representing abstract ideas; for example, symbols such as feathers or crystal balls.

Reasons for using the sand tray

As counsellors of adolescents, we need to remember the importance of keeping the young person interested and engaged in the counselling process. Most adolescents enjoy trying out new ways of expressing themselves. Using the sand tray provides a novel way for them to do this.

When using the sand tray some adolescents enjoy getting back in touch with their childhood experiences and happily regress into childlike behaviours. However, for most adolescents, the use of the sand tray involves very different behaviour from this as it presents an interesting challenge for them. They will work in a very mature and early adult way in setting up and processing the contents of the tray. Generally, with adolescents, the sand tray can be used to help the young person:

- tell their story
- explore feelings, thoughts, situations and issues relating to their story
- explore past, present and future situations and events
- gain a cognitive understanding of the elements or events occurring in their life.

Using the sand tray

A good way to start is by inviting the adolescent to choose and use any symbols they wish to make a scene or picture in the sand to represent the life events or story which they wish to describe. Sometimes an adolescent will start to tell the story without initially selecting any symbols. In this case the counsellor can interrupt and say, 'OK, you've just told me that you were riding your bike over to your mate's place. Would you like to put a symbol in the sand to represent your bike and another one to represent your mate's place?' In this way the adolescent is encouraged to symbolize the story as it is told.

Some adolescents will spontaneously describe the story they are telling, as it develops in the sand tray. Other adolescents may start to build a picture, by placing symbols in the sand, without speaking. The counsellor then has a choice and can either just observe until the picture is complete, or can ask the adolescent to describe the story as it is created. The counsellor might say, 'Would you like to talk about what you are doing as you build your picture?' However, while the picture is being constructed, it is important to observe the process carefully and to allow it to develop without unnecessary interpretation or intrusion. Some adolescents may prefer to complete their work before discussing their picture. With other young people, counselling skills may be used to help process information, feelings and issues related to the picture, as the picture develops. Once the picture is complete, it needs to be fully processed by using counselling skills.

In processing a sand-tray picture it is important not to go beyond the meaning that is understood and used by the adolescent in connection with either the symbols or the picture. Feedback of observations about the placement of symbols in relation to each other is particularly useful when processing sand-tray work. For example, a counsellor might say, 'I notice that your story has developed in this corner of the sand tray. Can you tell me what happens in the rest of the space?' In this way the counsellor can explore absences or omissions in the adolescent's picture as these may have significant relevance to the adolescent's story. Additionally, reflective skills are of value when responding to thoughts and feelings expressed by the client.

The purpose of sand-tray work is to encourage disclosure of material that will help adolescents gain a greater understanding of themselves and of their current life situations. With this disclosure, and with heightened awareness of their situation, comes growth and the opportunity to feel empowered, make choices and have control over the direction of their lives. Readers who wish to learn more about sand-tray work may wish to read Ryce-Menuhin (1992) or Mitchell and Friedman (1994).

The use of miniature animals

This technique has a high level of appeal to most adolescents. If it is introduced casually, but with enthusiasm, it can be very useful for initial ice-breaking and joining. When adolescents are invited to use this technique, they become engaged in a task which may be treated light-heartedly or with seriousness. Often, when they start using a light-hearted approach, important information of a serious nature will emerge, with the young person becoming actively engaged in the counselling process. The technique involves the use of miniature animals which are used as symbols to represent people in the client's family or social system. It is a projective technique which focuses specifically on exploring the interpersonal relationships of the adolescent.

The advantages of using a projective technique

There are considerable advantages in using projective techniques with adolescents:

1   Clark (1995) points out that projective techniques enhance the client–counsellor relationship, help in the understanding of the client and can be useful in clarifying goals and determining the course of counselling.
2   Reyes (1994) talks about the usefulness of symbols in shifting the perspective of a counselling conversation from an outside-in to an inside-out perspective. Using an outside-in perspective, the client and counsellor try to look from the outside at what is happening within the client, whereas, by using an inside-out perspective, the client reveals through projection what is happening inside, so that it can be outwardly observed.
3   Waiswol (1995) points out that not only do projective methods facilitate communication, but they also allow for the overcoming of inhibitions, in effect bypassing resistance.
4   Projective techniques are less threatening for the young person because of the indirect way in which they access personal information.

The use of miniature animals allows sensitive material to be discussed in relation to the symbols used, rather than in direct relation to the young person's real-life situation. The adolescent is, during this process, able to compare information related to the symbols, with real life, selecting what fits and rejecting what does not fit and what is too painful or risky to own. By using this technique, we believe that we often identify important things which need to be addressed in the adolescent's life which may not have been disclosed using other strategies.

In this technique the adolescent projects ideas from her family, peer group or other social system on to the miniature animals which are used as symbols, but has the freedom to exaggerate or modify these projections. The young person may access ideas and beliefs which have been suppressed into the unconscious because of fears about the consequences of recognizing and/or owning those ideas and beliefs. Additionally, the method allows the adolescent to attribute characteristics and behaviours to the symbols which the adolescent might initially be unable to own with regard to the real-life situation. In so doing, the adolescent is likely to make important discoveries about relationships within her social environment and to take advantage of the opportunity to talk about them.

Materials

A variety of small toy animals and other creatures, such as the following, are used in this technique:

- domestic animals
- farm animals
- jungle animals
- zoo animals
- dinosaurs
- reptiles
- insects
- sea creatures.

The animals and other creatures should preferably be made of plastic, and be as representational as possible of those animals. The appearance and nature of the animals will suggest particular behavioural and personality characteristics for them, enabling the adolescent to choose particular animals to represent particular people. This can occur more easily if the miniature animals look realistic, rather than being caricatures of animals.

Method

The method involves four well-defined stages:

1 Choosing animals.
2 Arranging the animals in a picture.
3 Exploring various configurations.
4 Rearranging the animals so that they are comfortable.

By using this structured process, the work moves from initial engagement through to active exploration of relationships, and then to satisfying closure involving processing of the projective work so that use can be made of the information disclosed.

Choosing animals   The counsellor begins by inviting the adolescent to choose an animal to represent themself. The counsellor will do this by saying 'Choose the animal that is most like you.' The wording of this instruction is critical. The aim is to encourage the adolescent to choose an animal that is most truly representative of themselves, rather than the animal that they would most like to be.

Once the animal is chosen, the counsellor encourages the adolescent to describe the characteristics of the animal which they have chosen as most like them. The counsellor might say 'What is this animal like?' or 'What can you tell me about this lion [or whatever animal the adolescent has chosen]?' It is often useful for the counsellor to follow up the adolescent's response to such questions by asking the adolescent to elaborate on their description. The counsellor might say 'Tell me more.' Finally, the counsellor might elicit more detailed information by asking the question 'Is there anything else you can tell me about this animal?' These supplementary questions often bring out significantly more useful information as these questions encourage the young person to think more deeply about the animal's characteristics. Often, when they do this, they will discover characteristics of themselves that have not been previously recognized.

Once the adolescent has chosen an animal to represent themself, they are invited to choose animals to represent other people in their social system. The counsellor might say, 'Choose an animal that is most like your mother/father/brother [and so on].' As each animal is chosen, the counsellor will invite discussion of that animal, using the same questions as were used when the animal chosen to represent the adolescent was discussed.

Arranging the animals in a picture   The counsellor then invites the adolescent to arrange all the animals in a picture. This is not unlike the process used in family sculpting in family therapy. Once the adolescent has arranged the animals in the picture the counsellor can use statements to feed back to the adolescent what they notice about the arrangement. The counsellor might say, 'I notice that the giraffe is a long way away from the lion', or 'All the animals are in a circle.' These feedback statements are likely to encourage the adolescent to explain the reasons why the animals have been positioned as they have.

Exploring various configurations   In this stage, the counsellor instructs the adolescent to move the animals into different positions. For example, the counsellor might say 'Move the lion so that it is facing the zebra' or 'Put the monkey next to the elephant.' Each time the adolescent moves an animal, the counsellor can make use of circular questions to invite the client to explore the emotional responses of the animals to the changes in position. For example, the counsellor might ask, 'How does the rabbit feel with the dinosaur standing close to it?' or 'How does the elephant feel when he sees the rabbit and the dinosaur together?' Throughout the process, the counsellor continues to give the adolescent feedback by making statements of observations of the arrangement of the animals. Through this process, the counsellor can explore various configurations of closeness and distance between animals, and can help the client to think about and discuss alliances, alignments, absences and hierarchical structures within the animal group.

During this process, and throughout the use of the miniature animals, it is important for the counsellor to maintain the projective nature of the technique. The counsellor does this by referring to 'that animal' or using its name (for example, 'the lion'). The counsellor does not call an animal by the name of the person it represents and does not imply that the animal is that person. Referring to the animal as 'that animal', or by its name, allows the adolescent to distance themself from the chosen animal, so that although it represents the adolescent or a member of their family in some way, it is not the same as they are. The adolescent can then project qualities, characteristics and behaviours on to the animal with safety. The animal, and not the person represented, becomes the owner of negative, positive, acceptable and unacceptable attributes. This enables the adolescent to feel freer in attributing negative and undesirable behaviours which they may recognize in themselves and others but may not be ready to own.

To enable the adolescent to stay connected with the projective process, it is also advisable for the counsellor never to touch or move the animals. Instead, the counsellor instructs the adolescent to move the animals during the process, and observes how the adolescent touches and moves the animals. By using this approach, valuable information may be observed which can then be fed back to the adolescent. For example, the counsellor might say 'I noticed that when you moved the rabbit near the dinosaur, you hesitated and eventually moved the rabbit a little further away.' The feedback of this observation might help the young person recognize suppressed information about the relevant relationships.

Rearranging the animals so that they are comfortable   Finally, the counsellor will terminate the projective process by inviting the adolescent to arrange the animals in a new picture so that they all feel comfortable. This allows the adolescent to close the process in a way which, it is hoped, leaves them feeling comfortable. There are usually differences between the termination picture and the initial picture. Sometimes it can be useful to explore the differences between these pictures. This may help bring into focus internal processes which may have taken place, during the work with the animals, in the adolescent's perceptions of the interpersonal relationships concerned.

In summary

Symbolic techniques are particularly suitable for adolescents, as many are restless and like to do things that maintain their interest and concentration. Symbolic techniques particularly appeal to them because they involve choice of visual objects as symbols and also activity in the use of those symbols. Consequently, it is easy to keep the adolescent engaged, interested and enthusiastic with regard to the counselling process.

Using symbols also challenges the adolescent's new-found cognitive skills of abstraction and the use of imagery. It helps the adolescent to disclose material that may otherwise be inaccessible or difficult for the adolescent to talk about. Working with symbols, however, will not suit all adolescents. The counsellor therefore needs to be proactive in deliberately and actively selecting the appropriate strategy for each adolescent.

13   Creative strategies

Adolescents are in a phase of their lives where they are experimenting with new and complex cognitions. They are able to think more abstractly than before and consequently are generally able to understand and use symbols, metaphors and other forms of creative representation. Many adolescents use artistic methods to express themselves and convey meaning about their lives to others. For example, young people are often seen sketching and/or using graffiti to express themselves, release emotions and convey messages to other people. In this chapter we will discuss a number of creative strategies under the following headings:

- art
- role play
- journals
- relaxation
- imagination
- dream work.

These creative strategies are particularly appealing to adolescents because they involve activities which are interesting and dynamic. Each type of creative strategy is suitable for achieving particular primary counselling functions, as illustrated in Figure 13.1. This figure can be used as a guide when selecting suitable strategies.

Counsellors need to be sensitive to an adolescent's personal preference when selecting creative strategies. Some adolescents will readily engage in art or drawing activities, whereas others will feel threatened. Similarly, some adolescents will feel relaxed and comfortable when writing or using journals, whereas

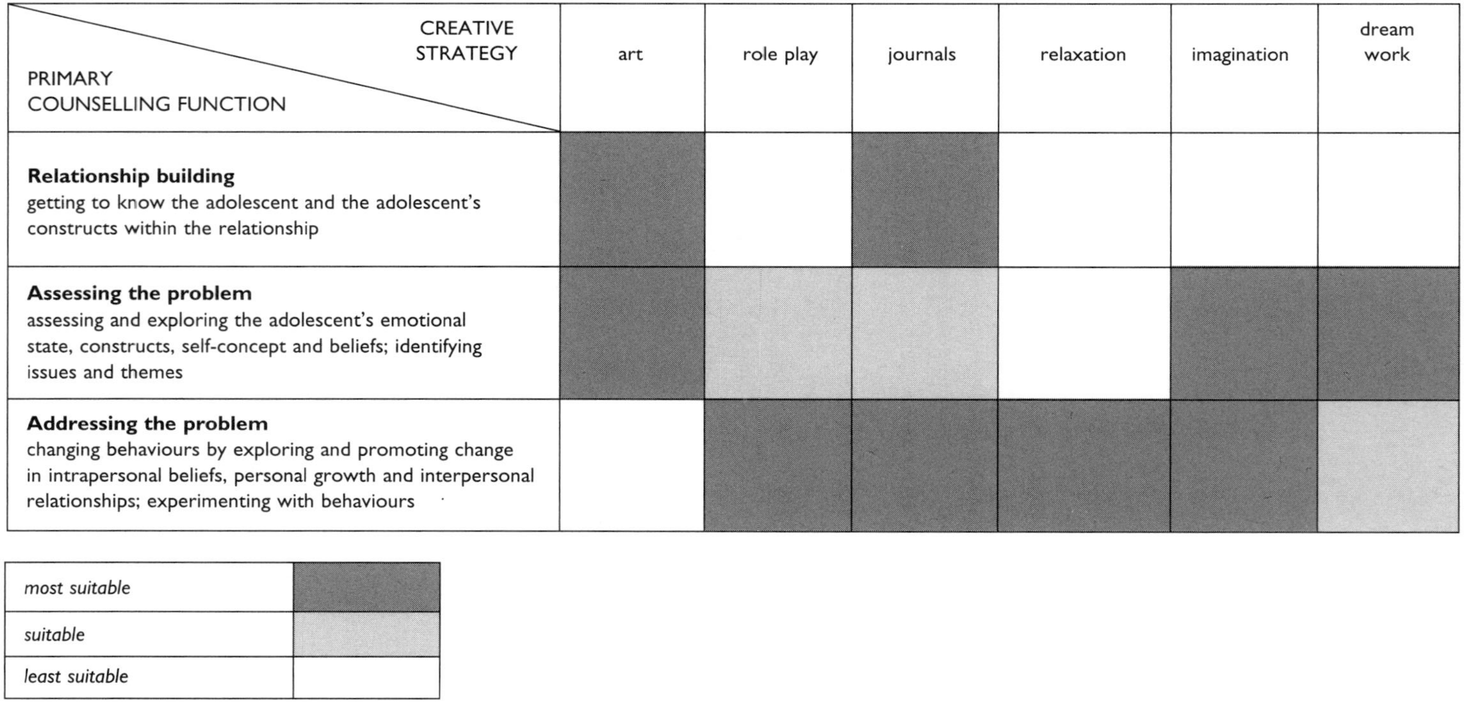

PRIMARY COUNSELLING FUNCTION \ CREATIVE STRATEGY	art	role play	journals	relaxation	imagination	dream work
Relationship building getting to know the adolescent and the adolescent's constructs within the relationship	most suitable	least suitable	most suitable	least suitable	least suitable	least suitable
Assessing the problem assessing and exploring the adolescent's emotional state, constructs, self-concept and beliefs; identifying issues and themes	most suitable	suitable	suitable	least suitable	most suitable	most suitable
Addressing the problem changing behaviours by exploring and promoting change in intrapersonal beliefs, personal growth and interpersonal relationships; experimenting with behaviours	least suitable	most suitable	most suitable	most suitable	most suitable	suitable

most suitable
suitable
least suitable

Figure 13.1   *Suitability of creative strategies for achieving primary counselling functions*

others will not. Role play and drama may be threatening for some adolescents, who may fear embarrassment and exposure, whereas others will enjoy the dynamic and energized processes involved.

Art

Visual arts are non-threatening for most adolescents and provide a way for them to express innermost thoughts, feelings and ideas. Drawing a picture can enable young people to externalize thoughts or feelings, by placing them in a picture, so that they can be observed as separate from themselves. Doing this is generally less threatening than owning painful thoughts and feelings directly. There is safety in the use of a picture, provided that interpretation of the picture is done by the young person so that they have control over what they choose to disclose.

Art can be used in counselling to:

- understand current issues and problems
- explore feelings
- develop insight.

There are many different ways of achieving these purposes by using visual art. We have selected, and will describe, a few methods which we have found to be useful in our work with adolescents.

We recognize that some art therapists hold strong beliefs about their ability to be interpretative when using art in counselling. However, we prefer to leave interpretation to our young clients. We believe that it is true that the presence of some commonly identifiable features in works of visual art may be an indication of particular issues or psychological problems. However, we believe that, generally, it is unwise for counsellors to attempt to be interpretative. It is better for them to invite their adolescent clients to interpret their own work and to disclose whatever meanings are relevant for them and safe for them to disclose. If we become interpreters of our clients' work, we run the risk of contaminating their work through projection on to their work of our own ideas, beliefs, feelings and issues.

Use of art to understand current issues and problems

Three ways to use art to help a young person to understand their current issues and problems are:

1   The use of free drawing.
2   The use of a family picture.
3   The use of shapes, lines and colours.

The use of free drawing   In the course of getting to know an adolescent a counsellor might discover that the adolescent has an interest in drawing and/or art. The young person's own art work may be a valuable source of information concerning their current issues and problems. It can be useful for a counsellor to invite an adolescent to bring art work, such as drawings and paintings, to a counselling session. The young person can then be invited to talk about their art and to share the feelings, thoughts, ideas and beliefs associated with it and the responses which it evokes. The counsellor may then be able to give the adolescent positive feedback with regard to their talents and skills and affirm their ability to use art as a means of personal expression.

Art allows the adolescent to make strong statements which may be either socially acceptable or unacceptable. Currently, in Western society, there is considerable emphasis in the media, which targets the adolescent population, on violence, surrealism, sadistic and cruel themes, domination and Satanic and other undesirable rituals and practices. The covers of compact disks, videos and magazines, which target adolescents, often reflect negative and socially unacceptable practices. The same is true of some advertisements. Adolescents are likely to reflect this current cultural bias in their own art work. As counsellors, we need to recognize the cultural influences at work in our society so that we do not incorrectly impose sinister or dysfunctional interpretations on our young clients' work. Instead, we need to invite our adolescent clients to explain the meaning of their work.

A useful way for a counsellor to begin to process a drawing or painting is to ask 'Can you tell me about your drawing?' This might be followed up by the question 'Can you tell me more?' The second question may seem unnecessary, but is often extremely useful because it encourages the young person to think more deeply. As a consequence, important information may emerge. It can be useful for counsellors to give concrete feedback, without interpretation, about attributes or features which they notice in a drawing or painting. For example, a counsellor might say 'I notice that this section of your picture is brightly coloured', or 'There is a lot of detail in this shape.' Such non-interpretative feedback will often result in a young person getting more fully in touch with feelings, meanings and ideas which are being expressed through her art.

If a drawing (or painting) contains pictures of figures or people it can be useful for a counsellor to invite the adolescent to imagine that they are a person or figure within the picture. The counsellor might say 'Imagine that you are this monster. What are you like? Describe yourself to me.' A Gestalt therapy technique can then be used to invite the young person to continue imagining that they are the monster and, as the monster, to say something to another creature or part of the picture. For example, a counsellor might say, 'As the monster, what would you like to say to the baby [or the clock] in the picture?' This might be followed up by asking, 'As the baby [or the clock], what would you like to say in reply?' Thus, a dialogue can be created between various parts of the picture, enabling the young person to enter, in their imagination, into the underlying story. By doing this, they are likely to discover feelings and issues related to the story. Sometimes, when a picture is processed in this way, information may emerge which the young person spontaneously relates to their own life and issues. When this does not occur, the counsellor might ask questions such as, 'Does this fit with anything that is happening in your life at the moment?' or 'Do you ever feel that way?' By asking these questions, information about the current issues relevant for the adolescent may emerge.

The use of a family picture   Inviting an adolescent to draw a family picture helps her to explore current family relationship issues and talk about them. There are two different ways of drawing a family picture: either a traditional representational picture of the family can be drawn, or the family can be depicted in an abstract picture, where shapes, colour and symbols are used to represent family members. Having provided coloured felt pens and paper, a counsellor might say, 'Draw a picture of your family.' In response, some adolescents will ask questions about the type of picture required, in which case the counsellor might say, 'When you think of your family what comes to mind?' and 'Just draw your family as you picture it.'

Sometimes a counsellor might ask an adolescent to use symbols, lines, shapes and colours to draw a picture of their family. The counsellor might say, 'Draw a picture of your family using just lines, shapes and colours but nothing real', or 'Draw a picture of your family and use symbols to represent each member of your family.' Some adolescents may have difficulty understanding a request to use symbols in their drawing, and for them it can be useful to give examples of the use of symbols. For example, a member of the family could be drawn as a soft, cuddly cushion if that fitted her personality and behaviour, or a member of the family could be drawn as a worm if they were sneaky.

Processing an adolescent's drawing is critical in understanding her perception of relationships within the family. As noted above, the most essential part of processing a picture is to give specific, non-interpretative feedback about things which the counsellor observes or notices. It can be useful to feed back information regarding the arrangement of family members in the picture. The closeness or distance between family members and the alignment of some with others are relevant. In giving feedback, a counsellor might say, for example, 'I notice that the blue shape which is your mother and the pink shape which is your father are on opposite sides of the page.' The counsellor might also find it useful to comment on absences and additions within a family picture. For example, 'I notice that there is a big space in this part of your picture', or 'I notice that your younger brother is missing from this picture.'

Significant information about the adolescent's family and about how the adolescent perceives relationships within the family can be gained through discussion which evolves in response to non-interpretative feedback. Most importantly, using this approach gives the young person an opportunity to talk about their family, without feeling vulnerable as a consequence of premature discussion of sensitive material. The young person has control over what is disclosed, so that they do not feel threatened but perceive the counselling environment as safe.

The use of shapes, lines and colours   The use of shapes, lines and colours combines many of the features of the previous methods of using art. The adolescent is asked to create a picture that represents her world just by drawing lines, shapes and colours, but nothing real. During the drawing the adolescent is invited to put herself in the picture. The counsellor might say 'Where will you put yourself in this picture?' Once the drawing is completed, the counsellor may invite the adolescent to imagine that they are the shape which has been drawn to represent self and to talk to other shapes in the picture. The counsellor might say, 'I'd like you to talk to the shapes around you. Tell them who you are and what you would like to say to them.' In response an adolescent might reply by saying, 'I'm a solid, strong shape and none of you can get inside me.' The counsellor can then encourage the adolescent to imagine being another shape in the picture, and to reply to what was previously said. Thus, a dialogue can be created between parts of the picture. Finally, the adolescent can be invited to explore whether the dialogue between shapes in the picture relates in any way to her current life.

Use of art to explore feelings

Research confirms that drawing can be used to help an adolescent to get in touch with emotional feelings and explore them. Jolley and Thomas (1994) explored adolescent sensitivity to metaphorical expression of mood in abstract art. Their results confirm that adolescents can associate formal properties of painting with the correct labelling and comprehension of mood. Additionally, Morra et al. (1994) found that adolescents could successfully draw symbols to represent emotions. Two ways of using art to explore feelings are:

1 Drawing a picture of how you feel now.
2 Drawing parts of yourself.

Drawing a picture of how you feel now   At times, during a counselling session, an adolescent is likely to experience strong feelings. At these times, a counsellor can invite the adolescent to draw a picture of how they feel at that point in time. The counsellor can begin by reflecting back to the adolescent observations about their behaviour. The counsellor might say 'You sound angry. Draw a picture of how you feel emotionally now.' When the drawing is complete the counsellor can invite the young person to talk about the drawing. Drawing the emotional feeling currently being experienced can help an adolescent to talk about that feeling and the things which contribute to it. By expressing feelings, the adolescent is likely to feel better, with more positive feelings emerging.

Drawing parts of self   Adolescents often experience conflicting feelings which relate to different parts of self. For example, a young person might feel both ashamed and proud of a particular behaviour as described in the following example:

• Being ashamed might be because the behaviour contravenes socially acceptable norms. Knowing this might bring the young person in touch with the part of self that wants to be seen as responsible and mature.
• Being proud might be because part of the young person wants to confront and challenge society's norms.

Conflicting feelings such as these can be confusing and troubling to an adolescent who is attempting to make sense of their world. In such a situation, encouraging the adolescent to draw the two conflicting parts of the self can be useful. There are three ways in which this can be done:

1   Lines, shapes and colours might be used to represent the conflicting parts of self.
2   Symbols might be used to represent conflicting parts of self (for example, a hammer and a sea shell might be drawn).
3   Two self-portraits showing differing expressions might be used.

Usually, we give a general instruction which allows the young person to choose freely how to depict the parts of the self. Drawing conflicting parts of the self allows the adolescent to visualize, explore and discuss them. If appropriate, a dialogue can be created between the two parts of the self as described in Chapter 12 in the discussion of the use of symbols to anchor alternatives for comparison. As a consequence, the conflicting parts of the self will, it is hoped, be understood and accepted, so that they can coexist comfortably.

Use of art to develop insight

The following strategies can be useful in enabling an adolescent to gain personal insight:

1   Drawing a fruit tree to represent self.
2   Drawing a self-portrait.

Drawing a fruit tree to represent yourself   As discussed in Chapter 12, the use of metaphor is a safe and easy way to enable an adolescent to get in touch with, and talk about, personal information. A fruit tree can be used as a metaphor for the self to enable an adolescent to gain personal insight and disclose personal constructs, beliefs, feelings and issues.

When using this technique, the counsellor might begin by inviting the adolescent to imagine himself as a fruit tree, prompting him with regard to features of the tree which might be included. For example, the counsellor might say, 'How big are you?', 'What shape are you?', 'What colour are you?', 'Do you have fruit?', 'Do you have leaves?' and 'Where are your roots?' Processing the adolescent's drawing of a fruit tree requires the skills used when processing other metaphors (see Chapter 12). It is important for the counsellor to remain with the metaphor until it has been fully explored. Doing this enables the adolescent to feel safe and, if they feel safe, they are more likely to be able to disclose information.

While processing the drawing, the counsellor might ask the young person to continue imagining that they are the tree by saying, 'You are that fruit tree.' Then the counsellor might ask questions such as: 'Where are you?', 'Do you have fruit all the time?', 'What happens to your fruit?', 'What happens to the fruit that falls from the tree?', or 'When the wind blows strongly how does the fruit tree feel?'

During processing of the drawing of the fruit tree it can be useful for the counsellor to observe the verbal and non-verbal behaviour of the young person, and give feedback about this. For example, a young person might appear to be very sad when saying that flocks of birds had eaten all the fruit. Feeding back what had been observed, the counsellor might say 'Fruit tree, you seem to be sad when you say that birds have eaten your fruit.' After hearing the response to this statement, the counsellor might continue by asking if there was anything the tree would like to say to the birds. This might be followed by encouraging dialogue between the tree and the birds.

To finish processing the drawing of the fruit tree the counsellor might ask the adolescent whether anything that was said about the fruit tree fits with their own life. It is likely that this will be the case because the young person will have inevitably projected ideas from their own life on to the tree. If the young person has attributed feelings to the fruit tree, the counsellor might ask, 'Do you ever feel that way?'

Drawing a self-portrait   Sometimes inviting adolescents to draw pictures of themselves can be useful in helping them to gain insight and to explore personal attributes, including strengths and weaknesses. As with art generally, interpretation is best done by the young client. This is encouraged by the counsellor feeding back specific aspects of the picture, such as 'You have drawn yourself as a very small person on a very large page', or 'Your hands are coloured in green.'

Role play

Role play can involve the use of specific techniques from a variety of therapeutic models, including psychodrama, Gestalt therapy and rational emotive behaviour therapy. When counselling adolescents, role play is an excellent way of keeping the energy flowing. When role playing, many adolescents become actively involved in a very dynamic process. They can play out parts of their lives in a highly charged and physical way, which for many young people is easier than sitting down and talking through issues.

Engaging in role playing does not suit all adolescents. Some are too self-conscious to allow themselves to play a role creatively. It is therefore essential for counsellors to check out whether an adolescent client is willing or not to use role play. Sometimes adolescents will be willing to try out role playing if it is made clear to them that they may withdraw if they find that role play is not comfortable or useful for them. It is often helpful, in setting up a role play, for the counsellor to model role-playing behaviour and then encourage the adolescent to join in. When using role play it is essential for the young person to feel in control of the process and also to feel supported in what they do. Thus, the counsellor needs to provide a balance between allowing the adolescent to take risks in the role play, and giving support.

Role play can be used for the following purposes:

- to gain an understanding of roles and relationships
- to get in touch with feelings
- to explore parts of the self
- to make choices
- to externalize beliefs or feelings
- to practise and experiment with new behaviours.

Sometimes these purposes will overlap. It is part of the proactive counsellor's job to set up role plays opportunistically, at points in the counselling process where they are likely to achieve useful purposes and/or positive outcomes.

When a young person is involved in role play it is important for the counsellor continually to observe their verbal and non-verbal behaviour in order to detect underlying emotional feelings. When a counsellor notices behaviours that suggest underlying emotions, which are not being openly acknowledged, it can be useful to feed back the observed information to the young person. For example, the counsellor might say, 'I noticed that, as you spoke, you clenched your fists very tightly, clenched your mouth and closed your eyes', or the counsellor might say 'As you said that your voice sounded sad.' Such observational feedback is extremely important because it enables the young person to get in touch with emotional feelings which otherwise might not be recognized and might be being avoided because they are painful. Unfortunately, issues related to such painful emotions cannot be resolved unless the emotions are first accepted and released.

Use of role play to gain an understanding of roles and relationships

Role play can be useful in helping adolescents explore their relationships with others and gain a better understanding of the issues involved in these relationships, both from their own point of view and from the perspectives of others. During role play adolescents can act out, both verbally and non-verbally, ways in which they behave in their relationships with others. By reversing roles – that is, by taking the role of the other person within a role-play situation – they may be better able to observe their own behaviours more objectively, and understand the behaviours of other people.

Role play can be used to help adolescents recognize the difference between roles which they believe are functional and productive and roles which are dysfunctional and unproductive. They then have the opportunity to expand their repertoires of roles by learning to play new roles which have not been used previously.

The Gestalt two-chair approach   In helping to explore issues connected with relationships, role-play methods from Gestalt therapy, using two or more chairs, can be valuable. In the two-chair approach, if an adolescent has relationship issues with another person, that other person is imagined to be in an empty chair facing the adolescent's chair. The adolescent is then encouraged to talk to the imagined person in the empty chair, and to say to him whatever they wish. Some adolescents will initially be reluctant to talk to an empty chair. In order to support and encourage the client in this process, the counsellor can stand beside them and model the appropriate behaviour by making a statement on behalf of the adolescent to the imagined person in the empty chair. In doing this, the counsellor needs to use the first person and, speaking on behalf of the client, say, for example, 'Mary, I'm furious with you because …' (where Mary is the imagined person in the empty chair). The adolescent can then be invited to add to that statement.

Once an adolescent has spoken to the imagined person in the empty chair, they can be invited to experiment, by changing over and sitting in the other chair, and imagining that they are the other person. They can then be invited to reply, as though they were the other person, to the message that was given. Thus, a dialogue can then be created with the counsellor directing the role play by indicating to the adolescent when to move from one chair to the other. This movement from chair to chair is necessary so that the adolescent anchors both herself and the other person in the correct chairs and speaks on behalf of the person they are representing at any particular time. At all times during this process, the adolescent must be encouraged to use 'I' statements. For example, when in the other person's chair, the adolescent may be tempted to say, 'Well, Mary would say ...'. If that happens, the counsellor needs to give a clear instruction that this is a role play, and say, 'I would like you to imagine that you are Mary and to talk on her behalf.' The counsellor might then model an 'I' statement which could be made by Mary, such as 'I disagree with what you have said ...'.

From the role-play experience, it is likely that the adolescent will gain an understanding of her own issues, feelings and thoughts, and will also gain some level of understanding of the other person's perspective. It is often not necessary to do any processing of the role play while using the two-chair approach, although it is likely to be useful to feed back non-verbal indications of emotional feelings and to explore them. During role play the adolescent will experience something of what it is like to be the other person, and that experience may be sufficient in itself.

After the role play is completed, the adolescent may be encouraged, through the use of counselling micro-skills, to deal with current feelings and thoughts. In this stage of the process it is likely to be counterproductive to ask the client questions about how the other person in the role play might have felt or thought. To do that would take the client away from their own experience and invite them to try to do something which might be both difficult and threatening. They have already role played that other person and have some sense of what that person's perspective might be, and that is sufficient. Pushing the young client to talk about the other person's perspective might lead to resistance and possible unwillingness to return for further counselling.

The psychodrama approach using cushions   An alternative to using the two-chair, Gestalt therapy approach is to use a technique derived from *psychodrama*. Psychodrama originated in the work of Moreno in the 1940s (Vondracek and Corneal, 1995). In this approach, the adolescent is initially invited to choose from a pile of assorted cushions of various colours and styles. Some cushions may have patterns on them, while others are plain, some may have fringes, some may be soft and fluffy and others thin and hard, some may be small and some large. The adolescent is asked initially 'Choose a cushion to represent you.' Having chosen the cushion, the young person is then asked to describe the cushion. The cushion is effectively a symbol for the young person so, by describing the cushion, the young person may well discover information about themselves which they have not previously recognized. Clearly, this is a projective technique.

The adolescent is next invited to put the cushion somewhere on the floor and to choose another cushion for the other person with whom there is a problem. It may be that there is more than one other person involved. If this is the case, the young person can be invited to choose cushions for each of the people concerned. Having chosen each cushion, the adolescent can be invited, if the counsellor wishes, to describe each of the cushions and, in doing so, the attributes of the person represented by that cushion may be discovered. Once the cushions are selected, the young person can be invited to place them in an arrangement on the floor to demonstrate their relationships. Thus, a relationships sculpture is formed. This sometimes involves one cushion being on top of another.

The young person is then coached in the use of the cushions, each of which represents a person. Initially, the young person is invited to stand behind their own cushion and to face another cushion representing the person who will be the target of whatever the young person wishes to say. As in two-chair work, the counsellor may stand beside the client and act as their alter ego, adding to what the client says and repeating what is said with more energy and emotional feeling. The adolescent can then be invited to stand in a new position behind the cushion of the person who was addressed, to role play that person, and to respond verbally to what was said. The process can continue with the counsellor directing a drama by moving the young person into playing the roles of different people represented by the cushions. When playing a particular role, the adolescent is encouraged to stand behind the relevant cushion.

This process is very similar to two-chair work but has the following advantages:

- It is more flexible because it allows for easy movement of cushions as relationships change in the adolescent's perceptions.
- Using cushions instead of chairs enables the drama to unfold more quickly, because rather than having to stand up and sit down each time a role change occurs, the adolescent can quickly move across from one cushion to another.
- Experiments can easily be done with regard to changes in relationships. For example, the counsellor may move a cushion nearer to another and check out the young person's response.

In this process the counsellor needs to direct the drama proactively. Thus, the adolescent is moved from cushion to cushion so that energy is maintained and a useful dialogue is created among the imagined participants. At some point in the process, the counsellor may observe that resolution of issues has occurred. The young person can then be invited to leave the cushions, sit down and talk about their current emotional feelings. When resolution does not occur, the counsellor can summarize the process so that the young person's awareness of feelings and issues is raised. By doing this, the possibility of future change is promoted.

It is important to note that it is generally not useful to talk about the drama itself because that would involve an attempt to re-run what has already been experienced. What is required is for current 'here and now' feelings to be explored after the drama has been completed. Dramas created using cushions provide an opportunity for a counsellor proactively to introduce paradoxical counselling skills and to make use of humour in the counselling process. Properly directed dramas may be energized, lively and, at times, very amusing, capturing the young person's interest and imagination. Equally, it is possible for dramas to be intense and/or charged with emotion, with the young person displaying strong emotions by shouting or crying.

The use of role play to get in touch with feelings

Role play as described above, using either Gestalt two-chair work or the psychodramatic method with cushions, can be used effectively to help young people explore and express emotional feelings. A technique which can be used when encouraging expression of feelings during role plays is the psychodramatic technique of *doubling*. In doubling, the counsellor stands beside the adolescent and acts as the adolescent's alter ego (as described in the examples above). If the adolescent is extremely angry with a friend called Martin, for example, it may be that the adolescent, standing beside her own cushion, will say 'I am very angry with you, Martin', using a low, flat and quiet tone of voice. If this were to occur, the counsellor could stand beside the adolescent and shout in a loud, energy-charged voice, 'I am furious with you, Martin!' The counsellor might also add words, including expletives, from the adolescent's own declared vocabulary. Through this, the adolescent may be able to model on the counsellor and express feelings with energy and congruence. Thus, a dynamic role play can be created. This can be very cathartic for the young person because it can help in the release of strong feelings which may have been bottled up.

Some counsellors worry about using the techniques described with young people. They argue that modelling such behaviour in drama might encourage adolescents to behave disrespectfully or abusively in real life. Clearly, this is not the intention, so counsellors need to make sensible decisions about the suitability of this method for particular clients. Generally, when adolescents are allowed to express their feelings powerfully in a safe therapeutic environment, catharsis occurs with the consequence that the young person re-enters the outside world feeling more relaxed and thus more able to respond appropriately.

The use of powerful role plays needs to be seen in context. After completion of such role plays, a satisfactory counselling process will continue by encouraging the young person to explore adaptive options for dealing with the relationship problems in the future. These options will not be abusive or provocative, but will include the use of assertive behaviour and conflict-resolution skills. Strategies to enable young people to learn such behaviours and skills are described in Chapter 14.

The use of role play to explore parts of self

Adolescents often become troubled and confused because they are striving to establish an individual and unique identity which is consistent and congruent, but while doing this they are almost certain to experience different parts of themselves which are in conflict and appear to be inconsistent with each other. Adolescents are naturally complex, and have to deal with opposing desires and with conflicting beliefs and emotional feelings, which are certain to trouble them.

These different parts of self, although appearing to be in conflict, comprise the individual uniqueness of the adolescent. Adolescents who are able to discover and accept that their personalities are not homogeneous, but are made up of various differing parts, may experience a sense of relief which will enable them to integrate the differences within themselves. To help adolescents in the processes of discovery and integration, counsellors can use strategies similar to those described in Chapter 12, where the use of symbols to represent polarities within the self was described (see p. 138).

In order to explore conflicting parts of the self, or polarities within the self, cushions can be selected to represent these conflicting parts or polarities. For example, a young person may recognize their ability to be both vindictive and forgiving, and may be confused about how to integrate these two conflicting parts of self. In this case it could be useful to ask the adolescent to choose a cushion to represent the vindictive part of self and a cushion to represent the forgiving part of self. The cushions can then be placed on the floor on opposite sides of the room. Role play, as described in the previous section, can be encouraged to enable the adolescent to role play each of the parts of self. Thus, the adolescent can be supported in creating a dialogue between the two parts of self, standing behind one cushion and arguing for that part of self, and then moving to the other.

As the role-played argument continues, the counsellor might suggest that the adolescent experiment with taking up various positions on the line joining the two cushions. The young person can then be asked to describe what it is like to be in a particular position on that line and can be encouraged to move along the line to experience what it is like to move along a continuum between opposites. This process can help the young person to integrate the opposites by accepting them both as being available for use. The adolescent may then recognize that they do not need to be locked into either extreme, but can exercise personal control in making use of parts of self. Thus, they can move to a position on the continuum which suits them best at a particular time in a particular situation.

The use of role play to make choices

This strategy is similar to the strategy described in Chapter 12 on using symbols to anchor alternatives for comparison (see p. 137). However, in place of symbols, cushions are used to represent the various options. The adolescent is then encouraged to move from cushion to cushion. While standing behind a cushion, the young person argues for that option, as well as talking about both its advantages and disadvantages. During the role play the counsellor may help the young person challenge irrational beliefs, as described in Chapter 14.

The use of role play to externalize beliefs or feelings

Often messages from the past influence how adolescents believe they should behave in the present. These messages may be connected to cultural and spiritual beliefs, and may be very strong. For example, an adolescent may have incorporated a belief that they need to be nice to everybody regardless of the treatment they receive from others, but may be experiencing inner conflict because that belief is causing them to allow other people to be abusive towards them. Beliefs (or feelings) such as this can be externalized by encouraging the adolescent to choose a cushion to represent themself and a cushion to represent the belief or feeling. A dialogue is then created between the adolescent and the externalized belief.

The counsellor may take part in this dialogue and use paradoxical statements, in conjunction with humour, in order to challenge the young person into reviewing particular beliefs. For example, in the case described, the counsellor might take up a position behind the 'belief' cushion which represents 'being nice to everyone at all times'. The counsellor might then say to the adolescent who is behind their own cushion, 'Look, mate, if someone pours red paint all over you, you should smile, shake their hand and say thank you.' The young person is almost certain to challenge this provocative and humorous statement. The adolescent then has choice about the degree to which they hold on to the belief, give up the belief or integrate part of the belief into a revised construct.

The use of role play to practise and experiment with new behaviours

Role play can help adolescents to gain better control over their lives by learning new behaviours (Gladding, 1991). During role plays the counsellor can use a technique from psychodrama called *mirroring*. Mirroring requires the counsellor to replace the adolescent during the role play. The role play is then continued, so that the adolescent can watch the drama unfold and gain a more objective awareness of themself with regard to interactions with others.

It can also be useful to video-tape role plays. This enables the adolescent to get instant feedback about their behaviour through observation of video-tapes. Consequently, they may become more involved in changing their behaviours (Furman, 1990). Adolescents can be encouraged to repeat role plays using new and different behaviours which have been learnt through previous role-play experiences. This provides the adolescent with the opportunity to rehearse and practise new behaviours. Additionally, video-taped role plays have been found to increase significantly the ability of adolescents to maintain an internal locus of control (Dequine and Pearson-Davis, 1983).

Journals

Many adolescents like writing. They enjoy writing diaries, lyrics and poetry, so that keeping journals is a task which is interesting, familiar and satisfying for them. This can be very useful in conjunction with counselling because it has been found that adolescent diaries provide an opportunity to disclose personal and intimate information (Rotenberg, 1995). They can record reflections about, and emotional responses to, present and past personal experiences. Journals can be written in a variety of ways, as described by Weinhold (1987). When counselling adolescents, *daily logs* and *dream logs* are especially useful.

The daily log

The daily log closely resembles a diary and serves as a running record of the adolescent's subjective experience of daily life. It is important for the daily log to be reviewed regularly so that the adolescent can reflect, gain insight and explore opportunities for positive change.

   We find it useful to follow guidelines which are adapted from those of Nelson (1992). The adolescent is invited to record the events of each day using particular headings as follows:

- *What I did*   Under this heading the adolescent simply records the content of the day's events. For example, 'I got up', 'I had a shower', 'I had breakfast', 'I went to school', and so on.
- *How I viewed the day*   Under this heading the adolescent is encouraged to pretend that they are looking through a window at the day and to make comments such as 'Today was a disgusting day', or 'Today I got lots done.'
- *How I felt emotionally*   Under this heading the adolescent is encouraged to write down the positive, negative or mixed emotional feelings that were experienced during the day. For example, 'Felt great when I was eating my cereal, but felt depressed when I thought about going to school, but was happy when I arrived there.'
- *Relationships or lack of relationships*   Under this heading the adolescent is encouraged to record information about relationships with others, including both contact and lack of contact with others, and also the influences of others during the day. For example, 'I didn't see my father all day and wasn't allowed to go and visit my friends, but had an argument with Paula which made things worse.'
- *Things I learnt from today*   Under this heading the young person is encouraged to record anything they learnt from the day's events. For example, 'Today I learnt that not having any social contact with my friends is just as bad as not having any contact with my father.'

   By looking at places in the journal where different choices could have been made the adolescent may be able to identify possibilities regarding the use of different behaviours and/or the achievement of different outcomes. If used over a period of time, the adolescent may identify patterns of behaviour that have been either useful or unhelpful, and may identify goals for the future. Through discussion with the counsellor, the young person may also be enabled to explore underlying motivations for particular unsatisfactory behaviours, allowing change to occur.

The dream log

Adolescents often show great interest in their dreams. Sometimes they are troubled by them, particularly if they are continually recurring. Dreams can be a very useful way of helping a young person to access important personal information. In order to be able to use the information from a dream, it is helpful if as much detail about the dream as possible can be remembered.

In cases where it is likely that a young person will return for further counselling, and it is clear that the young person would like to explore a dream, it can be useful to invite them to keep a log of the dream. To keep a log of the dream, the young person needs to keep a pad of paper and a pen beside the bed. On waking, whenever they remember a dream or part of a dream, they need to write details in the log immediately. The log should preferably be written in three parts as follows:

Part 1: the content of the dream, including a full description of what happened in the dream.
Part 2: the emotional feelings experienced during the dream.
Part 3: thoughts about the dream.

The log can then be used as described later under the heading 'Dream work' (see p. 167).

Relaxation

Some adolescents find it helpful to learn relaxation techniques. However, it needs to be recognized that not all adolescents find this useful. For some, relaxation performed in a structured way is not helpful because they are unable to enter happily and comfortably into the experience. Relaxation training can be useful for the following:

1 To help adolescents who are troubled by anxiety and/or tension.
2 To teach adolescents how to cope actively with anxiety and a variety of other problems that result from stressful situations (Forman, 1993).
3 As a prerequisite to the use of guided imagery.

How to help an adolescent learn to relax

First, it is important to determine the adolescent's attitude to taking part in a relaxation exercise. Many adolescents will have already been exposed to some form of relaxation exercise. Some of them will have found this useful, and others will not. There may be little point in trying to help a young person learn relaxation techniques if they have previously had bad experiences with them.

When undergoing any relaxation technique, it is important for adolescents to feel that they are in control, rather than the adult who is helping them to learn the relaxation process. Failure to observe this requirement disempowers the adolescent and might lead them to believe that they need to be dependent on the help of an adult in order to achieve their goals.

Before starting the relaxation procedure, the adolescent needs to be informed that they have a choice about whether to observe the instructions given by the counsellor or not. They also need to be told that they have a choice about whether to continue with the exercise or not. There needs to be some rehearsal of the way in which the young person would stop the relaxation exercise, if that was what they wanted to do. It is insufficient for a counsellor just to say, 'If you want to discontinue this exercise, discontinue it.' It is important to ask how they will stop the exercise. Will they raise a hand, will they open their eyes and say 'Stop' or will they just get up and say 'I don't want to do this any more'? Failure to go through this process of checking out how the adolescent will discontinue, if they want to, may make it difficult for some young people to feel that they are in control.

Relaxation cannot easily occur in a brightly lit, noisy environment. For relaxation training to be most effective, the environment needs to be one in which there are no intrusive noises and where the lighting is subdued. Adolescents undergoing relaxation training need to be seated in a comfortable position. We prefer to ask them to make themselves as comfortable as possible on a bean bag. Asking them to lie on the floor would not be appropriate because for some adolescents, particularly those who have been abused, lying on the floor may make them feel vulnerable and unsafe. With a bean bag, they have more control; they can shape the bean bag so that they are reclining, if they wish, or sit in a more upright position, if that is what they prefer.

Giving the relaxation instructions

In giving relaxation instructions, the counsellor needs to talk in a fairly monotonous, flat tone of voice. There needs to be a pause between all statements to allow time for the young person to respond to instructions and continue relaxing. The relaxation process can be started in the following way:

> Make yourself comfortable on the bean bag by shuffling yourself around.
> When you are ready, close your eyes. Notice the way you are sitting and recognize any part of you that is not comfortable.
> If any part of your body is not comfortable, move it.
> Check your feet and your legs. Are they comfortable? If not, shuffle them into a better position.
> Check your body. Is it comfortable? If not, move it.
> Check your arms, your neck and your head. Make them comfortable.
> If necessary, move completely to get more comfortable.

Once the young person is comfortable, the relaxation process continues as the counsellor says words such as:

> During this exercise breathe naturally, and silently say to yourself the word *relax* every time you breathe out.
> Whenever there is silence, you might want to focus on your breathing, and say *relax* silently to yourself, each time you breathe out.
> If intruding thoughts come into your head, don't worry about them, but focus again on your natural breathing.

The counsellor can then observe the young person for a short while and, whenever they breathe out, say quietly 'relax'. The young person is then helped to relax their body progressively from their feet to the top of their head as the following instructions are given:

Wiggle your toes and your feet and allow them to feel relaxed.

Notice your breathing. [The counsellor now says 'relax' each time the person breathes out for a few breaths.]

Now notice your feet. Wiggle your toes, and as you breathe out allow them to relax. Notice your legs. Tighten the muscles in them gently. As you breathe out say 'relax' to yourself, allowing your legs to relax. Let the relaxed feeling flow from your legs down through your feet into the floor.

Notice your lower back and your stomach. Gently tighten the muscles in them, and as you breathe out, silently say 'relax' as you let the muscles relax.

Allow a relaxed feeling to flow from your stomach, through your lower back, your legs and your feet into the floor.

Relax, relax, relax [said quietly in time with breathing].

Notice your chest and your arms, tighten the muscles in them gently and let them relax as you breathe out. Allow the relaxed feeling to flow from your arms, down your chest into your legs and your feet and into the floor.

Notice your hands, tighten the muscles gently, let them relax and allow the relaxed feeling to flow from your hands through your arms, your body, your legs to the floor.

Allow yourself to sink deeper into the bean bag, and focus on your breathing, saying 'relax' every time you breathe out.

Tighten the muscles in your head and neck slightly, and allow yourself to relax as you breathe out, notice the relaxed feeling flowing from your head down through your body to your feet and out into the floor.

You can continue relaxing by saying 'relax' each time you breathe out.

The counsellor can now allow some time for the young person to experience being relaxed and should say, 'I won't say anything for the next two or three minutes. I'll just let you practise focusing on your breathing and on saying "relax" to yourself. If intruding thoughts come into your head, don't worry about them, just focus on your breathing.' After a while the counsellor can say, 'It is time for you to start to move towards finishing this relaxation exercise. I'd like you to start preparing yourself for becoming alert and active again.' Then, with a pause between statements, the counsellor can continue by saying:

Instead of noticing your breathing and saying 'relax', notice that you are sitting on the bean bag.

Shuffle around a bit on the bag to become aware of the bag.

Move your head and neck, and open your eyes.

Look around and notice things that are in the room with us.

When you are ready, get up carefully, remembering that you have been relaxed, so it might not be a good idea to stand up suddenly.

After teaching relaxation, it is sensible to tell the young person that they may be feeling more relaxed than usual, and that it may therefore be inadvisable to engage in any activity which demands a high level of alertness. For example, if the adolescent has become very relaxed, it would not be sensible to send them off to ride a bike through traffic, along a busy street, because they may not be alert enough to cope properly. This could result in an accident.

Once a young person has learnt to relax it can be useful to help her to generalize this relaxed behaviour to situations which are anxiety-provoking or stressful.

This can be done by getting the adolescent to stand upright, and then suggesting that they take a few deep breaths (do not allow hyperventilation to occur). While taking these breaths, tell them to allow their body to relax. Thus, in a standing position, they learn to relax the muscles in their hands, arms, neck, shoulders, body and legs so that, although they are standing, they become relaxed by taking a few deep breaths. This ability to relax when standing may be useful when confronting stressful situations.

Imagination

Four important ways to use imagination are:

1   To change self-perceptions.
2   To establish new emotional and behavioural patterns.
3   To reconstruct negative memories.
4   To go on an imaginary journey.

In achieving the above goals, imagination enables the adolescent to replace old memories with new memories which are more helpful and adaptive.

Use of imagination to change self-perceptions

The self-perceptions of a young person originate from childhood but will change and develop during adolescence. Unfortunately, past self-perceptions tend to continue to influence the way adolescents think about themselves and to affect their relationships with other people.

Traumatic and/or abusive experiences in childhood and adolescence often lead to dysfunctional and unhelpful self-perceptions. For example, adolescents who have been abused might believe that they are undesirable, unworthy of affection, helpless, untrustworthy and unreliable. Such negative self-perceptions may mean that they continue to behave in ways which are consistent with, and support, these beliefs. Imagination can be used to help adolescents change such perceptions and beliefs.

The first step, in using imagination to change self-perceptions, is to bring the influence of unhelpful beliefs into full awareness. This is done by discussing current behaviours and the way in which they are influenced by entrenched thinking. The counsellor also needs to raise adolescent awareness of behaviours that are used to avoid painful thoughts about themselves. For example, a young person might present a façade of being tough and robust, but this façade might be a way of hiding feelings of helplessness and vulnerability.

Once negative self-perceptions and their origins have been identified, guided imagery can be used to bring about change. The adolescent is encouraged to remember the negative past experiences (where, for example, they may have felt victimized or helpless). Then, in a guided imagery exercise, they are encouraged to re-live those experiences but to change the way they behaved so that they can feel good about themself.

The process used is as follows. First, the counsellor uses a relaxation exercise and then, when relaxed, the adolescent is invited to remember a negative experience from the past. Then, while continuing to stay relaxed with their eyes closed, they are invited to describe the scene and events which they are imagining from the past. Next, the counsellor asks the young person to suggest ways in which they might change that picture, or the events, so that their feelings and the outcomes would be different. The young person is then invited to return to the beginning of the imagined scenario and to re-run the script, so that events occur differently with positive outcomes and so that they experience good feelings about themself.

In such an exercise, an adolescent might imagine events from the past where they were bullied in the playground as a young child by several older and bigger children. During the re-experiencing of these memories, the adolescent might be encouraged by the counsellor to replace the aggressive and violent behaviours of the bullies with behaviours which would indicate that the young person was accepted and valued by peers in the playground. This would allow the adolescent to get in touch with their positive attributes such as friendliness, helpfulness, sense of humour and loyalty. The counsellor might then highlight these attributes, make them newsworthy and help the adolescent to construct a new, different and positive perception of themself. This new perception might, in the future, enable the adolescent to engage in positive social relationships.

Use of imagination to establish new emotional and behavioural patterns

This is a rational emotive behaviour therapy approach (Dryden and DiGiuseppe, 1990). Sometimes adolescents are troubled by failures from their past. These may be either recent past experiences or experiences which occurred some time ago. For example, an adolescent might remember an episode in the playground at school, involving three or four other students, which resulted in an abusive exchange. As a consequence, the young person may have been called to the principal's office, along with the students involved and a teacher who witnessed the event. During the discussion in the principal's office the adolescent may not have found an opportunity to explain their perceptions of the event. They may have been prevented, through interruption, directions by the more powerful members in the meeting and their own ignorance of the procedures of the meeting, from putting their point of view forward. This encounter may have left the young person feeling powerless, disrespected and inadequate.

In order to change the young person's feelings about the event, the counsellor might first use a relaxation exercise. While relaxed, the young person might be invited to imagine the events as they actually occurred and to talk about them as they are imagined. The counsellor might then invite the young person to re-run the story in their imagination and to describe it so that events occurred differently and in a way that was satisfying for the young person. By re-running the revised story several times, it is hoped that the adolescent will become less troubled by the past memories. The adolescent may also begin to feel more comfortable and confident that in the future they will have the skills to deal with similar situations in an appropriate and empowering way.

Use of imagination to reconstruct negative memories

Often adolescents who have been traumatized have difficulty putting their story together in a sequence which makes sense to them. This may be because some pieces of information are missing from their memories. The fragmentation of their stories prevents them from feeling a sense of completion of their experiences, resulting in anxiety. In addition, as their stories are fragmented, they may experience a sense of not having been able to control events, because the events are not remembered as following a logical and understandable sequence. They may also be troubled by flashbacks which result from triggers which are difficult to identify. If traumatic events can be reconstructed so that they follow a complete sequence which is fully understood, then a sense of control may be achieved, and triggers may be identified and reduced in power. Additionally, ways to manage responses to triggers may be explored.

A good way to help such young people to reconstruct their story, so that it makes sense for them, is to help them to imagine the story when relaxed, and to talk about it as they imagined it, so that the story flows from beginning to end. In this way the young person can make sense of what happened. It does need to be remembered, however, that the story as recounted may not in fact be completely accurate, but may include material which has been invented.

The first step in the process is for the counsellor to invite the adolescent to relax and, while relaxed, to recall their memory of the traumatic experience. During the adolescent's recollection the counsellor might promote exploration of the event by asking questions such as, 'When you remember what happened, do you see any pictures in your mind?', 'What are you wearing?', 'Are you aware of any sounds, smells or activity around you?' The purpose of asking such questions is to help the adolescent to get in touch with the more sensory components of their experience because triggers associated with traumatic events are often related to sensory experiences. Once such triggers are recognized, the adolescent is likely to be better able to deal with them. After this exercise, the adolescent is encouraged to identify any new or enlightening information which may have changed their original perceptions of the event. These new insights may help the adolescent make sense of the original trauma.

Use of imagination to go on an imaginary journey

Imaginary journeys can be used either to take adolescents into a pleasant place which they might like to visit in their imagination in the future, or to help them get in touch with past troubling experiences.

To get in touch with a pleasant place   In helping a young person to get in touch with a pleasant place, continue a relaxation exercise by inviting them to move, in their imagination, to a place which they find pleasant and enjoyable. Consequently, they have the opportunity to choose a place, which for them, will be comfortable and pleasant. While they are imagining the pleasant place with their eyes closed, the counsellor might invite the young person to talk about their imagined experience.

To get in touch with past troubling experiences   When the imaginary journey is used to enable a young person to get in touch with past experiences which may have been troubling, the counsellor takes them on an imaginary journey which leads them back to a time and place where the events occurred. The young person may then be invited to imagine, as a sequence, that:

1   They are looking at the troubling scene from the past.
2   They are part of the scene.
3   They are able to say anything they like to anyone in the scene, to hear responses from those people and to do anything which they would have liked to have done at the time of the actual event.
4   They can complete their imaginary journey by doing or saying anything which they wish to do or say before leaving the journey.
5   Finally, they are invited to leave the imaginary journey and be fully aware of their actual situation in the counselling room.

After the journey has been completed and the person has been invited to open their eyes and leave the journey, they may be invited to draw or sketch, using coloured felt pens, anything which comes into their mind with regard to the journey. After completing the drawing, the young person may be invited to talk about it. The counsellor may comment on the picture, with statements such as, 'I notice that there is a large red blotch over here', or 'I notice that there is a space in this part of the picture.' Thus, by making non-interpretative statements of fact about the picture, the young person is invited to disclose information about their picture, if they wish, without being troubled by intrusive questions.

An alternative is to use a more open and less structured imaginary journey, so that the young person has freedom to choose where they go in their imagination. For example, a counsellor might suggest to a young person that they imagine they are standing in front of a door, and that when they open the door they will see a scene which they remember. This sets a very open agenda, but often the scene remembered will be a very significant one. The numbered sequence described above can be used so that the young person is invited to look at the scene, move into the scene, talk to people in the scene and do anything which they wish to do before leaving the scene. It is important that the young person be invited to leave the scene, in their imagination, in the same way as they entered. Thus, they should be invited to come back through the door, close the door and leave. By doing this, in their imagination, they have completed their journey and are able to resume life within the counselling situation rather than being invited to stay in the imaginary situation.

The journey can be processed by drawing a picture, as described above. It is likely that, when a counsellor processes the experience of going on an imaginary journey of this type, the adolescent will disclose information about real-life situations. This provides an easy opportunity for the sharing of personal information.

Dream work

Most adolescents are very interested in their dreams. They tend to be intrigued by them and often attach particular significance and importance to them. Sometimes they will believe that their dreams are almost prophetic in nature and consequently will wish to have them interpreted. We believe that the only people competent and able to interpret adolescents' dreams are the adolescents themselves. It is their own interpretation which matters.

As discussed on pp. 159–60, adolescents who wish to work with their dreams may be encouraged to keep a dream record, made immediately on waking. Sometimes, however, adolescents will come to a session without a journal, but remembering a dream quite clearly and wishing to discuss it.

Two different ways of processing dreams will be discussed: one is through the use of art, and the other is a psychodramatic or Gestalt therapy approach (there is considerable overlap between psychodrama and Gestalt therapy).

Use of art to process dreams   When using art, the young person is invited to draw or sketch a picture of her dream, using coloured felt pens. This picture may be a representational picture or it may be an abstract with just shapes and colours. Sometimes, while the picture is being drawn, the adolescent will talk spontaneously about the dream. At other times, the client will draw silently and, after the picture is complete, the counsellor might say 'Tell me about your picture.' This question can be followed up by the useful statement 'Tell me more', which encourages the young person to think more deeply and disclose important information which comes into her awareness. Further processing can occur by the counsellor inviting the adolescent to imagine they are an object or person within the picture. As that object or person, the young person can be invited to describe how they feel and what they are thinking. They may also be asked if they would like to say anything as the object or person. While imagining that they are the object or person, the young person might be asked to say something to another object, person or animal in the picture. They can then be invited to imagine that they are the object, other person or animal, and respond to what was said. Thus a dialogue can be created between two parts of the picture. This dialogue will often raise new and unexpected information for the adolescent which can contribute insight into a troubling issue or event.

Psychodramatic processing of a dream   In the psychodramatic approach to processing dreams, the adolescent is first invited to describe the dream. Next they are invited to choose cushions to represent significant items or people in the dream. The story is then re-told with the cushions being placed on the floor in an arrangement which creates a picture of the dream. The adolescent is then invited to take up positions by standing behind relevant cushions. When at a cushion the adolescent is asked to experience what it would be like to be that item, object or person within the dream, and talk on behalf of the item, object or person. By moving from cushion to cushion, dialogue is created between various parts of the dream. During the psychodramatic process, the counsellor needs to observe and give feedback about both verbal and non-verbal behaviour. Thus, the young person's awareness of emotions and associated thoughts is raised and these can be processed.

In summary

We have described a number of creative strategies which can be used in helping young people to explore issues, deal with their feelings and make changes. All of these creative strategies require activity on the part of the adolescent, and must therefore be chosen to suit the abilities and needs of the young person. We strongly believe that it is essential to give young people choice about participation in activities during counselling. With all the strategies discussed, the technique itself is of limited value unless the work done is properly processed by exploring thoughts, emotional feelings, attitudes and beliefs which emerge during the process.

14   Behavioural and cognitive behavioural strategies

In Chapters 12 and 13 we looked at symbolic and creative strategies, which can help adolescents to understand and gain insight into themselves and change their behaviours by becoming more fully aware of troubling emotions and underlying issues. Symbolic and creative strategies are also useful in helping adolescents to define, understand and change beliefs and values, as a consequence of which changes in behaviours will often occur. In this chapter we will discuss behavioural and cognitive behavioural strategies. These methods rely on structured, goal-oriented approaches, collaboration between an active counsellor and an active adolescent and emphasis on current issues (Kutcher and Marton, 1990). Behavioural and cognitive behavioural strategies specifically target behaviours, whereas symbolic and creative strategies influence behaviour indirectly. In targeting behaviours directly, there is an assumption that when behaviours change, emotional feelings will also be positively influenced.

Behavioural and cognitive behavioural strategies have been successful, to varying degrees, when working with adolescents who are anxious, depressed, aggressive, oppositional and unmotivated, and with adolescents who have difficulty with interpersonal and social skills (Valliant and Antonowicz, 1991; Finch et al., 1993; Wilkes et al., 1994; Biswas et al., 1995). Behavioural and cognitive behavioural strategies can be used to address primary counselling functions (see Figure 8.2) as shown in Figure 14.1. It will be seen from Figure 14.1 that these strategies are most useful for those primary counselling functions concerned with addressing the problem. They are least suitable for use in conjunction with

PRIMARY COUNSELLING FUNCTION \ BEHAVIOURAL OR COGNITIVE BEHAVIOURAL STRATEGY	self-control	challenging self-destructive beliefs	anger management	assertiveness training	setting lifestyle goals	making decisions
Relationship building getting to know the adolescent and the adolescent's constructs within the relationship						
Assessing the problem assessing and exploring the adolescent's emotional state, constructs, self-concept and beliefs; identifying issues and themes	suitable	suitable	suitable	suitable	suitable	suitable
Addressing the problem changing behaviours by exploring and promoting change in intrapersonal beliefs, personal growth and interpersonal relationships; experimenting with behaviours	most suitable	most suitable	most suitable	most suitable	most suitable	most suitable

▓	most suitable
░	suitable
☐	least suitable

Figure 14.1 *Suitability of behavioural and cognitive behavioural strategies for achieving primary counselling functions*

primary counselling functions concerned with developing a relationship. It is interesting to compare Figure 14.1 with Figures 12.1 and 13.1, where it is shown that the symbolic and creative strategies can be used to address a wider range of primary counselling functions.

Behavioural and cognitive behavioural strategies will be discussed under the following headings:

- self-control
- challenging self-destructive beliefs
- anger management
- assertiveness training
- setting lifestyle goals
- making decisions.

Self-control

There are four stages involved in learning behavioural self-control:

1   Identification of problem behaviour.
2   Observation of behaviour.
3   Evaluation of behaviour.
4   Setting consequences for behaviour.

When self-control issues need to be addressed it can be useful for a counsellor to describe these stages to the adolescent, so that, together, they can plan a programme for behavioural change.

Identification of problem behaviour

In counselling, an adolescent may be able to identify one or more behaviours which have been causing problems. For example, the young person may be fighting with a younger sibling and getting into trouble as a consequence of this. An adolescent with this sort of problem might initially complain about a younger brother's behaviour and blame him for what is happening. It is the proactive counsellor's responsibility to help the young person recognize that they cannot change other people's behaviours. To help a young person acknowledge this, a counsellor might ask questions such as 'Do you think your brother is likely to change?' and/or 'Do you think that you can change your brother's behaviour?' As a consequence of these questions, which challenge the young person's beliefs, the young person will perhaps recognize that the only behaviours they can change are their own.

Observation of behaviour

If adolescents wish to change their behaviours, the first thing they need to do is observe their current behaviours so that they can fully understand them and their consequences. Often, simply observing when an unwanted behaviour occurs, and when it does not occur, will result in change in that behaviour. For example, if an adolescent notices each time conflict arises with a younger sibling, then the very act of observing this may decrease the conflict. This is because, as soon as the targeted behaviour starts to occur, the young person's awareness of it will be raised, so that action can be taken immediately to change what is happening.

The use of a diary may be helpful to adolescents who wish to observe unwanted behaviour. They can record situations and/or events where the unwanted behaviour occurs, and record both antecedent behaviours and the consequences of the unwanted behaviour. A good way to keep a diary for this purpose is to use a notepad where the pages are divided into three columns headed:

1   The behaviour of others and self prior to the situation/event (and my feelings).
2   Description of the situation/event (and my feelings).
3   The outcome for self (and my feelings).

Thus, under each heading, the young person is invited to describe their feelings at the time.

It can also be helpful for an adolescent to divide each day in the diary into parts so that changes in the frequency of the targeted behaviour can be determined. Suitable parts might be:

- before school
- during the morning
- during the afternoon
- after school.

The number of times the unwanted behaviour happens in each of these parts of the day may give useful information about times and situations where problems in management of the unwanted behaviour occur. Keeping a diary in this way can be 'homework' for the adolescent between counselling sessions. It needs to be remembered that young people will only do homework of this kind if they find the task interesting and useful.

Evaluation of behaviour

In this stage adolescents evaluate their own behaviour against criteria which they set for themselves. For example, an adolescent may make a decision to try to reduce the number of times he fights with his younger brother by 50 per cent. Setting a level of 50 per cent is more realistic than trying to extinguish the behaviour completely, which might set the young person up for failure.

Adolescents often become discouraged if they believe that they are not making good progress in achieving change. To avoid this and provide motivation and incentive for continuing change, the adolescent can be encouraged to monitor quantitatively the success actually being achieved in meeting predetermined goals. To make the exercise more interesting, the adolescent can be helped to chart or graph the targeted behaviour so that comparison can be made with a baseline established during an observation stage.

Setting consequences for behaviour

If an adolescent is to be motivated to achieve self-control, there will need to be rewards for the achievement of goals. Often, rewards occur naturally because, as undesirable behaviours change, negative consequences diminish and positive consequences are experienced. However, in the early stages of change, such naturally occurring consequences may not be noticeable. It is therefore sensible to put in place formally a system of positive rewards. These rewards can take a variety of forms. They may be specific rewards, such as a new possession or participation in a desired activity, for achieving target criteria, or they might be in the form of tokens which can be cashed in later for a specific reward.

As an important goal is to encourage self-control in young people, it is preferable for adolescents to be in control of determining what kinds of reinforcement or reward they should receive. In some cases, parents or significant others can be involved in the process of reward-giving. For example, a young person might negotiate a deal with his father by saying, 'Dad, if I'm able to cut down my fighting with Bill so that I only fight with him three times a week, will you drive me to soccer on Saturday?' Thus, the young person has an external incentive, which they were personally responsible for establishing, thereby demonstrating their own ability to take responsibility for change.

Challenging self-destructive beliefs

Adolescents commonly hold a range of beliefs which lead them to behave, or think, in ways which are destructive for them. Albert Ellis, the originator of rational emotive therapy, which is now more commonly known as rational emotive behaviour therapy (REBT), drew attention to the need for counsellors to challenge what he described as clients' 'irrational beliefs'. Readers who would like to make significant use of rational emotive behaviour therapy may wish to read Dryden and DiGiuseppe (1990). Ellis's ideas, and the way in which they have been developed, are extremely useful when working with adolescents.

Irrational beliefs (renamed 'self-destructive beliefs') when counselling adolescents

In rational emotive therapy, beliefs are considered to be 'irrational' if they prevent people from achieving their basic goals and purposes, are illogical (especially, dogmatic) and are empirically inconsistent with reality. Labelling beliefs this way appeals to many adults, but adolescents tend to be less convinced. Many adolescents are simplistically logical and like to argue. If we use Ellis's term 'irrational beliefs', they may argue that some so-called 'irrational beliefs' are not irrational, but do have a logical rational base. Thus, calling these beliefs 'irrational' invites unnecessary argument. However, if we call these beliefs 'self-destructive beliefs' there is unlikely to be any argument and most young people will understand the concept and agree with the definition. We believe that counsellors are therefore on safer ground, when working with adolescents, if they use the term 'self-destructive beliefs'.

The REBT theory of change

Rational emotive behaviour therapy (REBT) theory regarding change is very useful when working with adolescents. This is sometimes described as the ABC framework where:

A   is the *Activating* event.
B   is the *Belief* which conditions the response to the event.
C   is the *Consequence* of the response.

When an *activating event* occurs, the young person responds automatically by using current beliefs. These beliefs condition the person's response and there are consequences related to this response. Thus, when a young person has self-destructive beliefs, these will condition their responses to external events and are likely to result in negative consequences for them, so that they will feel bad.

If the young person changes a self-destructive belief, and replaces it with a more useful constructive belief (or, in REBT language, a 'rational belief') then they will respond differently to an activating event, as a result of the new belief. Having behaved differently, there will be a positive emotional consequence for the young person, who will be more likely to feel good, than to feel bad, in the way they did when they responded in accordance with the self-destructive belief.

Types of self-destructive belief

Table 14.1 shows a list of self-destructive beliefs compared with a list of useful constructive beliefs. Self-destructive beliefs fit into the following categories:

* should, must, ought-to and have-to beliefs
* catastrophizing beliefs
* 'always' and 'never' beliefs
* intolerance-of-others beliefs
* blaming beliefs
* negative self-perception beliefs.

Should, must, ought-to and have-to beliefs   These beliefs are demonstrated by the use of statements such as:

Other people *should* always be responsible.
I *must* conform to my peers.
I *ought to* please my brother rather than do what I want.
I *have to* visit my dying uncle every day.

Table 14.1 *Self-destructive beliefs and constructive beliefs*

Self-destructive beliefs	Constructive beliefs
Should, must, ought-to and have-to beliefs	
My friends *should* be loyal to me.	Sometimes my friends won't be loyal to me; that's the way it is. It doesn't mean there's something wrong with me.
Other people *should* live up to my expectations.	Other people won't live up to my expectations.
I *must* conform to my peers.	I can be an individual and do my own thing.
I *must* win.	According to the law of averages most people only win 50 per cent of the time. I don't need to win to feel OK.
I *ought to* please my brother rather than do what I want.	I need to attend to my own needs so that I feel OK. Then if I feel OK, I can care about other people too.
I *have to* visit my dying uncle every day.	I have a choice. I can choose whether or not to visit my dying uncle every day.
Catastrophizing beliefs	
I can never go back to school again. It would be too embarrassing. I wouldn't be able to face the other students.	I am me, I am OK, Everybody makes mistakes at times, so I'm normal and proud to be me.
I might as well stop work on the project altogether because it is a total failure.	I've done really well to take on such a hard project. It's not a *total* failure. I can still get some positives out of it.
It's all too much. I just can't cope any more.	I can cope. I always have in the past, and I will now.
Nobody will ever respect me again.	I don't need other people's respect to feel good about myself. I am OK.
Always and never beliefs	
I'm not going to ask my mother because she *always* says 'no'.	I am going to ask my mother because she might say 'yes'.
I *never* succeed in anything.	Sometimes I succeed and sometimes I fail. I'm human and I'm OK.
Everybody *always* criticizes me.	People sometimes criticize me, but that's OK because it's impossible to please everybody all the time.
I should *never* make mistakes.	Everybody makes mistakes. The only way to avoid making mistakes is to do nothing, and that's not me.
Intolerance of others beliefs	
She makes me mad because she borrows my library books and then returns them late. She deliberately gets me into trouble.	She's just careless. I know that and I have a choice about whether to lend her my library books or not.
He didn't turn up to meet me after class as we arranged. He deliberately stood me up to make me look foolish.	He probably forgot – that's the way he is, and there is nothing I can do about that. He's the one who's made the mistake. I can feel OK about me.
My little brother makes me mad because he never does his share of the work.	My brother is lazy. I can't change him, so I'll ignore his behaviour and be proud of being a hard worker myself.
Blaming beliefs	
I can't do my homework because my sister keeps asking me to play with her.	I don't have to play with my sister when I have important things to do for me.

(Continued)

Table 14.1   *(Continued)*

Self-destructive beliefs	Constructive beliefs
If he didn't keep annoying me I wouldn't hit him. It's his fault that I get into trouble.	I can choose other ways to deal with his annoying behaviour so that I don't get into trouble.
I am always late for class because they are so slow at the tuckshop.	I can only blame myself if I'm late because I don't get to the tuckshop earlier. I am in control of what happens.
Negative self-perception beliefs	
I'm a victim	I'm powerful
I'm a loser	I'm a winner
I'm no good	I'm OK
I'm worthless	I'm worthwhile
I'm helpless	I'm resourceful
I'm a bad person	I'm a good person
I'm incapable	I'm capable
I'm stupid	I'm smart
I'm unlovable	I'm lovable

A printable version of this table is available to download from the Sage website (www.sagepublications.com)

At times, these beliefs may be self-destructive for adolescents. The beliefs set them up to have expectations which may not be met and/or to do things which other people want done rather than to attend to their own needs.

Catastrophizing beliefs   Catastrophizing beliefs lead the young person to believe that they have few options left, and that a disaster of enormous proportions has occurred, or will occur. For example, an adolescent may believe:

> I can never go back to school again. It would be too embarrassing. I wouldn't be able to face the other students.
> I might as well stop work on the project altogether because it is a total failure.
> It's all too much, I just can't cope any more.
> Nobody will ever respect me again.

These statements are clearly very destructive because they leave no options for the future and inevitably lead the young person to feel hopeless and depressed.

Always and never beliefs   *Always* and *never* beliefs are an exaggeration of the truth and leave the young person feeling bad because times when positive things do occur are ignored or denied. Typical *always* and *never* statements are:

> I'm not going to ask my mother because she *always* says 'no'.
> I *never* succeed in anything.
> Everybody *always* criticizes me.
> I should *never* make mistakes. [This is a combination of a 'should' and a 'never' belief.]
> I must *always* complete my assignments on time. [This is combination of a 'must' and an 'always' belief.]
> I never get any free time. I *always* have to work.

Intolerance of others beliefs   These beliefs are beliefs which suggest that other people are intrinsically hopeless, bad or malevolent, don't do as they should and generally don't live up to the adolescent's expectations. For example:

> She makes me mad because she borrows my library books and then returns them late. She deliberately gets me into trouble.
>
> He didn't turn up to meet me after class as we arranged. He deliberately stood me up to make me look foolish.
>
> My little brother makes me mad because he never does his share of the work.

These beliefs lead to negative feelings and damage relationships.

Blaming beliefs   With these beliefs young people blame other people for their situation. By blaming, the people who blame excuse themselves from the need to change, and want someone else to change. This is clearly self-destructive because no one can make another person change, so the unsatisfactory situation is certain to continue. Typical examples of blaming beliefs are:

> I can't do my homework because my sister keeps asking me to play with her.
>
> I am always late for class because they are so slow at the tuckshop.
>
> If he didn't keep annoying me I wouldn't hit him. It's his fault that I get into trouble.

Negative self-perception beliefs   These are beliefs where people describe themselves in negative ways. Examples are:

> I'm a victim.
>
> I'm a loser.
>
> I'm no good.
>
> I'm worthless.
>
> I'm helpless.
>
> I'm a bad person.
>
> I'm incapable.
>
> I'm stupid.
>
> I'm unlovable.

Constructive beliefs

Constructive beliefs to replace all of the examples of self-destructive beliefs described in this section are given in Table 14.1.

The origins of self-destructive beliefs in adolescents

When counselling adolescents it is important to understand the origins of their self-destructive beliefs because it is the origins of these beliefs which give them validity in their minds. Most adolescent self-destructive beliefs are accumulated during childhood as a consequence of messages given directly and indirectly by adults in the child's environment. Some of these messages are appropriate during childhood and provide a framework for social and moral development, but later in life become self-destructive and most unhelpful.

Most children are continually told that they *should, must, ought to* and *have to* do things that adults require them to do. They are often told that things *always* or *never* happen, and they are frequently led to believe that if they do not do the right thing a *catastrophe* will happen. Additionally, they are often treated with intolerance if they do not behave in ways that are acceptable for adults. Consequently, they learn to be *intolerant* of others themselves. Children are often blamed for things that go wrong when they make mistakes. This is inevitable. However, it leads them to start engaging in beliefs which rely on *blaming* other people for their behaviours. Children model on the behaviours they observe in adults, and for most children the modelling behaviour of adults suggests that beliefs which will later be unhelpful for them are the ones that they should have.

How to challenge self-destructive beliefs when counselling adolescents

When using rational emotive behaviour therapy techniques with adolescents, we need to modify the challenging processes that are normally used with adults by taking account of the adolescent developmental process. As counsellors, we need to recognize that adolescents are different from adults. They are in a process of moving out of childhood where they have naturally and inevitably absorbed beliefs that now need to be changed.

If a counsellor, working with an adolescent, uses the usual rational emotive behaviour therapy technique of directly and actively disputing self-destructive beliefs there is a risk that the adolescent will be alienated. This is because beliefs that the young person has rightly held for years will be treated disrespectfully and will not be validated.

When counselling adolescents, challenging self-destructive beliefs needs to involve two stages:

1   The adolescent needs to be complimented for existing beliefs. These need to be validated as having been useful in the past, during childhood.
2   Existing beliefs need to be challenged as now being self-destructive and needing to change as a consequence of the adolescent's movement from childhood into adulthood. The young person no longer needs to be constrained by these beliefs but is free to reject them if they choose.

The challenging needs to be done by debating the issues in a way which parallels the way in which adolescents debate issues. This debate, in paralleling adolescent communication, may involve a level of self-disclosure. It is appropriate for a counsellor to disclose and share with an adolescent their views and beliefs in a way that allows the adolescent to integrate these beliefs into their own belief system. For example, a counsellor might say 'I have some difficulty when people tell me that I *should* do things. I prefer to do things that I *choose* to do rather than necessarily doing things that other people believe I should do.' By making a statement such as this, the counsellor is disclosing their own need for individuation, and their desire to take responsibility for their own decisions without being excessively influenced by other people's expectations.

Having made a statement such as that described, the counsellor has a responsibility to help the adolescent to fit in with the demands of the real world where we cannot do exactly as we like, but have to make choices about when and where to conform to other people's expectations. The counsellor might continue by saying, 'Sometimes, I choose to do what other people want. For example, because I choose to work at a school I have to comply with the rules here.' Thus the message is given that as a general rule it can be self-destructive to use *should* beliefs, but that there are times when we might choose to comply with other people's expectations because we want to avoid the consequences of not doing so.

Modelling a process for dealing with self-destructive beliefs may also be helpful for an adolescent. The counsellor might talk about having held a certain set of beliefs in the past, and having changed them because they were unhelpful. A counsellor might usefully ask 'Where does that belief come from? Who told you that you always had to perform to the highest standards?' By doing this, the counsellor is inviting the young person to recognize that the beliefs they hold may have been appropriate for them as a child. As a child, their parents had the right to tell them what to do, and to teach them particular values and standards. However, these beliefs, values and standards may need to be amended because their parents are no longer running their life as they once did.

In challenging self-destructive beliefs with adolescents, a conversational style is used, where the beliefs of each member in the conversation are respected, existing beliefs and values are validated as having been useful, but then questioned in terms of their current usefulness. By discussing beliefs and their origins, the adolescent is given permission to become more flexible in their thinking. The counsellor's goal is not to replace the adolescent's beliefs immediately with a new set of beliefs. Rather, it is to leave the adolescent feeling freer to think about alternative beliefs and with an openness and readiness to explore and change those beliefs which are self-destructive. Thus, the proactive counsellor does not try to impose new ways of thinking on an adolescent, but sets up a challenge and leaves the young person to deal with it in their own way.

To help in the development of new beliefs, a white-board may be used to list constructive beliefs which could replace particular self-destructive beliefs. Additionally, if the young person is willing to participate, role play and the use of imagination, as described in Chapter 13, can help the adolescent explore the outcomes of adopting new beliefs, holding on to current beliefs or rejecting part of an old belief while maintaining some part of that belief.

Anger management

A number of authors have contributed to our knowledge of the management of anger in adolescents, including Feindler and Ecton (1986), Fodor (1992) and Forman (1993). There is a general consensus that adolescents who have a problem with anger control need to externalize the problem and understand their own personal triggers and beliefs which may result in inappropriate angry behaviour. There are five clearly identifiable stages in anger management for adolescents:

1 Identifying the angry response pattern.
2 Externalizing the anger and the catalysts.
3 Identifying personal triggers and catalysts.
4 Focusing on personal power.
5 Choosing control options.

Identifying the angry response pattern

Each adolescent is unique, so that the pattern of behaviours which results in an angry response will be different for each individual. Before the undesired behaviour pattern can be changed, the adolescent needs to recognize and understand it. To help a young person do this, a counsellor might invite them to describe the following:

1 The antecedents to an angry outburst, including triggers, their own behaviour and feelings and the behaviour of others before the outburst occurs.
2 Behaviours displayed during the angry outburst. For example, being verbally or physically abusive. When describing these behaviours, the adolescent can be encouraged to talk about their reactions and also their physiological and emotional feelings.
3 Consequences that arise from the angry episode. Here, the adolescent is encouraged to examine whether the consequences make them feel good, bad or otherwise, in both the short term and the long term.

By discussing all of the above, the young person may recognize influences which are reinforcing the undesired behaviour and/or making it harder for change to occur.

Externalizing the anger and the catalysts

To help the adolescent understand their behaviour patterns the counsellor may wish to use a white-board and felt pens to draw the model shown in Figure 14.2. This model externalizes the adolescent's anger, describing the anger and the adolescent as separate identities.

Triggers, which have been triggering off the anger, do not act directly on the anger. They act on the adolescent. The adolescent has control of whether or not these triggers are allowed to activate the anger and cause a damaging explosion. Between the adolescent and the externalized anger is a space filled with catalysts (Figure 14.2). These catalysts are things which cleverly trick the young person into passing the trigger on so that it activates the anger. Additionally, the catalysts give extra power to the triggers.

The anger model shown in Figure 14.2 presents the adolescent with a dilemma. They can either choose to be powerful and take control of the triggers, the

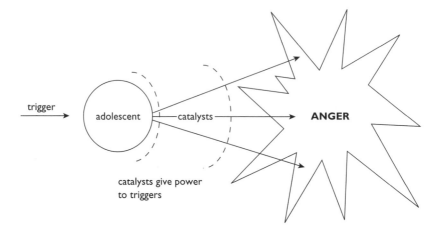

Figure 14.2   *Externalizing anger*

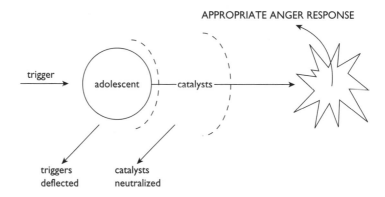

Figure 14.3   *Triggers and catalysts deflected*

catalysts and the anger, or they can give their power away so that the triggers, catalysts and anger take control. If the adolescent chooses to be powerful, triggers will be deflected, catalysts will be neutralized and the expression of anger will be appropriate, non-abusive and less damaging, as shown in Figure 14.3.

In reviewing the personal dilemma of the anger model, the adolescent needs to recognize that they can, if they choose, be the most powerful component in this model. The counsellor might ask questions such as, 'Do you want to be controlled by your anger or do you want to control your anger?', 'Who is the stronger, you or your anger?' and 'Are you going to let the triggers and catalysts trick you into letting the anger take control, or are you going to be ready to deflect the triggers and neutralize the catalysts?' The adolescent is likely to recognize that, if they take control, consequences that are better for them can be achieved, whereas if the triggers and catalysts are allowed to give power to the anger, and the anger is allowed to take control, negative consequences will inevitably result.

Table 14.2 *Triggers catalysts and alternative beliefs*

Triggers (The activating event)	Catalysts (The self-destructive belief)	Alternative belief (To neutralize the catalyst)
Being teased	Other people should always respect me	Sometimes people are disrespectful; I can cope with that because I know that I'm OK
Someone tries to get me to do something that I don't want to do	They are trying to take advantage of me	I am me and I can make my own decisions about what to do
Being pushed	Other people don't respect me	I respect myself and I will be assertive when other people try to push me around
Being shamed	Other people are better than me	I am me, and I am OK
Making a mistake	Making mistakes is a disaster	Everybody makes mistakes; that's normal, so I am normal
Waiting in a queue	I should be served first	It would be nice if I were served first but everybody has to queue up, not just me
Not being able to do something competently	I'm useless	There are some things I'm really good at doing and other things I need more practice at; nobody's perfect
When something is lost	Someone has taken it	It's just mislaid; I can find it if I stay calm and take time to look
Accidental intrusion by others	They don't respect my rights	They are careless; I am capable of telling them what I need
Someone else doesn't do what I want them to do	Other people should live up to my expectations	Other people don't need to live up to my expectations
Being unfairly treated	I should always be treated fairly	Life is not always fair and just
Losing in a game	I must always win	If I win 50 per cent of the time I'm doing well
Being told what to do by someone in authority	People in authority do not have the right to tell me what to do	I can accept that in some situations I will be told what to do and that is appropriate

A printable version of this table is available to download from the Sage website (www.sagepublications.com)

Identifying personal triggers and catalysts

Triggers are external events and precede the angry aggressive outburst. Examples of triggers are given in Table 14.2. Initially, a counsellor might invite an adolescent client to make a personal list of triggers that are commonly associated with their angry outbursts. It can then be useful for the counsellor to explore with the adolescent whether or not they believe that triggers are inevitably going to occur from time to time in their life. Recognition that triggers are inevitable is an essential part of anger control. Adolescents need to understand that triggers cannot be stopped, but are a natural part of life. What is important is the young person's response, which they can control if they choose.

Triggers are given power by catalysts. Catalysts are self-destructive beliefs, and examples of these are given in Table 14.2. Consider, for example, the trigger of 'someone trying to get you to do something you don't want to do'. A catalyst which would be likely to give this trigger more power might be the belief that they were trying to take advantage of you. This belief needs to be challenged because it is self-destructive (see discussion above on challenging self-destructive beliefs). Counsellors need to help adolescents to identify both triggers and catalysts. Catalysts can then be reviewed, challenged, and replaced by more helpful beliefs which will not give power to triggers.

Focusing on personal power

As adolescents are at a stage of life where they want to have control over their lives, so issues of power and control are important to them. The anger-control model shown in Figure 14.3 is therefore likely to appeal to adolescents because generally they will recognize that they do, if they wish, have the ability to exercise power and control over the influence of triggers and that they can neutralize catalysts by replacing self-destructive beliefs with more helpful ones. Additionally, adolescents generally don't like being controlled, so they may be motivated to control their anger rather than be controlled by it.

Some adolescents are reluctant to let go of abusive ways of expressing anger because being abusive gives them a feeling of power. It can therefore be helpful for an adolescent to identify what the pay-offs are from being powerful. By identifying these pay-offs, they may find other ways of obtaining them without being abusive. For example, a pay-off, as a consequence of being aggressive, might be that an adolescent gains a sense of being respected by others. If they are to give up aggressive behaviour, they will need to explore other ways of achieving respect. Through discussion in counselling, they may realize that as a result of being powerful in a different way, by taking control of their anger, they might gain in respect from others as a consequence of the following:

- increased self-respect
- increased confidence
- being seen as mature
- being seen as tough and in control
- being able to stand up for values and beliefs.

By contrast, when an adolescent engages in unacceptable ways of expressing anger, there are certain to be negative consequences. The young person may get into a great deal of conflict and trouble with both peers and adults, and particularly with adults who are in authority positions. In such cases, it may be useful for a counsellor to say, 'It seems to me that your anger gets you into a lot of trouble when it gets control. When you're able to control your anger, you seem to be able to avoid trouble.' Clearly, the issue of power and control in anger management needs to be presented in terms of who has the control: does the anger have control of the young person, or does the young person have control of the anger?

Choosing control options

There are a number of strategies which an adolescent can use in order to deal with triggers and/or catalysts so that they don't fire off unacceptable levels of angry behaviour. These strategies are:

- avoiding triggers
- recognizing symptoms of arousal
- using thought-stopping
- using relaxation
- challenging self-destructive beliefs
- dealing with internalized anger
- using appropriate expression of anger
- finding constructive ways to get needs met.

Avoiding triggers   Once an adolescent has been able to identify triggers that result in angry or aggressive behaviour, they may be able to identify situations where triggers might occur more often than in other situations. During the process of learning improved anger-management strategies, it may be useful for an adolescent to plan to avoid situations deliberately where triggers are likely to occur. For example, going to a particular spot on the school sports field might be likely to bring the young person into contact with others who have in the past succeeded in triggering unacceptably angry behaviour. In other situations, an adolescent might find it useful to leave a scene where their anger has been triggered in order to prevent an aggressive outburst occurring. Although avoiding triggers is a useful strategy, it may lead to the young person internalizing anger, which will need to be dealt with later (see below).

Recognizing symptoms of arousal   Adolescents need to learn to recognize the physiological symptoms of arousal which occur in situations that are likely to provoke angry responses. Young people who are starting to get angry may exhibit some, or all, of the following physiological symptoms. Sweating; increase in heart rate; clenching of jaw or fists; tensing of muscles; hair standing on end; knots in the stomach; face going red or white; increasingly rapid breathing or difficulty in getting breath. Once the physiological symptoms of arousal have been recognized, they can be used as a signal to enable the adolescent to use strategies to prevent triggers from setting off an angry outburst.

Using thought-stopping   Thought-stopping can be useful in helping an adolescent to intercept a trigger quickly to prevent it having effect or to reduce its effect. To do this, the young person is taught to use thought-stopping as soon as physiological symptoms of arousal are recognized. If someone slams a book down on a desk and simultaneously shouts 'Stop!', anyone near will have their thoughts interrupted by the 'Stop' message. In the same way, young people can be taught to interrupt their thoughts suddenly, as soon as they recognize the physiological cues of anger arousal.

It can be useful to pair thought-stopping with one specific physical behaviour. For example, some people, when learning to thought stop, will wear a loose elastic band around their wrist. When they notice that the physiological cues of arousal are starting to occur, they stretch the elastic band with their other hand so that it flicks back on to their wrist as they silently say to themselves 'Stop!' This provides an interruption to thoughts associated with the anger-arousal process. A relaxation strategy can then be used. Additionally, self-destructive beliefs which might be catalysts for triggering anger can be challenged.

Using relaxation   The use of relaxation can reduce the level of emotional arousal, making it easier for an adolescent to deflect a trigger, neutralize the power of a catalyst and take control of anger. Relaxation can be used immediately after thought-stopping, which will have occurred following the recognition of the physiological symptoms of arousal.

A relaxation exercise, as described in Chapter 13, can be used to teach an adolescent to relax. Having learnt how to relax in this way, the adolescent can then be taught how to do brief relaxation exercises in a standing or sitting position. To model brief relaxation, first show the adolescent how to take a deep breath and encourage them to try the technique themselves. You might say, for example, 'Place your hand on your stomach, breathe in slowly through your nose, feel your lungs fill completely with air, and, as you breathe in, your hand should move outward. Once your lungs are completely filled with air, breathe out completely through your mouth.' While doing the breathing exercise two or three times, the young person can be encouraged to allow their muscles to relax each time they breathe out, while silently saying calming words, such as 'relax', 'calm down', 'slow down' or 'keep cool'. The deep breathing, muscle relaxation and calming words help to reduce tension and shift the adolescent's attention away from whatever is triggering their anger and on to their own self-control (Feindler and Ecton, 1986). Clearly, when doing this exercise, excessive breathing which might create hyperventilation must be avoided.

Challenging self-destructive beliefs   As discussed, catalysts are generally the result of self-destructive beliefs and need to be challenged and replaced with more helpful beliefs (see p. 174).

Dealing with internalized anger   It is not sensible to teach a young person to control anger by merely suppressing it, because this is likely to result in a high level of internalized anger. Internalized anger can have psychological and behavioural consequences. It may lead to depression and/or the anger may be expressed in subtle ways which will cause undesirable consequences. It is therefore important that young people have ways of dealing directly with their anger, rather than just suppressing it, so that they can feel better.

One way of dealing with internalized anger is by talking through the issues related to the angry feelings with a counsellor or friend. By doing this, catharsis might occur naturally. Alternatively, a cathartic process might be deliberately planned to enable the adolescent to release the anger. In counselling, this might be through the use of two-chair work, or in the wider environment the young person might act their feelings out in a cathartic and safe way without the involvement of other people. For example, this might be done by going into an open space and yelling out things that need to be said and released. Another way to deal with internalized angry feelings is through the expression of physical energy. For example, a young person might go on a long run or engage energetically in sport. By doing this, they will release natural endorphins which will have a soothing effect. Finally, internalized anger can be released by directly expressing it to the person concerned as described in the following section.

Using appropriate expression of anger   There are times when it is appropriate for adolescents to express their anger directly. Role playing can be used, as described in Chapter 13, to help a young person to learn non-abusive ways of expressing anger. These will generally involve the adolescent learning to make statements beginning,'I feel angry because ...', followed by non-interpretative statements of fact, such as '... you have accused me of something that I didn't do.' Sometimes, feelings other than anger will be involved. For example, a young person might say, 'I feel angry and humiliated because in front of my friends you have accused me of something I didn't do.'

In teaching adolescents to make appropriate expressions of anger it is important to help them to recognize:

1   That having made a clear statement of their feelings, as described, they need to listen to and validate any response from the other person, rather than becoming involved in counterproductive argument. Being able to let the other person have the last word is a sign of maturity.
2   That there may be undesirable consequences for them if they directly express their anger to the person they feel angry towards. Hence they have to weigh up the likely consequences when deciding whether, or not, to express their anger directly in this way.

Finding constructive ways to get needs met   In teaching adolescents to control their anger it is essential to help them find socially acceptable ways to get their needs met. If they are not able to do this they will inevitably build up angry and resentful feelings, and their efforts at anger control may be undermined. They therefore need to learn assertiveness skills which will enable them to communicate with others so that they can get their needs met.

Assertiveness training

Assertiveness is a non-defensive way of presenting a point of view, and being heard, without offending others. Being assertive involves the following steps:

1   Listening to the other person.
2   Validating what the other person has said.
3   Believing in your right to present a point of view.
4   Expressing a point of view.
5   Being prepared to negotiate a compromise.
6   Being prepared to accept that differences do exist.

We believe that, for adolescents, 5 and 6 in the above list are particularly important. If these are not respected, conflict may occur. In seeking individuation for themselves, adolescents sometimes lose sight of the need for others to be individuals. However, when this is drawn to their attention they are usually quick to accept and respect the rights of others to have different opinions, because this fits with the adolescent frame of reference regarding individuation.

Teaching assertiveness to young people is best done through the use of a combination of didactic teaching on a white-board and role-playing rehearsal as described in Chapter 13.

Listening to the other person

Listening to another person involves (a) attending to the content of the message that is being verbally communicated; and (b) observing and taking account of any non-verbal messages which accompany the verbal communication. It is particularly important for adolescents to learn to pay attention to incongruence between verbal and non-verbal messages, and to check out whether information being received is correctly understood or not. Often, misunderstandings between adolescents occur because they do not get the true message being communicated. As counsellors, we need to remember that adolescents are not experienced in adult communication methods.

Adolescents need to learn to check out that they have correctly heard and understood the other person's message. For example, an adolescent might practise asking questions such as, 'Are you saying that ...?' Similarly, adolescents need to learn to check out incongruence between verbal and non-verbal messages. For example, they might practise making statements like, 'I'm confused because you are telling me to go ahead but you sound disappointed. I am not sure what you would really like.' Rehearsing statements of this type, which begin with an 'I' statement of personal feelings, can be very useful.

Validating what the other person has said

It is important for an adolescent to learn to validate what the other person has said by letting them know that they have been heard and understood. Role play can be used to practise making statements which reflect back the content of what has been heard. Typical validating statements are:

I've heard you say that ...
You would like it if ...
You think that it is important ...
You think that I ...
You are saying that ....

Validating involves being sensitive to the other person's needs and/or point of view, while continuing to stay in touch with your own needs and/or point of view.

Believing in your right to present a point of view

Adolescents need to feel confident that they have a right to present an alternative point of view, while at the same time recognizing that other people have the right to have different points of view. This inevitably means that they have to accept the possibility that their own point of view may not necessarily be accepted. Adolescents often find this difficult because of their tendency to be egocentric. However, because adolescents have a strong belief in their right to be respected as individuals, they can usually understand and accept that other people may also want to be respected as individuals with their own points of view. In this regard, it can be useful for counsellors positively to promote the right to be different.

Expressing a point of view

When expressing a particular point of view it is helpful for the adolescent to state things from their point of view by making 'I' statements. Coaching in the use of 'I' statements, particularly those which express feelings, can be useful. For example, a counsellor might coach an adolescent to make statements such as 'I feel embarrassed about asking for money, but I want to get to the job interview and I need money so that I can catch the bus.' Adolescents need to learn that when expressing a point of view, it is important to stay focused and not be distracted by side issues. Additionally, there is a need to be specific, and to avoid making assumptions about the other person's feelings or motives without checking these out.

Being prepared to negotiate a compromise

Some counsellors, who teach assertiveness training with adults, will suggest that assertive behaviour requires the person to continue making their request without deviating, and that this may involve behaving like a cracked record, by repeatedly restating the request. For adolescents, this approach to assertiveness training can be destructive as it may set them up for failure. Other people are likely to become angered by constant repetitions of a request, particularly when coming from a young person. It is better to teach adolescents to try to make sure that their message has been heard correctly, and then to negotiate so that compromise can be achieved, if this is possible, in situations where their requests are not going to be granted in full.

Being prepared to accept that differences do exist

There will be times when adolescents will not get their requests met in any way. Such situations may present strong triggers for anger. Adolescents therefore need to be prepared for such situations and to rehearse behaviours for dealing with triggers when these occur. Where there are unresolvable differences, the adolescent needs to learn to be able to back off by saying something such as, 'You and I don't think the same, so we may as well stop discussing it.' In saying this, the young person needs to recognize that expecting that they will always get their needs met is unrealistic and constitutes a self-destructive belief.

Success in assertive skills training depends on good modelling, coaching in specific skills, rehearsal through role play and reinforcement when positive outcomes occur. Readers who wish to seek further information on assertiveness training for adolescents might consult Forman (1993).

Setting lifestyle goals

Adolescents are at a stage in their lives when they are confronted by new experiences and situations. In addition, they have an unknown future which threatens to present them with unexpected challenges. Because they are moving through unknown territory in their lives, they often have problems in finding an overall direction which makes sense for them. If they lack an overall sense of direction, and do not have clear lifestyle goals, they may become excessively troubled by the uncertainty of their lives.

Lifestyle goals provide a general sense of direction within which other less global decisions can be made. They also help to provide motivation. This is important because if adolescents are to be successful in achieving satisfaction for themselves, they need to be motivated.

Types of lifestyle goals

Goals can be divided into categories as follows (Ford, 1992):

1   *Affective*: where goals are described in terms of feelings.
2   *Cognitive*: where goals are described in terms of creativity or knowledge.
3   *Subjective*: where goals are described as fulfilling spiritual needs.
4   *Relationship*: where goals are described in terms of relationships with one's self and others.
5   *Task-oriented*: where goals are described as meeting material or mastery needs.

When adolescents are exploring their goals, it can be useful for counsellors to identify the categories into which possible goals fall.

Selecting goals

It can be useful for adolescents to list their goals and then develop a hierarchy which prioritizes the goals which are most important for them. Sometimes, when they do this, they will be surprised to find that their priorities are not what they would have expected.

The simultaneous pursuit of more than one type of goal will be the most motivating. For example, combining the affective goal of feeling happy, with a relationship goal of being with friends, might lead an adolescent to choose activities, experiences or an occupation which involves working and interacting with others. Thus, it can be helpful for an adolescent to explore lifestyle possibilities in which more than one type of goal might be achieved simultaneously.

As an adolescent begins to isolate particular goals, a counsellor might encourage him to consider sub-goals, or targets, which will help him to achieve these goals. This is useful, because self-motivation is sustained by the achievement of obtainable sub-goals which lead to larger goals. Success in achieving sub-goals provides reinforcement and incentive to proceed further. It is the proactive counsellor's task to help the adolescent try to design a lifestyle that offers opportunities for achieving a number of types of goal. Unfortunately, environmental and personal constraints sometimes preclude the possibility of meeting multiple goals.

Once sub-goals have been achieved, it is useful to provide the young person with feedback to help them continue. Feedback should include information which enables them to evaluate their progress and identify hurdles. It should reinforce the young person's beliefs with regard to achieving desired outcomes. Feedback should also provide the adolescent with information about whether or not they have the skills required to achieve targeted goals.

Suicide and goals

Baumeister (1990) believes that helping to identify goals is essential for adolescents who attempt or threaten suicide. He has formulated the 'escape theory' which suggests that adolescents who attempt suicide intentionally fail to attend to the broader goals and values that normally provide meaning to a person's thoughts, feelings and actions. Changes in goals, emotions and personal beliefs are often precursors to suicide. Helping adolescents to identify both short- and long-term goals can therefore be helpful in suicide prevention.

Making decisions

As adolescents are moving from a stage of being dependent on their parents and family to being independent, they are required to make many decisions for themselves. For many adults, making decisions can be difficult, and for most adolescents even more difficult. This is because they do not have a body of experience from past decisions on which to base their current judgements. Additionally, they often do not have information about the options available to them or the likely consequences of these options. Sometimes, even though they will understand cognitively what the consequences of particular actions are likely to be, because they have not personally experienced such consequences they may underestimate their importance or severity. Alternatively, they may exaggerate their importance and be afraid to choose alternatives because they believe that the associated consequences will be too severe for them.

Adolescent decision-making processes are often influenced by pressure from peer groups to conform; they may also be influenced by beliefs about other people's motives, abilities and characteristics, where these people's co-operation might be required to facilitate or implement decisions. Adolescents can often be over-optimistic in their estimates of the outcomes and consequences of their decisions. Because an adolescent feels optimistic, they may have an illusion of being in control in situations where this is unrealistic.

Adolescents are likely to make decisions impulsively and/or defensively in response to situational demands without carefully following a properly thought-out decision-making process. Counsellors need to help them use their own resources for arriving at decisions but, in the process, to provide them with information which they do not have because of lack of experience. They need to be encouraged to make the best possible choices, taking account of their personal values and the objectives they wish to achieve (Janis and Mann, 1982).

In helping adolescents to make decisions it can be useful for a counsellor to identify, for them, the following stages of decision-making:

1   Identifying unhelpful decision-making response patterns.
2   Exploring risks associated with change or with not changing.
3   Exploring lifestyle goals.
4   Identifying losses involved in choosing.
5   Examining alternatives.
6   Informing others of a decision.
7   Maintaining a commitment to a decision.

For most important decisions, all of these stages will be required. If any of them are missed out, then it may be that decisions will be reached that cannot be maintained.

Identifying unhelpful decision-making response patterns

It is helpful for adolescents to be able to identify ways in which they behave when they need to make decisions. Stress is almost always associated with decision-making because of anxiety related to the losses involved. Some common ways in which adolescents respond to the stress of making decisions are as follows:

1   They may continue doing what is already happening.
2   They may adopt a new course of action without any prior thought or planning.
3   They may hastily adopt a solution that provides immediate relief without looking at the consequences.
4   They may procrastinate and try to shift the responsibility of the decision-making on to somebody else.
5   They may search for information, assimilate the information in an unbiased way and appraise the alternatives to arrive at a decision.

Clearly, the last response is the most useful. Counsellors can help adolescents identify their responses to the stress associated with decision-making. This can be useful in enabling them to recognize unsatisfactory responses in the future.

Exploring risks associated with change or with not changing

When adolescents are trying to make decisions regarding change, counsellors may need to help them to explore their expectations about the risks involved in changing, or not changing.

Risks in changing   There are often problems for adolescents when they do decide to change their behaviour, even if the changes are for the better. First, they have to cope with their own emotional feelings with regard to change. Whenever change occurs there are likely to be some losses, and there may be feelings of apprehension and uncertainty about the change.

Not only do young people have to cope with their own feelings, but they also have to cope with other people's responses to any change. Unfortunately, sometimes when adolescents make decisions which will lead to positive outcomes for themselves and/or others, parents, other adults and peers will be troubled by the change and will resist it.

When changing, there is usually uncertainty because adolescents may not have previously experienced using the behaviours which have been chosen. Consequently, they cannot be sure whether the outcomes of these behaviours will be positive or not.

Risks in not changing   Adolescents often make decisions because their current behaviours are causing problems for them. They are, therefore, usually very aware of the risks associated with not changing. However, it can be useful for a counsellor to ask about these risks so that they are brought into focus in the adolescent's mind, thus encouraging a decision which will result in positive change.

Exploring the adolescent's optimism   Risk-taking is very much a part of adolescent behaviour, so adolescents will often look forward to new and exciting changes, even though they may be stressful. Thus, many adolescents will view change with enthusiasm and optimism. However, some adolescents will feel excessively anxious when making decisions. For them, exploring the risks associated with making a decision to change is an important step in the process of decision-making.

Exploring lifestyle goals

As explained above, counsellors can help adolescents to explore lifestyle goals which are important for them. Once goals are identified, these will influence current decisions.

Identifying losses involved in choosing

In making decisions, adolescents need to be able to recognize losses which are associated with the alternatives available to them. Almost all decisions involve losses. For example, consider a situation where an adolescent makes a decision to leave home. As a consequence, the young person will experience the loss of guidance and support from parents, as well as material comfort and security. Typical losses associated with decisions may include the loss of such things as:

- a relationship
- closeness in a relationship
- intensity of a relationship
- support

- security
- freedom
- personal control
- leadership
- power
- material possessions
- personal faith
- previously held values and/or beliefs.

Sometimes adolescents may be able to compensate for personal losses such as loss of freedom, loss of control, loss of leadership and loss of power by making decisions which provide other rewards in these areas. At other times, adolescents will need to accept losses without being able to compensate for them. This is particularly so with regard to losses which involve the emotions, such as relationship losses.

Once losses are identified, it may be possible to find ways to minimize them. For example, an adolescent who is wanting to leave home may recognize the loss of material comforts and security, and as a consequence consider ways to earn money to make up for the loss.

Examining alternatives

Alternatives may be explored using symbolic strategies as described in Chapter 12 (see p. 137) or the creative strategy of role play as described in Chapter 13 (p. 152). However, some adolescents do not enjoy the use of symbolic or creative strategies and may wish to work in a more cognitive way. Sometimes it is possible to combine creative and/or symbolic strategies with cognitive strategies.

It can be helpful for an adolescent to write up on a white-board alternatives that need to be considered when making a particular decision. While this list is being drawn up, the counsellor might encourage the young person to think of as many options as possible. The options can then be explored by allowing the adolescent to talk about them in a general way. After this the counsellor may wish to summarize the alternatives clearly and encourage the young person to explore each option individually. By doing this, the positive and negative aspects of each option should be discussed so that the alternatives can be narrowed down to a shorter list. There may be some advantage in encouraging the adolescent to deal with the most unlikely or least preferred options first. This helps in shortening the list of alternatives, making it easier for a decision to be reached.

When examining alternatives, it is helpful to encourage the adolescent not only to look carefully at the consequences, both negative and positive, of each alternative, but also to take account of their emotional or gut feelings connected with each alternative.

There are some risks for adolescents when examining alternatives. These are:

1   The adolescent needs to understand the difference between decisions which are based on fact and also sit comfortably emotionally, and those which are

only based on emotional preference and have little factual basis. Often, because of lack of experience, adolescents will be carried away by strong emotional preferences and make decisions which may have doubtful or negative outcomes.

2   The adolescent might get distracted by irrelevant aspects of the alternatives which lead to an unrealistic prediction of outcomes. To guard against this, the counsellor needs to help the young person to focus on the most significant aspects of each option.

3   The adolescent's level of stress, self-perception, confidence and self-esteem will often influence their ability to look at alternatives clearly.

4   An adolescent may be pulled in one direction by thinking which depends on past values and beliefs. In this case, it is important to check out whether these beliefs and values are still important for them. Where a decision fits with the adolescent's current values and beliefs, it is more likely that there will be commitment to the decision.

After proper consideration of alternatives, the final choice must be the adolescent's, rather than a choice which is influenced by the counsellor. It is to be hoped that, with careful consideration of the advantages, disadvantages and consequences of choosing each alternative, the adolescent will be able to make a decision which is best for him. However, this decision may not be the one that the counsellor believes to be the most desirable, sensible or appropriate.

Informing others of a decision

Once a decision has been made it needs to be acted on. However, this may not be immediate. The timing needs to be suitable for the adolescent and it is sensible to discuss this in counselling.

With many decisions, other people will need to be informed. Often an adolescent will deliberate about implementing a decision because they are uncertain about how to manage the responses of other people. To deal with this uncertainty, a counsellor might help an adolescent to anticipate the possible reactions of others and to decide on possible responses to these reactions. When doing this, it might be helpful for the counsellor to encourage the adolescent to rehearse the way in which they intend to tell others of their decision. This rehearsal can be done through the use of role play as described in Chapter 13, if desired. Additionally, role play can be used to allow the adolescent to experience what it would be like to be the recipient of the intended message. To help the adolescent in informing others of their decision, the counsellor might also coach the adolescent in the use of 'I' statements and assertiveness skills.

Maintaining a commitment to a decision

Adhering to a decision is often difficult for an adolescent, who may be constantly confronted with challenges and pressures that are contrary to the decision and the chosen direction. In particular, the young person may receive negative feedback from others regarding the decision.

Following an initial honeymoon period, where the adolescent is excited about a new decision, there will often be a period of renewed stress in response to the decision. However, young people can often cope with stress at this time more easily than when the decision was initially made. They are often more resilient, having dealt with the earlier stress, so they may be able to continue with their commitment to the decision.

The stability of the adolescent's decision will be significantly affected by the intensity of feedback, both positive and negative, which the adolescent receives from others regarding the decision. In the face of strong and consistent negative feedback, the adolescent may abandon a decision and seek an alternative. When this happens, it is important for a counsellor to give the young person positive feedback in connection with having tried out the original decision. The young person can be told that, in effect, an experiment has been done, with information from the experiment showing that the decision needs to be altered. By framing feedback in terms of a useful experiment, the young person may feel good rather than feel that they are poor at making decisions.

In summary

In this chapter we have discussed cognitive strategies which can be used with adolescents. These strategies can often be employed in conjunction with the psycho-educational strategies discussed in Chapter 15.

15   Psycho-educational strategies

In this chapter we will discuss a range of educational strategies which teach adolescents about life and may also help them to gain more control over their behaviours. Adolescents are on a journey of self-discovery and are mostly hungry to learn about themselves and their relationships with others. Gaining such knowledge helps them to develop an identity and make sense of the world around them. Figure 15.1 shows the ways in which various psycho-educational strategies can be used to achieve particular primary counselling functions. The psycho-educational strategies which will be discussed encourage adolescents to participate actively in ways of learning new information. The processes used are largely ones of self-discovery.

Most adolescents see counsellors as people who have knowledge and skills in the area of intrapersonal and interpersonal relationships (Gibson-Cline, 1996).

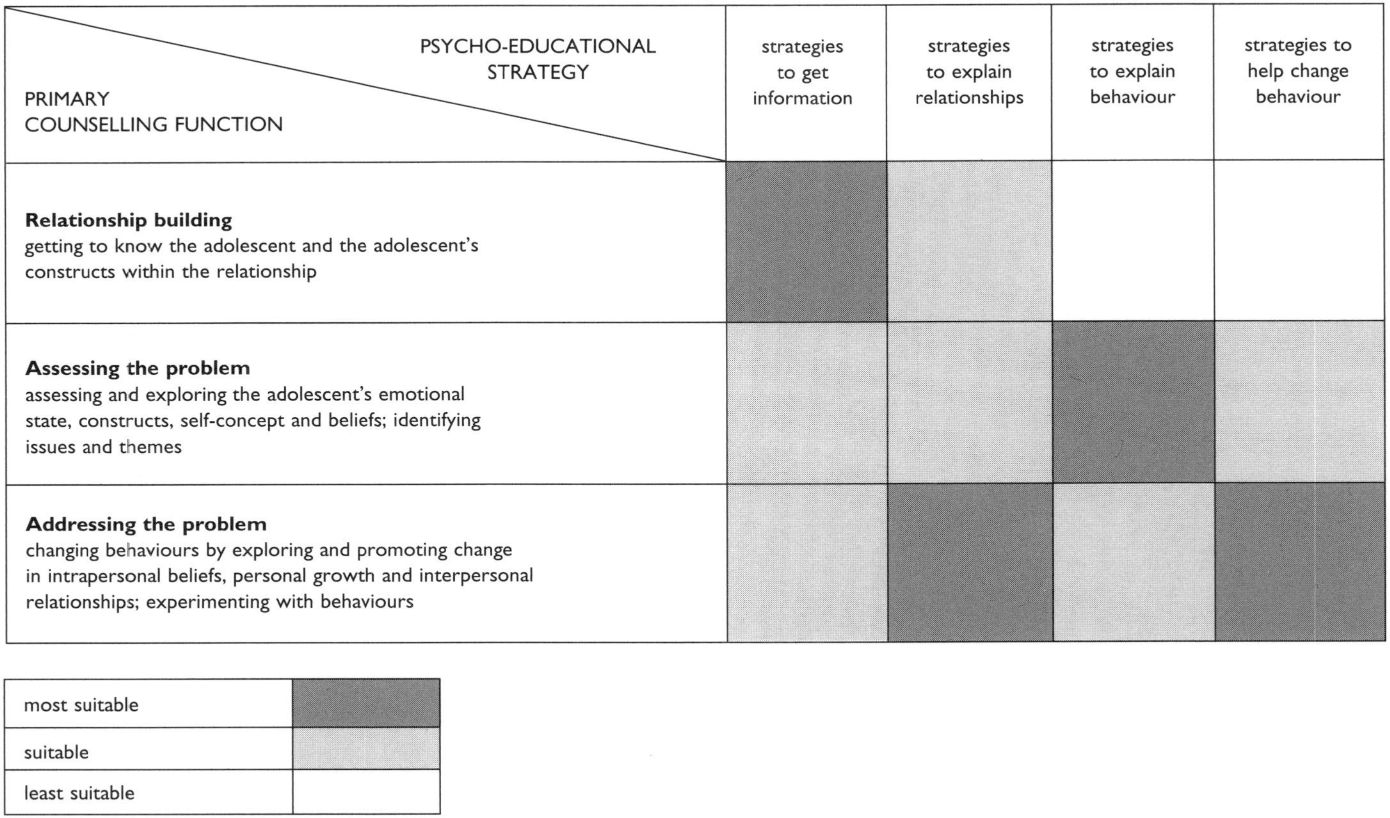

PRIMARY COUNSELLING FUNCTION \ PSYCHO-EDUCATIONAL STRATEGY	strategies to get information	strategies to explain relationships	strategies to explain behaviour	strategies to help change behaviour
Relationship building getting to know the adolescent and the adolescent's constructs within the relationship	most suitable	suitable	least suitable	least suitable
Assessing the problem assessing and exploring the adolescent's emotional state, constructs, self-concept and beliefs; identifying issues and themes	suitable	suitable	most suitable	suitable
Addressing the problem changing behaviours by exploring and promoting change in intrapersonal beliefs, personal growth and interpersonal relationships; experimenting with behaviours	suitable	most suitable	suitable	most suitable

Legend:
- most suitable
- suitable
- least suitable

Figure 15.1 *Suitability of psycho-educational strategies for achieving primary counselling functions*

Consequently, while learning mainly through self-discovery by using psycho-educational strategies, adolescents are also likely to gain if they can make use of the personal knowledge and experience of the counsellor, about human relationships. Thus, it is useful for counsellors to share relevant knowledge and experience so that young people can integrate information that fits into their own body of knowledge.

When using psycho-educational strategies, a counsellor needs constantly to observe the young person's non-verbal behaviour and verbal responses. Through this observation, new material may be discovered about the young person's emotional feelings, beliefs, issues and attitudes. Quite often, a counsellor will need to interrupt the use of a psycho-educational strategy in order to explore issues which are spontaneously emerging for the adolescent. In this respect, it needs to be remembered that a strategy is only a tool which is used to enhance the counselling process. It is more important for a counsellor to continually watch for, and deal with, underlying issues as they emerge, than to stay with a particular psycho-educational strategy.

There is a risk when using psycho-educational models, that an adolescent may uncritically accept a complete psycho-educational model and try to fit themself into that model. It is more important that the adolescent should be encouraged to examine critically and modify the model so that it suits them.

Psycho-educational strategies will be described under four headings:

- strategies to get information
- strategies to explain relationships
- strategies to explain behaviour
- strategies to help change behaviour.

Strategies to get information

Two simple psycho-educational strategies, which can be used to enable adolescents to find out and share information about themselves, are rating scales and inventories.

Rating scales

When using rating scales, a white-board or poster paper is needed so that information is visually presented. Rating scales are linear models which depict a range of items from one extreme to another. They can use either numerical ratings, such as 1 to 7, as indicators, or qualitative ratings, such as 'very much' and 'not at all'. Rating scales can be used to rate and monitor intensity, severity or frequency of behaviours.

Qualitative rating scales   Imagine that an adolescent is complaining about the restrictive behaviour of parents. A counsellor might draw a rating scale on a white-board as shown in Figure 15.2. The young person could then be asked to put marks on that rating scale to indicate exactly where their mother fits and exactly where their father fits on the scale. Discussion can then follow to help the young person recognize variations in parental behaviour. For example, the

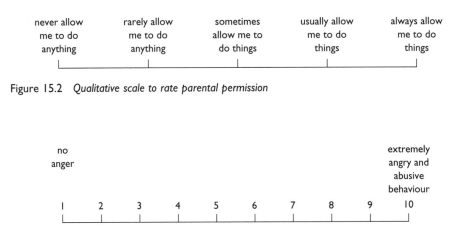

never allow	rarely allow	sometimes	usually allow	always allow
me to do	me to do	allow me to	me to do	me to do
anything	anything	do things	things	things

Figure 15.2   *Qualitative scale to rate parental permission*

no anger

extremely angry and abusive behaviour

1   2   3   4   5   6   7   8   9   10

Figure 15.3   *Numerical scale to rate behaviour in terms of severity*

young person might have put the marks at the extreme left-hand end, 'Never allow me to do anything', but it might emerge in discussion that, at times, this is not correct. The young person could also be asked to mark where they would like their parents to be on the scale. As a consequence, discussion of issues relating to control and responsibility might emerge.

Numerical rating scales   Sometimes it can be useful to draw rating scales using numerical values, ranging from 1 to 10, for example. Rating scales using numerical values are particularly useful for rating behaviour in terms of severity or intensity. For example, it might be useful for an adolescent to rate their level of anger on a scale of 1–10 as shown in Figure 15.3. Numerical scales can also be useful in rating the frequency of occurrence of behaviours; for example, the number of times each week a young person intervenes in a dispute between their parents. Such rating scales can be used to provide base-line measures and then monitor change. Thus, they may be useful in promoting change and in providing information required for setting goals.

The use of rating scales to monitor feeling   Rating scales can be used to monitor feelings, at a point in time or over a period of time, using a scale such as that shown in Figure 15.4.

The use of rating scales to give feedback   Rating scales can help a young person to stop and think about their behaviours. Often young people tend to think of their own and other people's behaviours in terms of extremes. When processing the responses of an adolescent on a rating scale, a counsellor may be able to help the young person to recognize the way in which behaviours often vary along a continuum between two extremes. This can be done by encouraging the adolescent to identify times when exceptions to the extremes on the continuum occur.

Inventories

Inventories, or questionnaires, are used by mental health workers in assessing a range of mental health problems. In addition, when counselling adolescents, it can be useful to use informal questionnaires such as those found in popular

	unhappy most of the time	unhappy some of the time	sometimes happy, sometimes unhappy	happy some of the time	happy most of the time	happy all the time
unhappy all the time						

Figure 15.4   *Scale to rate feelings*

magazines and those which specifically target adolescents. Such inventories can be used in a serious or a humorous way to help young people identify informa-tion which is consistently true about their perceptions of themselves.

A typical questionnaire is shown in Figure 15.5. The 'How friendly are you?' questionnaire explores an adolescent's perceptions of their ability to be friendly towards others. Processing of the completed questionnaire can facilitate discus-sion and exploration of self-perceptions and related issues. The scoring key can also be used for discussion. For example, what does a score of 20 actually mean for the individual concerned?

Even though a counsellor may not believe in astrology, numerology or other new age concepts, horoscopes are popular with many adolescents, and may be useful to help them explore their perceptions of themselves. Similarly, more con-ventional, established methods of categorizing people and their personalities can be used, such as the Myers–Briggs type indicator (McCaulley, 1990).

Strategies to explain relationships

Three ways of exploring relationship issues, and helping adolescents under-stand the nature of relationships, involve the use of:

* genograms
* ideas from transactional analysis
* strategies for understanding boundaries.

Genograms

Figure 15.6 shows a typical genogram where females are drawn as ellipses, males as rectangles, and the lines are used to indicate various relationships as described in the key. (The genograms shown in Figures 15.6 and 15.7 are invented: any similarity to a real family is purely coincidental.)

Adolescents like to be engaged in activity. Many of them, therefore, will enjoy drawing genograms of their extended families on white-boards or on poster paper using coloured felt pens. Genograms are a useful way of collecting and organizing information about a family. This information might include the extended family, including grandparents, uncles, aunts and so on. A genogram provides a pictorial layout of a family which can help adolescents to recognize their position within the family. This is something that is important for adoles-cents because they are trying to find a personal identity, and part of their per-sonal identity is likely to be framed in the context of their family.

HOW FRIENDLY ARE YOU?: circle your answer and check your score!	
1 When other people invite you out, you go … (a) Sometimes (b) Always (c) Not usually	5 Your friends indicate they would like to celebrate your recent athletic win. You … (a) Match their lively behaviour and respond cheerfully (b) Ignore their attempts to engage you (c) Wish that you were at home
2 You remember a friend's birthday so you … (a) Send flowers (b) Call them (c) Call them only if they remembered your last birthday (d) Say 'Happy Birthday' next time you meet	6 When going for your regular walk in your neighbourhood, you usually … (a) Say 'hello' only to people that you recognize (b) Say 'hello' to everyone that you pass (c) Say 'hello' to no one
3 You haven't heard from a friend since your last outing, during which you had a slight disagreement, you … (a) Call and ignore the issue of the disagreement (b) Call, acknowledge the disagreement by owning your part in it and suggest you both meet at the place you like to hang out (c) Wait until your friend calls you	7 You know that a classmate has been involved in a weekend sporting accident. You … (a) Drop in to see how they are and hear about their ordeal (b) Wait for them to recover fully before you ask them how they're feeling (c) Stop by quickly to let them know that if they need anything you're available to help
4 You are sorting through photos and come across one of an old school friend you have lost contact with. You … (a) Remember the good times you had together (b) Try to get back in touch with them (c) Prefer to remember them as someone from your past	8 You are going on a school excursion by bus. You are likely to … (a) Talk with the person who sits in the vacant seat next to you (b) Take advantage of looking at the scenery (c) Find a seat next to someone already on the bus so that you can chat

HOW DID YOU SCORE?

(1) a = 2, b = 5, c = 0; (2) a = 5, b = 2, c = 0 d = 1; (3) a = 2, b = 5, c = 0; (4) a = 2, b = 5, c = 0; (5) a = 5, b = 2, c = 0; (6) a = 2, b = 5, c = 0; (7) a = 2, b = 0, c = 5; (8) a = 2, b = 0, c = 5.

25–40 points: being friendly is important to you
You consider friendliness high on your list of priorities in relationships. You try to make other people feel valued and liked in relationships and are willing to persevere in relationships. You will do so even if others don't want to!

10–24 points; you see being friendly as a two-way street
Being friendly is important to you; however, you need feedback from others to continue to be friendly. You are conscious of not intruding on others' privacy.

9 points or less: friendliness is not a priority for you
You are one of the world's rare people who is comfortable with his or her own company, while not being unfriendly. There are other things that capture your interest.

Figure 15.5   *Example of an inventory*
A printable version of this figure is available to download from the Sage website (www.sagepublications.com)

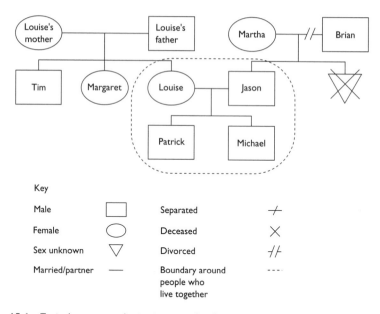

Figure 15.6 *Typical genogram: Louise is married to Jason and they have two children, Patrick and Michael. Jason's mother and father, Martha and Brian, are divorced, Jason had a sibling of unknown sex who died.*

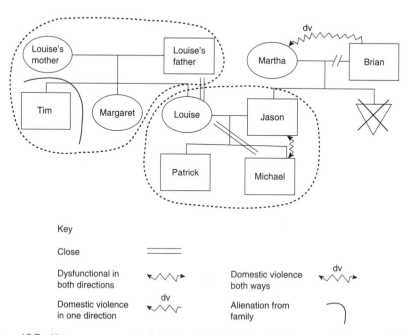

Figure 15.7 *Using a genogram to illustrate relationships: Jason's father was violent towards his mother during their marriage. Jason has a dysfunctional relationship with his son Michael. Louise has a close relationship with Michael. Louise is also close to her father. While Louise's parents and siblings live together, her brother Tim is alienated from the rest of the family.*

While an adolescent is drawing a genogram, discussion is likely to revolve around family characteristics and relationships within the family. Consequently, a genogram may enable a young person to talk about their family in a way which is likely to reveal personal issues. A genogram can indicate the closeness and distance of family members in relation to each other. Additional lines may be added to indicate particular relationships. As shown in Figure 15.7, the double line between Louise and Michael indicates a close relationship, whereas the wavy line between Jason and Michael, indicates an unsatisfactory relationship. Where the wavy line has the small letters 'dv' written beside it, as on the line from Brian to Martha, domestic violence has occurred or is occurring. The dotted lines around clusters of family members indicate those who are living together.

From a genogram, a young person may be able to recognize patterns of behaviour and particular influences which come from generation to generation. For example, the young person may recognize that there has been an inter-generational dependency on alcohol within the family. Once this behaviour has been recognized, the young person may be able to make a decision, either to continue the family tradition and become an alcoholic, or to make a new and different life for herself by choosing a different path.

Ideas from transactional analysis

Transactional analysis was originated by Berne (1964) and developed by Harris (1973). Ideas from transactional analysis tend to appeal to adolescents because they provide easy-to-follow explanations of behaviours within relationships and within people. Transactional analysis models can be represented by pictorial drawings which can be put on to a white-board or poster paper. These drawings provide an anchor for the ideas which are being presented and allow the young person to participate by modifying the drawings to suit their own situation.

In Chapter 7 we described a modified version of the transactional analysis model by showing the inner components of a person as including parent, adult, adolescent and child. We believe that the modified model given in Chapter 7 is most useful in helping counsellors understand the needs of adolescents in counselling. However, when the transactional analysis model is used with adolescents as a psycho-educational tool, we believe that it is better to return to the original model, as proposed by Berne (1964), in which there are only three inner components identified within an individual, as follows:

1   *Inner parent*: The inner parent can be either a critical parent or a nurturing parent. The critical parent is powerful, dominating, rigid and controlling, whereas the nurturing parent is warm, protective and caring. The parent role has a high level of responsibility, including responsibility not only for self, but also for others, when the communication is directed from the inner parent to the other person's child.
2   *Inner adult*: The inner adult:

   - is reality-based and logical
   - is respectful of others rather than seeking to control them

inner parent	The *critical parent*: powerful, dominating, rigid, controlling, coercive and restrictive. The *nurturing parent*: caring, permissive, protective and with a high level of reponsibility for self and others.
inner adult	The *adult*: able to choose responses, self-directed, reality-based and logical. Respectful of others, seeks information before making decisions, independent and self-sufficient. Flexible and able to change in response to new information
inner child	The *child*: dependent, childlike, helpless, submissive or rebellious. Responds without thought to emotional feelings. Easily takes the victim role, experiences high levels of emotion and is prone to tantrum.

Figure 15.8   *The transactional analysis model of personality*

- seeks information before making decisions, rather than being governed by emotional responses
  - is not submissive but independent and self-sufficient
  - is flexible and able to change in response to new information.

3 *Inner child*: The inner child is childlike and helpless. It may be submissive or rebellious. It is dependent, responds reactively and without thought to emotional feelings, easily takes the victim role, may experience high levels of emotion and is prone to tantrum.

In using this model of personality with an adolescent, a diagram such as that shown in Figure 15.8 can be used. As this diagram is constructed, the adolescent can be involved in discussion of the characteristics that apply to a critical parent, a nurturing parent, an adult and an inner child. By doing this, the adolescent will inevitably become involved in an exploration of parts of herself.

The adolescent can next be invited to explore the ways in which relationships are influenced by communications which come from differing parts of the inner self and go to various parts of the inner self of the other person, as shown in Figure 15.9. Figures 15.9a and 15.9b show examples of communication patterns which are dysfunctional and unsatisfactory because the communication lines cross each other. Many patterns such as these were described by Harris (1973). Parallel communications, as shown in Figures 15.9c and 15.9d tend to be more satisfactory, although they may still cause problems. For example, if one person

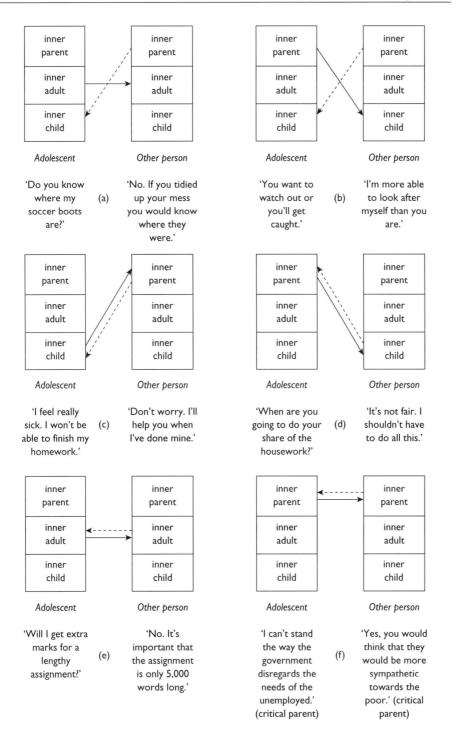

Figure 15.9 *Communication interaction patterns (the solid arrows designate the first message and the dotted arrows indicate the response)*

is behaving as a child talking to a parent and the other is responding as a parent talking to a child, as shown in Figure 15.9c, then there is effectively collaboration between the two parties to play particular roles. However, this arrangement may be uncomfortable for both, particularly over a long period of time. The communication pattern between a person who is behaving like an angry critical parent and the other person responding as a dissatisfied child will also be uncomfortable (Figure 15.9d).

Generally, people are more satisfied if the communication lines are parallel and horizontal as shown in Figures 15.9e and 15.9f. Parent–parent and child–child communications can be quite enjoyable and satisfying at times. However, there could sometimes be disastrous consequences from these communications because both parties might collude in undesirable behaviour. The optimum mode of communication is that between adult and adult, as shown in Figure 15.9e.

Clearly, every person has choice about which inner part they use in communicating with others. This choice is certain to influence the outcome of communication and also to impact on the relationship. Teaching adolescents the transactional analysis model can help them to understand more about the ways in which they relate to, and communicate with, other people. They may, in addition, become more aware of the likely consequences of their behaviour on relationships. Readers who wish to learn more about transactional analysis might like to read Berne (1964), Berne et al. (1996) and Harris (1973).

Strategies for understanding boundaries

As described in Chapter 1, adolescents have a heightened awareness of biological and physical needs. They are changing physically, and becoming aware of the sexual changes in their bodies and of their heightened sexual arousal. For many adolescents this can be a period of intense discomfort, while at the same time being exciting. They are continually faced with making decisions about personal closeness and intimacy in situations that may be new for them. Consequently, it is often necessary in counselling to help adolescents explore issues related to closeness and distance in relationships.

During childhood, relationships and friendships are often governed and controlled by parental decisions. This usually changes during adolescence, as the young person starts to have more freedom in choosing, maintaining and relinquishing friendships. Adolescents also learn that there are different types of relationship. Whereas, for a child, another child is either a friend or not a friend, in adolescence there is a growing recognition of the development of a range of relationships. This range varies along a continuum, as follows:

- not a friend
- an acquaintance
- marginally a friend
- one of a number of friends (or part of a group of friends)
- a close friend
- a special friend in an intimate personal relationship.

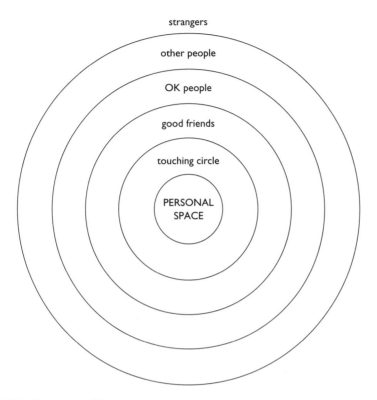

Figure 15.10 *The circle model*

Managing and maintaining such a range of friendships, and also allowing friendships to change, requires considerable skill, much of which has to be learnt during adolescence.

Adolescents often have problems in understanding what they perceive as, and what may actually be, rejection by others. Often rejection by others, or the perception of rejection, is a consequence of others setting boundaries that are important for them. If an adolescent is able to understand the nature of boundaries, then they will be better able to accept rejection when it occurs, as it inevitably will.

To help adolescents understand the concept of boundaries, a modified version of the circle concept suggested by Champagne and Walker-Hirsch (1982), can be used. Figure 15.10 shows the circle model, as we will call it, which can be drawn on a large sheet of paper using felt pens. The circles, in order of size, represent the following:

- *The central circle*: this circle is described as the adolescent's own personal space, which does not have to be shared with anyone else unless the adolescent decides to invite someone to do so. The adolescent may write their name in this circle. If another person is allowed into this circle, intimate behaviour will occur. This might involve the sharing of very private and personal information and/or touching. Sexual behaviour, which might include sexual intercourse, may also occur if that is what is mutually desired.

- *The touching circle*: this circle is one in which the adolescent might engage in some non-sexual physical contact such as hugging. Relatives and special friends may be invited into this circle.
- *The good friends circle*: this circle is for people with whom there are warm, positive and mutual feelings. Personal and intimate information might be shared with them. However, for many young people, there will be little or no touching or hugging.
- *The OK people circle*: this circle includes people who are in the young person's social system. Relationships with these people are comfortable, but they are not close friends. The adolescent may not particularly either like or dislike them. These people are part of the group to which the young person belongs. For a person to move from this 'OK people circle' to the 'good friends circle', they would need to spend more time with the young person, share more about themselves and participate more fully in common interests.
- *The other people circle*: this circle includes all of those people whom the young person might meet but who don't belong within the smaller circles. Thus, familiar faces such as shopkeepers, bus drivers and other people who are recognized, but with whom there are not generally conversations, are in this circle.
- Outside the outer circle is the space occupied by *strangers*.

When using the circle model, the adolescent is invited to describe the kinds of people who might be invited into each circle, and to write their descriptions or names within the correct circle. In addition, using a different coloured marker pen, behaviours which are appropriate for each circle are discussed and written in the relevant circle. The circle model can be used to teach behaviours that are connected with the development of appropriate boundaries and relationships with others. In particular, the young person might learn the following:

1   It is appropriate for young people to have boundaries, which they draw themselves, which set limits to the closeness of relationships with other people. On the circle model, no one has the right to move into a circle closer to the centre without mutual agreement.
2   Other people have their own boundaries, which can similarly be represented by sets of circles, and have the right to decide who may enter a particular circle. Consequently, young people will not be able to control where someone else will place them. Just as they control how close they will allow others to be, so other people will similarly set limits.
3   Relationships are not fixed, but are dynamic. If the adolescent wishes, they can, on their circle model, allow other people to move from one circle to another. They have the right to be in control of whether or not they allow a person to move from a larger circle to a smaller one. When inviting someone to move into a smaller circle, the adolescent needs to respect that other person's wishes. It may be that the other person will not wish to move in closer.
4   While young people have control over allowing others to move from one circle to another in their own model, they will not have control over whether they themselves are allowed to move from one circle to a smaller one in somebody else's set of circles.

5   There are different kinds of behaviours that are appropriate for relationships within each of the circles. If the adolescent wishes someone to move from a larger circle to a smaller circle, then they will need to display behaviours that are inviting and create a climate which encourages the other person to want to move. Equally, if the adolescent wishes to move from an outer circle to an inner circle, or from an inner circle to an outer circle in somebody else's model, they will need to develop behaviours that are appropriate for achieving this, subject to the other person's co-operation.

6   Behaviours must be developed which will give other people clear messages about where they belong, so that consistent relationships will be developed without unnecessary misunderstanding. These behaviours will involve social skills such as friendship-formation skills, assertiveness skills, negotiation skills and conflict-resolution skills. The ability to have some level of flexibility is also useful, provided that boundaries are not inappropriately transgressed.

7   Boundaries need to be respected and violations addressed. The young person needs to respect other people's rights to set their boundaries. Additionally, the adolescent needs to learn assertive behaviours to let other people know when their own boundaries are being infringed. For example, if someone who is not in the touching circle touches them, they need to be able to say clearly that this is not OK. In this regard, the counsellor may need to role play situations so that the young person can learn appropriate responses.

Strategies to explain behaviour

Under this heading we will deal with three different models, as follows:

1   The distracting role assignment model.
2   The goal-oriented role assignment model.
3   The cycle of violence model.

These models deal with repetitive maladaptive behaviour patterns that have been learnt. Often it will be difficult for an adolescent to recognize these repetitive patterns of behaviour because they are entrenched and habitual. If a young person is not able to recognize the repetitive pattern, they are unlikely to be able to learn to control its use, see that it is only used at appropriate times or change it altogether, if that is what they want to do. The first step, therefore, in dealing with repetitive behaviour patterns, is to help the young person to identify a pattern that fits personally.

The patterns that will be described are patterns that are frequently encountered, but will need to be modified to suit the particular behaviours of each individual adolescent. The process of using the role assignment model and the cycle of violence model invites the adolescent to develop a personal model that describes their own behaviour. However, the models shown in Figures 15.11 and 15.12 can be used as a general guide and adapted to suit the individual.

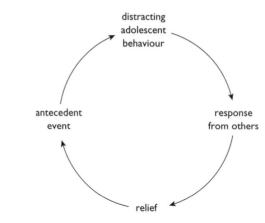

Figure 15.11   *The role assignment model*

The distracting role assignment model

The distracting role assignment model is illustrated in Figure 15.11. There are four stages in the circular process involved in this model:

- the antecedent event
- the distracting adolescent behaviour
- the response from others
- relief.

The antecedent event   This event marks the beginning of the cycle. It is usually an event which raises the young person's anxiety level. Examples of antecedent events are:

- a fight between the adolescent's parents
- a boyfriend consuming too much alcohol
- a friend doing something dangerous.

The distracting adolescent behaviour   During this stage of the cycle the adolescent engages in behaviour to distract, with the hope that by doing this the heat will be taken out of the situation. Distracting behaviour is usually behaviour which the adolescent has used in the past, and which has been successful in reducing tension and anxiety. As a consequence of the distracting behaviour, the adolescent assumes a particular role. Examples are:

- During a parental fight, an adolescent might distract their parents by behaving in a way that results in the parents disciplining them for unacceptable behaviour. Thus the focus has been shifted from the parental fight to the young person, who, as a consequence, has taken on the role of 'scapegoat' in order to reduce their anxiety concerning the parental fight.
- An adolescent might use humour as a distraction and consequently be assigned the role of 'clown'.

- An adolescent might become excessively protective of one parent and take on the role of 'rescuer'.
- An adolescent might become parental and mediate between fighting parents, thus adopting the role of 'parent'.

The response from others   During this stage there will be a response from others to the adolescent's distracting behaviour. This response usually deflects attention away from the antecedent event and shifts the focus from that event to the behaviour of the distracting adolescent. The adolescent's anxiety is consequently reduced, leading to the final stage of the cycle.

Relief   As a result of the adolescent engaging in a repetitive learnt behaviour pattern, the outcome is predictable. Both the adolescent and the other people involved may recognize the pattern, and respond in a consistent and predictable way to the adolescent's intervention. Relief from anxiety and tension is experienced by the adolescent and the other people involved in the interaction.

The goal-oriented role assignment model

In this model the adolescent becomes locked into an entrenched role in the family or wider environment. By playing this role, they provide safety and stability within the system in order to try to reduce their own anxiety, but are precluded from getting some of their own needs met and may become stressed by the responsibility of the role. Examples are:

- An adolescent might become locked into the 'protector' role because they believe that they need to rescue a young sister from the aggressive bullying tactics of an older brother. In doing this, they may need to be highly vigilant and protective of the younger sister. This vigilant behaviour will inevitably prevent the adolescent from pursuing their social needs and will result in them spending most of their social time with their younger sister rather than developing and forming relationships with their own peer group.
- An adolescent might be locked into a 'hero' role. The hero performs well at school, is good at sport and is socially adept. By doing this, the hero may believe that they will make their dysfunctional parents feel better because they will be able to be proud of having raised a successful child. The problem is that the hero feels driven to perform in order to avoid letting people down, and is constantly stressed by the performance expectations of others.
- An adolescent might take on, or be assigned, the role of 'peacemaker'. The peacemaker does not like people expressing strong emotions, but likes to negotiate solutions for others. Unless the peacemaker fulfils this role they will become anxious because of their fear of strong emotions being expressed, which may result in more intense levels of conflict.

Dealing with role assignment

The problem with the use of repetitive patterns, such as those described that result in role assignment, is that the young person gets locked into a particular role which may be extremely unsatisfactory for them in the long term. In particular, by using this role, they may be unable to get important needs of their own met. Instead of getting in touch with their own needs, and using their inner adult to step back from the situation and make logical decisions so that they can assertively state their own needs, the adolescent becomes engaged in behaviour that has been learnt, merely to bring about temporary relief from anxiety.

Clearly, the learnt repetitive behaviour helps in the immediate avoidance of tension. However, part of the process of adolescents growing up is for them to recognize that at times they need to face tension, so that they can make decisions that will enable them to get their own needs met. This may sometimes involve a recognition that others may have to take responsibility for looking after themselves.

When helping adolescents who have become locked into role assignments, either of the distracting or the goal-oriented type, the counsellor needs to find ways to help them to recognize the role they have assumed and the reasons why they have assumed that role. Self-destructive beliefs can then be challenged and ways to interrupt the repetitive behaviour can be explored. New skills can then be rehearsed so that more adaptive behaviours can be used.

The cycle of violence model

This model is illustrated in Figure 15.12, which shows the seven stages. Some adolescents become locked into the cycle of violence. This can have disastrous consequences for them, for their relationships with others and for others with whom they relate. Describing this model to an adolescent who is caught in the cycle may enable them to identify their repetitive pattern of behaviour and to recognize the early stages of the cycle. By recognizing the early stages, the adolescent has a choice about whether to continue around the cycle or to use an alternative behaviour. The cycle of violence model may be used in conjunction with the anger-management strategies described in Chapter 14.

The build-up phase   During the build-up phase the adolescent experiences increasing and rising levels of inner tension. The reasons for this build-up of

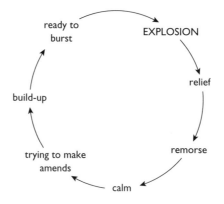

Figure 15.12   *The cycle of violence model*

tension can be usefully explored during counselling. In the build-up phase the adolescent may experience feelings of intolerance, impatience, frustration and may engage in the use of self-destructive beliefs with unrealistic expectations of others (see Chapter 14). Sometimes the build-up of angry feelings will be in response to the actions of a particular person or to a particular situation or event. However, for some adolescents it may be generalized, and may be a response to a wide range of situations. This is most likely to occur when an adolescent is experiencing high levels of anxiety or where there is a mental health problem. Where mental health problems are suspected, referral to a mental health professional for assessment is strongly recommended.

Ready to burst phase   Without the appropriate skills to deal adaptively with the tension experienced during the build-up phase, an adolescent is likely to become overwhelmed by their emotional state and have difficulty in monitoring and controlling their behaviour. During the ready-to-burst phase, the adolescent will probably give out verbal and non-verbal signals that demonstrate a very high level of angry feelings. Consequently, other people, who relate with the adolescent, may feel as though they are treading on eggshells and that they are waiting for an explosion. This is clearly damaging for relationships.

The explosion phase   In the explosion phase the adolescent acts out anger in a destructive way, either verbally or physically. However, the consequences for others are certain to be damaging, and there will be repercussions for relationships and the well-being of the young person.

The relief phase   Once the explosion is over, the adolescent experiences an immediate sense of relief from built-up energy and tension. It is the relief phase that reinforces the adolescent's cycle of violence behaviour.

The remorse phase   During the remorse phase the adolescent recognizes that their behaviour has been unacceptable, and feels guilty and apologetic. They may apologize to people, but will often attempt to minimize their behaviour by blaming others for what they perceive as provocation. They may believe that they do not have another way of dealing with their stress.

The calm phase   The calm phase is a phase in which the adolescent feels less emotional and is able to re-evaluate. It is in the calm stage that the adolescent is most likely to be able to recognize the repetitive behaviour pattern and to make decisions to avoid repetitions occurring. The young person needs to learn to recognize the physiological symptoms that indicate the build-up of anger (see anger management in Chapter 14).

The trying to make amends phase   During this phase the adolescent makes attempts to repair damaged relationships and restore comfortable relationships with others. Many adolescents do not have the repertoire of skills needed to do this, and experience increasing frustration as their attempts fail. This frustration tends to lock them into repeating the cycle.

Breaking the pattern   Whenever adolescents are locked into the cycle of violence, counsellors have a responsibility to be proactive in raising their awareness of this, so that they can learn new ways of behaving. By using the cycle of violence model, the adolescent can be helped to recognize that at any stage around the cycle, before the explosion occurs, they may use different behaviours, thought patterns and beliefs to break their repetitive pattern of violence. It is the counsellor's responsibility to teach the young person the skills of anger management as explained in Chapter 14. Additionally, the counsellor needs to be clear in letting the adolescent know that it is their responsibility to change their behaviour so that they don't continue going around the violence circle.

As part of the process of breaking the cycle of violence, education needs to be given regarding the following four important and essential messages:

1   *'Abuse is not OK'*: Abuse includes both verbal and non-verbal behaviour that is damaging or disrespectful of others, and it is never acceptable behaviour.
2   *'Provocation is not an excuse for abuse'*: Provocation is best dealt with through the use of non-abusive responses. These will vary with each particular situation. Suitable responses to provocation can be explored and rehearsed in counselling.
3   *'An abusive person is responsible for their abusive behaviour regardless of the behaviour of others'*: Taking responsibility is the key to changing abusive behaviour and it is sometimes hard for adolescents to recognize and accept this. When they were children, other people would have taken much of the responsibility for controlling their behaviour. They are now in the stage in life where they want more responsibility for controlling their lives but may still be reluctant to accept responsibility for making difficult changes. The issue of responsibility therefore needs to be explored fully, so that it is seen to extend to the control of unacceptable behaviour.
4   *'Provocation is abuse'*: Adolescents who are violent often like to blame their violence on other people's provocation, but often provoke other people themselves. This is not surprising because being provocative is a way, maladaptive though it is, of expressing frustration and anger. Young people therefore need to get two messages about provocation. First, as discussed, provocation does *not* justify an abusive response, and, secondly, being provocative is not OK, but is abusive.

Clearly, the negative messages about abuse, which the young person needs to learn in combating the cycle of violence, should be accompanied by skills training to enable positive relationships to be built.

Helping adolescent victims of the cycle of violence

Unfortunately, many adolescents are subjected to, or witness, violence in their homes. These young people need specialist help to deal with their post-traumatic stress and to enable them to make decisions to protect themselves in the future. In our work with both children and adolescents who have been traumatized in this way, we have found that the cycle of violence model can be useful in helping young people to understand the process they are experiencing or have experienced. Once they have recognized the process, it may be easier for them to devise a plan to protect themselves in the future.

Victims, during the build-up phase of the cycle, feel as though they are walking on eggshells. Often victims, unable to stand the emotional strain of the tension of the build-up phase, will precipitate the explosion by doing something provocative. Thus, they get the explosion over and can experience some relief, although they have risked serious injury in the process. As counsellors, we need to remember that children, adolescents and adults are killed each year through domestic violence. It is therefore important to ensure that all steps possible are taken to make young clients safe in ways that are acceptable to them.

Strategies to help change behaviour

Many of the strategies described in Chapters 12, 13 and 14 and earlier in this chapter can be used to change behaviour. In this section we will describe three additional strategies that can be useful in this regard:

* problem-solving
* the use of time-lines
* collapsing time.

Problem-solving

In Chapter 14 we discussed the process of decision-making with adolescents. While problem-solving follows similar lines, it is more helpful to use the problem-solving technique when discussing or exploring ways of dealing with everyday issues that require simple decisions. Figure 15.13 gives six steps that an adolescent can follow to solve problems.

Time-lines

Time-lines can help an adolescent gain a perception of changes that are occurring with time. They can be useful in conjunction with decision-making, as they provide a pictorial representation of the path along which the young person is travelling. A typical time-line is shown in Figure 15.14. Time-lines can be based on chronological age, beginning from childhood and moving through to adulthood, or may use dates to indicate positions along the line.

Time-lines can be used to chart the sequence of important events, and to evaluate the events in the adolescent's life that have been negatively or positively significant. They can be useful in enabling adolescents to recognize repetitive behaviours which have occurred over a period of time. By indicating on a time-line that the same behaviour has occurred on various dates over a long period, the adolescent may recognize repetitive behaviour and be encouraged to make decisions to break the cycle that causes the repetition. Time-lines can help adolescents gain a sense of where they have been and where they are going, and to highlight successes which can then be used to provide incentives for further change.

Collapsing time

Collapsing time can be useful in helping an adolescent recognize the need to make decisions and take action to change behaviour, rather than just allowing

STEP 1:   *Identify the problem*
Discuss the events and highlight the main troubling issue. Write down what you think is the main
problem.

_____

_____

_____

_____

STEP 2:   *List all the possible solutions*
Write down all the ideas you can think of to solve the problem. Be as creative as you like.

1 _____

2 _____

3 _____

4 _____

STEP 3:   *Make a list of the advantages and disadvantages of each solution*

	Advantages	Disadvantages
1		
2		
3		
4		

STEP 4:   *Choose the best solution* that takes into account your skills, money, time, resources. Write it
down.

_____

_____

_____

_____

STEP 5:   *List the steps you will take* to reach the desired result. List the things you need at each step to
help you carry out your solution.

	Steps	Things I need

STEP 6:   *Revise your progress* and make changes to your plan where necessary.

Change 1 _____

Change 2 _____

_____

_____

Figure 15.13   *Problem-solving steps*

*A printable version of this figure is available to download from the
Sage website (www.sagepublications.com)*

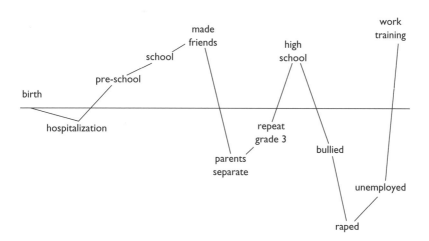

Figure 15.14   *Time-line to chart both positive and negative significant events*

things to continue as they are. In collapsing time, a counsellor might draw a horizontal line on a white-board or on a large sheet of poster paper to demonstrate time. The time-line might start, at the left-hand end, from some time in the past (say six months ago) and move to a point in the middle of the line representing the present and then to a point at the right-hand end representing a particular date in the future. Intermediate dates can be added to the line as discussion occurs.

After the time-line is drawn, the adolescent might be encouraged to talk about ways in which changes to their behaviour have occurred at various times. These changes can then be marked on the time-line. Discussion might then move to the behaviour which currently needs to be addressed. Time can be collapsed by encouraging the adolescent to think about whether the target behaviour will have changed in six months' time, a year's time, two years' time or five years' time. Thus, the timing of any proposed change is brought into focus.

The use of a time-line helps raise an adolescent's awareness of the need to make decisions and implement them in order for change to happen. As a consequence, there may be a recognition that it is not sufficient just to talk about wanting to change. If change is to occur, then there needs to be a specific target with regard to the timing of that change. Understanding this is particularly important for adolescents, many of whom are extremely good at procrastinating and not doing things which they do not feel pressured to do immediately.

PART FOUR

PROACTIVE COUNSELLING IN PRACTICE

16   Case studies

To illustrate the proactive counselling process we will describe two case studies:

Case 1: Max In this case the adolescent underwent a single session of counselling.
Case 2: Laura In this case the adolescent attended a programme involving six counselling sessions.

In the description of these case studies, the right-hand column indicates the skills and strategies used by the counsellor (as shown in Figure 8.2). They help to illustrate the proactive nature of the counselling. If the right-hand column is examined it will be apparent that the counsellor does not follow a set pattern in selecting skills and strategies but spontaneously and opportunistically responds to the current state of the client. The proactive counsellor is an eclectic and integrative counsellor, who deliberately seeks to introduce and employ strategies from differing theoretical frameworks, within one or a series of sessions, at specific times when the chosen strategies are likely to be most effective. However, this alone does not sufficiently describe the proactive process. The process needs to fit within the total framework which has been described in this book.

Case study 1: Max

Max, aged 15, is the youngest son and oldest surviving child of his mother Mary. Mary is in her third marriage. There are no children to this marriage. Max has a younger 12-year-old sister who has the same mother but a different father. Max's 18-year-old brother Trent committed suicide three months ago. Max and Trent were children of the same father. Mary's history is one of neglect and abuse as a child and abuse and violence in adult relationships. Her sons witnessed this violence. Mary has always had a close relationship with her children and sees herself as her children's friend.

Mary approached a counsellor requesting help for Max, following his brother's suicide by taking an overdose of pain-killers. Mary believed that Max needed help to deal with his responses to his brother's death. He dropped out of school after his brother's suicide. Mary is also concerned because Max has become increasingly withdrawn from the family. She believes that he may be using alcohol heavily because he frequently comes home appearing to be intoxicated. Mary describes Max's behaviours as similar to those of his deceased brother, but not typical of his behaviour before Trent's death. Mary says that Max has been wearing Trent's clothes, playing his music, adopting his mannerisms and socializing with Trent's friends more than with his own friends. Mary is worried that Max may also commit suicide. Attempts by Mary to talk with Max have failed. However, she believes that he is troubled and would be prepared to talk to someone else.

The counselling session

The following is a description of the counselling session that took place. This is not a verbatim report, but a summary of what happened in a session of about one hour's duration.

The counselling session	*Skills and strategies used by the counsellor (see Figure 8.2)*
The counsellor met Max in the waiting room, and by observing his mood and behaviour assessed that he appeared to be unhappy and anxious about being there.	*Observation*
The counsellor introduced herself informally and cheerfully.	*Relationship building*
To help Max feel at ease and join with him, she gave him a positive message about coming.	*Affirmation*
Once in the counselling room, the counsellor demonstrated her willingness to be honest in the relationship by disclosing that Max's mother had contacted her and that consequently she had some information regarding the background of what had happened in his family.	*Relationship building*
The counsellor invited Max to express what it was like for him to be there. The counsellor listened to his response and observed Max's accompanying non-verbal behaviour.	*Open questions, observation and active listening*
Despite his obvious restlessness, Max denied being anxious and believed he was only there because of his mother's request. This was not directly confronted as the emphasis was on building a trusting relationship at this stage. Instead, the counsellor agreed with Max's point of view and acknowledged that parents can sometimes be powerful influences on their children.	*Paralleled adolescent communication by agreeing with an adolescent point of view and mirroring Max's language*
The counsellor then talked with Max about confidentiality issues as part of the joining process and reached a mutually acceptable agreement with him.	*Relationship building*

The counsellor began to explore Max's beliefs about why his mother thought he should come to counselling. In an attempt to identify the major themes and issues for Max, the counsellor asked 'If your mother was here, what do you think she would say about why she thinks you need counselling?'

Assessing the problem through the use of active listening and circular questions

Max started to talk about how his mother was 'freaking out about him' since his brother's suicide. He stated that he had noticed her distress, and voiced his concerns about her ability to cope, since his brother's death. The counsellor used active listening skills to encourage Max to continue.

Active listening skills

In a further attempt to build a positive and honest relationship, the counsellor acknowledged that she had also gained the impression that Max's mother was extremely concerned about him. As a result of this disclosure, the counsellor was able to share openly in Max's opinion of his mother and agree with his perception of his mother's distraught behaviour.

Paralleled adolescent communication by open disclosure and agreement with the adolescent's point of view

The counsellor now moved the focus on to identifying the major issues for Max himself. She gave him feedback about his current emotional state as he talked about his mother, and invited him to talk about the issues related to his feelings. Max animatedly described how his mother behaved when she 'freaked out'.

Started to address the problem by using feedback statement to raise awareness of issues

Max explained that his mother's behaviour was not good for him. While listening to Max's story, the counsellor assessed Max's emotional state and observed how, as he spoke, he became agitated and sounded angry.

Used minimal responses and reflection

Max explained that his mother 'stressed out' when he behaved in certain ways. She cried, told him not to wear his brother's clothes and compared his behaviour to that of his dead brother (alcoholic binges and emotional withdrawal). Max said he felt that his mother depended on him too much. The counsellor summarized Max's comments and feelings regarding his mother's behaviours, and agreed that Max's mother was a problem for him.

Assessed the problem through the use of a summary

Max said that he did behave in the ways that his mother described, and that sometimes those behaviours of his were also uncomfortable for him, but that more importantly he was tired of his mother's behaviour and did not know what to do about it. Because Max felt as though the counsellor understood his position he was able to disclose his own feelings more openly.	*Joining with the adolescent by matching the adolescent style of communication*
During the course of conversation Max deflected and digressed. The counsellor followed his digressions.	*Paralleled adolescent communication*
Max made reference to many relatives and step-family members, and gave descriptions of his mother and extended family. He meandered through his story of a family exposed to violence, separations, losses and traumas.	*Used a range of active listening counselling micro-skills*
The counsellor suggested the use of a genogram to assist Max in his description.	*Psycho-educational strategy*
The counsellor observed and listened as Max talked at length about how he became stressed and angry when his mother behaved in the ways that he described in response to his behaviours.	*Used a range of counselling micro-skills*
The counsellor matched Max's emotional affect and said that she would feel the same as Max in the same situation.	*Paralleled adolescent communication*
The counsellor used scaling questions to explore Max's perspective of his mother's belief about his need for counselling. He was invited to indicate, on a scale drawn on a white-board, how he believed his mother saw him. He was asked 'On a scale of 1 to 10, where 1 corresponded to really needing help and 10 to not needing help at all, where do you think your mother thinks you are?' Max believed that his mother would place him at about 2 or 3 on the scale. In order to explore Max's own perceptions of his resilience and coping ability, he was asked 'Where do you think you are on the scale of 1 to 10?' He placed himself at about 6.	*Psycho-educational strategy*
The counsellor affirmed and validated Max's perceptions that he was coping better than his mother thought he was.	*Affirmation and validation*

To understand and assess Max's perceptions of his own coping ability more fully, the counsellor pointed out that she was puzzled because, although Max said that he believed he was coping better than his mother thought he was, he had not placed his own score near the top of the scale.

Assessing the problem through the use of a challenging question

As a consequence of the counsellor's challenge, Max began to relate the process of his own grieving from the time he first heard news of his brother's death. The counsellor actively listened while Max explained that he had completed his grieving and was getting on with his life.

Active listening

As he continued, the counsellor observed that Max became restless, less confident and finally became silent. The counsellor suspected that Max was getting in touch with emotions related to the death of his brother. She decided to focus on the immediate problem of Max's current emotional state.

Observation

The counsellor helped Max get in touch with his feelings and thoughts by identifying his bodily sensations and connecting these to his emotional feelings and thoughts.

Used feedback statement to raise awareness

Max cried, and talked about his brother and the loss of his brother. He identified his past dependency on his brother as a father figure and his fear about not being able to get support or advice from now on.

Minimal responses and reflection

The counsellor addressed the problem of Max's vulnerability and fear by using a psychodramatic technique to increase Max's awareness of his own innate strength, wisdom and ability to solve problems. The counsellor helped Max to externalize his fear, symbolized by a coloured cushion, and encouraged a dialogue between Max and his 'fear'.

Creative strategy

To complete the use of the creative strategy, the counsellor helped Max to explore current emotional feelings so that he could verbalize these and feel more in control.

Used range of counselling micro-skills

Max continued to talk about his regret at not having told his brother how much he had valued him as a role model and how he had relied on him.

Active listening

The counsellor helped Max to address the problem of his lost opportunity to talk with his brother. The counsellor made use of the two-chair technique to enable Max to role play a conversation between himself and his brother. In this conversation, Max expressed previously unexpressed feelings and thoughts.

Creative strategy

The use of this strategy enabled Max to access other thoughts. He explained that he believed that he was just like his brother. He also expressed emotional feelings towards his brother, and expressed anger towards him for committing suicide.

Reflection of content and feelings

Max suggested several alternative solutions that his brother could have taken, and implied that he himself would have behaved differently given the same circumstances. The counsellor challenged Max about conflicting information he had given as to whether he was the same as, or different from, his brother.

Used a challenging question

To explore the differences between Max and his brother, and to address Max's adolescent need to search for an individual and unique identity, the counsellor encouraged Max to draw up two lists. One list was of ways he was like his brother, and the other was of ways he was not like his brother. Max did this enthusiastically.

Used a cognitive strategy to anchor the differences through the use of a visual list

From this a discussion ensued about Max's predictions concerning his own future behaviours. The counsellor took the opportunity to help Max explore his lifestyle goals. He now seemed more relaxed and appeared to be pleased with himself.

Cognitive strategy

After this discussion had been completed, the counsellor took control by using a transitional question to return Max's attention to the earlier issue regarding his mother's perceptions of his need for help. Using the scale of 1 to 10, the counsellor asked Max to imagine how his mother would behave differently if she had a score of 10. Rather than answer this question, Max began to laugh and said that he would have to change into an almost entirely new person for his mother to be able to have a score of 10.

Counsellor took control by using a transitional question to return to an earlier issue

The counsellor made use of humour to maintain the positive relationship and energy of the conversation. She exaggerated by suggesting outrageous behaviours Max might need to use if his mother was to stop worrying (for example, stop wearing his brother's clothes but start wearing his sister's, stop playing his brother's music and listen to Mozart and so on).

Paralleled adolescent communication and made use of humour

The counsellor mirrored and matched Max's affect to validate and amplify his responses.

Paralleled adolescent communication

The counsellor asked 'Can you think of a time when your mother hasn't been stressed out by worrying about you?' Max was able to identify some exceptions to his mother's distressed behaviour. This included occasions when Max had worn his own clothes, and she had commented on how nice he looked. Max was able to recognize that at times when his mother was positive towards him he felt less hostile towards her.

Used exception-oriented question

However, wearing his brother's clothes and using his brother's possessions were comforting for him. Max identified a dilemma about how to meet his own needs and at the same time avoid conflict with his mother. He was encouraged to describe how he would like things to be with regard to wearing his brother's clothes, and with regard to his relationship with his mother.

Addressing the problem using future-oriented questions

The counsellor encouraged Max to use a problem-solving exercise to discover his options and choices in connection with his dilemma. Max continued by suggesting some compromises that he could put in place so that everyone might be happier.

Cognitive strategy

Max continued to express his uncertainty about the possibility of having 'a totally stress-free zone' when with his mother. He described his desire to become more independent of his mother and his family. The counsellor normalized Max's behaviour by suggesting that his wish to be separate and become an individual was normal for an adolescent.

Used normalizing

The counsellor shared with Max that when she was a teenager and wanted to be more separate her own mother had found this difficult to accept. This information allowed Max to explore how his mother might be feeling at a time when she had recently lost her eldest son. He was able to elaborate on and make sense of his mother's behaviours, and consequently felt more comfortable with his situation.

Counsellor self-disclosure to impart useful information

Max decided that it would be useful to return for one more counselling session. The counsellor agreed and negotiated a suitable time, but pointed out that if Max discovered later that this was unnecessary, then he could decide not to attend.

Maintaining a relationship

Follow-up

Although Max had decided that one more appointment would be helpful, he did not return for more counselling. Max's mother, Mary, did contact the counsellor to say that Max had been able to communicate with her more openly about his bereavement, and intended to return to school with a goal of becoming an apprentice. Mary also reported that Max was socializing with his own peer group and, while continuing to experiment with the use of alcohol, had been able to discontinue his previous bingeing behaviour. Max had begun to form a closer relationship with his stepfather, Brian.

While Mary felt that she and Max were not as close as they had previously been, she recognized that he was behaving normally 'for a boy of his age'. She noticed also that Max continued to wear his brother's clothes and use his brother's possessions. However, this behaviour now seemed less alarming to her because of the other positive changes she had noticed.

Comments on case study I

Because Max's brother had committed suicide it was important for the counsellor to be alert to any indications that might suggest that Max himself could be harbouring suicidal thoughts. In the absence of such indications the counsellor believed and accepted Max's construct that the problem belonged to his mother and not to him. By doing this, Max was able to revise his constructs regarding his own and his mother's behaviour, and access and address his own issues.

While proactively directing the counselling session by maintaining a focus on the primary counselling functions (Figure 8.2), the counsellor empowered Max to find his own solutions. Existential ideas about anxiety being a part of life were accepted and normalized through counsellor self-disclosure. A variety of strategies and counselling skills from differing frameworks were opportunistically selected and combined to meet Max's current needs. At different points in the process the counsellor selectively used her inner adolescent or inner adult to communicate effectively.

Case study 2: Laura

Laura was referred for counselling by a youth worker employed in a youth accommodation programme. Laura was a 16-year-old female referred because of concerns about her behaviour. Laura was described as having immature behaviour, lying, stealing, exhibiting poor hygiene, multiple somatic symptoms and low self-esteem. Laura was currently homeless. She had no reservations about attending counselling, believing that she probably needed help.

The counselling sessions

The following is a description of the counselling sessions. This is not a verbatim report, but a summary of what happened in sessions of about one hour's duration each.

The counselling sessions	*Skills and strategies used by the counsellor (see Figure 8.2)*
First session	
Laura arrived for her appointment early. In the waiting room she was talkative and on meeting the counsellor commented on the counsellor's clothes. The counsellor responded cheerfully, matching Laura's friendliness and tone.	*Paralleled adolescent communication and used relationship-building skills*
The counsellor observed that Laura continued to interact in a somewhat agitated but familiar way with her and in general seemed unconcerned about her own or other people's personal boundaries. The counsellor took note of Laura's lack of boundaries.	*Assessing the problem through observation*
The counsellor invited Laura into the counselling room, and in joining with Laura congratulated her on the apparent ease with which she was entering into a new situation, and stating that for many adolescents the counselling situation can be overwhelming. Laura appeared to be unimpressed with this feedback, believing that it was an expectation that she should disclose and communicate everything about herself, so that the counsellor could help her. She said that she had many problems and needed lots of help. The counsellor noted that this was inconsistent with what Laura had said to others before coming to counselling, and suspected that Laura was a very dependent teenager.	*Affirmed, normalized and paralleled adolescent communication*

The counsellor told Laura that she knew that there were many other people who were helping her, and asked what that was like for her. Laura believed that, with other people helping her, she might be able to stop behaving in ways that were getting her into trouble. The counsellor noted that Laura was relying on external controls to manage her behaviour and not taking personal responsibility for this.

Assessing the problem by using open questions

The counsellor then talked with Laura about confidentiality issues as part of the joining process, and reached a mutually acceptable agreement with her.

Relationship building

The counsellor actively listened while Laura spontaneously began to disclose information about her childhood experiences, and how she continued to have contact with her father and mother who had separated when she was young. This contact was always initiated by Laura.

Active listening

During this first session, Laura was talkative, articulate, anxious and confused, with regard to both recent and past memories. The counsellor observed that Laura needed to talk about herself and her experiences, and that she sometimes had difficulty separating past from current experiences.

Active listening and observation to assess the problem

During this session the counsellor invited Laura to draw a genogram to describe her complex family system.

Psycho-educational strategy

The counsellor used a time-line to help Laura describe her past and current events and circumstances.

Psycho-educational strategy

The counsellor then affirmed and congratulated Laura for her ability to describe in detail her personal experiences within her complicated family system.

Affirmation

As she shared this information, Laura's rapid speech and physical restlessness were observed. The counsellor provided feedback to Laura about her observation of this.

Observation and feedback

Laura was asked to identify her bodily sensations of physical restlessness, and through doing this to get in touch with her feelings and thoughts.

Used open questions

Laura described her restlessness as being due to excitement at meeting with a new person and talking about herself and her family. However, she admitted that the process was stressful for her. The counsellor helped Laura to explore her feelings by externalizing her anxiety. Using cushions as symbols, the counsellor helped Laura to create a dialogue between herself and her anxiety.

Creative strategy

During this exercise, it was clear to Laura and the counsellor that Laura felt too fragile emotionally to disclose further information. The counsellor gave Laura feedback statements about how apprehension and anxiety in the current situation were normal.

Normalizing

The counsellor shared personal experiences that reinforced this feedback statement.

Self-disclosure paralleling adolescent communication

Laura's heightened awareness of her anxiety helped her discover that, in order to disclose more personal information, a relationship of trust would need to be established. She said that her past experiences of trust in close relationships were not positive. The counsellor reminded Laura that she had a choice about whether to disclose or not. Discussion ensued regarding Laura's readiness for continuing counselling.

Various counselling micro-skills were used

The counsellor helped Laura to explore options and choices regarding further counselling by using a problem-solving technique. Laura contracted for four more sessions. She identified her goal for these sessions as the exploration of her issues with regard to trust in relationships.

Cognitive strategy

Second session

Laura arrived for her appointment appearing more reserved and tentative than last time. The counsellor asked her what it was like to come back for counselling. Laura likened the experience to going to the dentist.

Relationship building and assessing the problem through the use of open questions

The counsellor continued to use Laura's metaphor by disclosing her own fears of going to the dentist. Laura and the counsellor chatted together, mirrored each other's views and amplified each other's emotional feelings about visiting the dentist.

Symbolic strategy and paralleling of adolescent communication

The counsellor disclosed techniques she herself used, to make it less stressful, when going to the dentist and invited Laura to think about her own strategies. The counsellor explored with Laura whether she might be able to generalize these strategies to coping with the counselling situation. *Self-disclosure and use of cognitive strategy*

Laura identified that being in control was important for her and, together, the counsellor and Laura negotiated ways in which this could occur during counselling. *Addressing the problem*

The counsellor enquired about her mood and if things had been better or different since her last visit. *Question which presupposes change*

Laura had been able to recognize that in the last session she had made a decision to explore some important issues in her life and that she was now ambivalent about this decision. The counsellor encouraged Laura to explore the risks involved with regard to her decision by helping Laura identify the gains and losses associated with her decision. *Cognitive strategy*

Laura then felt comfortable enough to proceed with exploring the goal of trust and loyalty in relation-ships. The counsellor suggested that a start might be to explore her past and current relationships with her family by using miniature animals as symbols to represent her family. *Symbolic strategy*

From this session it emerged that: *Various counselling micro-skills were used*

1 Laura believed she was responsible for her parents' marriage failure.
2 Laura's experience of her early childhood was chaotic with multiple parental separations, which resulted in her living with each parent, at various times.
3 She believed that she had been sexually abused by her mother's partner over a two-to three-year period and had not been believed by her mother when she disclosed this.
4 Laura believed she was unwanted by both parents and that her siblings were preferred by her parents.
5 It emerged that Laura had a strong desire to be close to her father but not her mother. She believed that her mother could not be trusted.

Laura was able to identify the major issues for her as feelings of:

Summary

- being uncared for as a child
- being disempowered
- being neglected.

Third session

Laura arrived complaining of feeling sick. The counsellor explored Laura's 'sickness' and shared memories with Laura of being sick herself.

Self-disclosure and paralleling of adolescent communication

The counsellor explored what it was like for Laura being sick.

Use of questions, reflections and summarizing

The counsellor encouraged Laura to make a list of the advantages of being sick and the disadvantages of being sick. Laura saw the main advantage of being sick as having an opportunity to be cared for. She believed that the disadvantages of being sick were that being sick resulted in her being disempowered. She likened the experience of being sick to that of being a child.

Cognitive strategy

The counsellor asked whether Laura's experiences as a child might explain her ambivalence about trusting relationships with others. While, on the one hand, relationships might give her an opportunity to be looked after, on the other hand, they might result in her feeling anxious in case they became disempowering.

Used various counselling micro-skills including questions

Laura responded defensively by talking about the 'hundreds' of friends she had. During this conversation it appeared that Laura was unable to understand the difference between close relationships and newly formed relationships.

Various counselling micro-skills were used

The counsellor decided to use the circle model to help Laura recognize variations in closeness and distance in relationships and the need for differing boundaries. Laura was able to identify from her current social circle those people with whom she wanted closeness, and those with whom she wanted more distance. She was not confident of her ability to maintain the boundaries she wished to have. She decided to continue to explore related issues in the next counselling session.

Psycho-educational strategy

Fourth session

Laura arrived for her appointment and the counsellor observed that she was more measured and less effusive than at other times.	*Observation*

The counsellor explored Laura's level of comfort in continuing to have counselling and explored her current feelings and thoughts. *Relationship building*

Laura was keen to continue exploring the issues of trust in relationships and reminded the counsellor of the goal which had been set in the previous week. During this session the counsellor selected a creative strategy using coloured cushions to represent each end of a continuum. This was to help Laura to integrate the polarities of being totally trusting and of not trusting at all. The counsellor encouraged Laura to explore and experience her emotional responses while she physically moved along the continuum between the cushions. Further issues emerged regarding control over closeness with others. Laura began to understand that she had a choice about where she 'stood' on the continuum in relation to closeness. *Creative strategy*

The counsellor used cognitive behavioural strategies to help Laura explore the risks, and consequences, of being in control over closeness with others in relationships. This process raised further issues regarding Laura's self-esteem and self-worth in relationships with others. Laura identified exploration of her sense of self as a goal for the next counselling session. *Cognitive strategy*

Fifth session

The counsellor asked questions that presumed change had occurred during the week to discover how the week had been for Laura. *Questions presupposing change*

Laura was keen to relate how things had been different for her during the week. She had experimented with making choices about her level of involvement with others and had found the experience to be very empowering. The counsellor made her success newsworthy and congratulated her. *Cheer-leading and relationship building*

Laura admitted that there were times when her confidence had failed, and as a result she had felt unworthy and undeserving of some relationships. This had happened when she had tried to contact her father.

Active listening

The counsellor invited Laura to draw herself as a 'fruit tree' in order to use the metaphor to explore Laura's perceptions of herself. During the processing of the drawing it became clear to Laura that she had many negative perceptions of herself, which were related to helplessness and victimization.

Creative strategy

The counsellor helped Laura externalize her victimization and separate this from herself so that she could view it as a separate entity. The counsellor encouraged Laura to choose a symbol to represent her victimization and to create a dialogue with the symbol.

Symbolic strategy

The counsellor helped Laura focus on the problems caused by her victimization. Together, the counsellor and Laura spent time rediscovering times when she had not felt victimized. At this stage an alternative story began to emerge about Laura as a person who could be strong and independent.

Exception-oriented questions

The counsellor reminded Laura that the four counselling sessions in the contract, made at the end of the first session, were now over, but gave her the option of continuing, if she wished. Laura decided that she would like to come to one more counselling session. It was agreed that this would be a closing session.

Relationship maintenance

Sixth session

Laura presented with an elevated mood, increased sense of optimism, and described encounters with others during the previous week in a positive way.

Relationship maintenance

Laura had begun to make plans to move out of the youth shelter into shared accommodation. The counsellor reinforced Laura's goals and invited Laura to describe her plans to achieve these goals.

Cognitive strategy

At this point Laura decided not to continue with counselling. She described her life as currently too full. The counsellor affirmed her decision to terminate counselling.

Affirmation

Follow-up

While it was recognized that Laura might return for counselling at a later date, the counsellor believed that it was important for Laura to experience a period of integration and normal adolescent behaviour without counselling support. This would enable her in the future to continue to recognize her strengths, abilities and times when she was fully in charge of her life.

Comments on case study 2

This case was very different from that of Max in case study 1. In Max's case, a speedy counselling process could be used because entrenched personal issues had not developed over a long period of time. His problem was contained rather than generalized. In Laura's case, her problems were more global, affecting her self-perception and ability to cope and find solutions. She was much more fragile emotionally because her core constructs concerning her perceptions of self were easily threatened. Consequently, the counselling process needed to move more slowly.

By recognizing that Laura was struggling with the normal adolescent task of individuation and separation, the counsellor was able to use the counselling sessions as an arena in which Laura could practise making choices and being in control. In the first session, the counsellor made it clear to Laura that she had a choice about whether to disclose or not, and whether to come back for more counselling or not. In the second session, control issues were openly discussed, and ways in which Laura could have control during counselling were negotiated.

While proactively directing the counselling sessions by maintaining a focus on the primary counselling functions, the counsellor empowered Laura to find her own solutions. Counsellor self-disclosure was used to normalize Laura's anxieties regarding going to the dentist and memories of being sick. Throughout the counselling process a variety of strategies and counselling skills from differing frameworks were opportunistically selected and combined to meet Laura's current needs. At different points in the process the counsellor selectively used her inner adolescent or inner adult to communicate effectively.

References

Adams, G.R. and Marshall, S.K. (1996) 'A developmental social psychology of identity: understanding the person-in-context', *Journal of Adolescence*, 19: 429–42.

Afifi, W.A. and Guerrero, L.K. (1998) 'Some things are better left unsaid: topic avoidance in friendships', *Communication Quarterly*, 46 (3): 231–49.

Alexander, A. and Kempe, R. (1984) 'The role of the lay therapist in long term treatment', *Child Abuse and Neglect*, 6: 329–34.

Alexander, F. (1965) 'Psychoanalytic contributions to short term psychotherapy', in L.R. Wolberg (ed.), *Short Term Psychotherapy*. New York: Grune & Stratton.

American Psychiatric Association (2001) *Diagnostic and Statistical Manual of Mental Disorders*, 4th edn (revised). Washington, DC: American Psychiatric Association.

Anderson, D.A. (1993) 'Lesbian and gay adolescents: social and developmental considerations', *High School Journal*, 77: 13–19.

Angus, L. (1990) 'Metaphor and structure of meaning: the counselling client's subjective experience', First International Conference on Counselling Psychology (1988, Porto, Portugal), *Cadernos de Consulta Psicologica*, 6: 5–11.

Archer, Robert P. (1997) *MMPI-A: Assessing Adolescent Psychopathology* (2nd edn). Hillsdale, NJ: Lawrence Erlbaum.

Arnett, J. (1992) 'The soundtrack of recklessness: musical preferences and reckless behaviour among adolescents', *Journal of Adolescent Research*, 7: 313–31.

Arroyo, W. and Eth, S. (1985) 'Children traumatized by Central American warfare', in S. Eth and R.S. Pynoos (eds), *Post-traumatic Stress Disorder in Children*. Washington, DC: American Psychiatric Press. pp. 103–20.

Aseltine, R.H. (1996) 'Pathways linking parental divorce with adolescent depression', *Journal of Health and Social Behaviour*, 37: 133–48.

Atlas, J., Weissman, K. and Liebowitz, S. (1997) 'Adolescent inpatients' history of abuse and dissociative identity disorder', *Psychological Reports*, 80: 1086–92.

Bagley, C., Bolitho, F. and Bertrand, L. (1997) 'Sexual assault in school mental health and suicidal behaviours in adolescent women in Canada', *Adolescence*, 32: 341–66.

Bandler, R. and Grinder, J. (1979) *Frogs into Princes*. Moab, UT: Real People Press.

Barker, P. (1990) *Clinical Interviews with Children and Adolescents*. New York: Norton.

Bauman, K.E. and Ennett, S.T. (1996) 'On the importance of peer influence for adolescent drug use: commonly neglected considerations', *Addiction*, 91: 185–98.

Baumeister, R.F. (1990) 'Suicide as escape from self', *Psychological Review*, 97: 90–113.

Baumrind, D. (1971) 'Current patterns of parental authority', *Developmental Psychology Monographs*, 4, no. 1, pt 2.

Baumrind, D. (1991a) 'Effective parenting during the early adolescent transition', in P.A. Cowan and E.M. Hetherington (eds), *Family Transitions*. Hillsdale, NJ: Lawrence Erlbaum. pp. 219–44.

Baumrind, D. (1991b) 'The influence of parenting style on adolescent competence and substance use', *Journal of Early Adolescence*, 11: 56–95.

Berndt, T.J. (1995) 'Intimacy and self-disclosure in friendships', in K.J. Rotenberg (ed.), *Disclosure Processes in Children and Adolescents*. Cambridge: Cambridge University Press.

Berne, E. (1964) *Games People Play*. New York: Grove.

Berne, E., Steiner, C.M. and Dusay, J.M. (1996) 'Transactional analysis', in J.E. Groves (ed.), *Essential Papers in Short-term Dynamic Psychotherapy*. New York: New York University Press. pp. 149–70.

Bernet, W. (1993) 'Humor in evaluating and treating children and adolescents', *Journal of Psychotherapy Practice and Research*, 2: 307–17.

Billings, A.G. and Moos, R.H. (1981) 'The role of coping responses and social resources in attenuating stress of life events', *Journal of Behavioural Medicine*, 4: 139–57.

Biswas, A., Biswas, D. and Chattopadhyay, P.K. (1995) 'Cognitive behaviour therapy in generalised anxiety disorder', *Indian Journal of Clinical Psychology*, 22: 1–10.

Bjerregaard, B. and Smith, C. (1993) 'Gender differences in gang participation, delinquency, and substance abuse', *Journal of Quantitative Criminology*, 9: 329–55.

Blos, P. (1979) *The Adolescent Passage: Developmental Issue*. New York: International Universities Press.

Boldero, J. and Fallon, B. (1995) 'Adolescent help-seeking: what do they get help for and from whom?' *Journal of Adolescence*, 18: 193–209.

Borrine, N.L., Handal, P.J., Brown, N.Y. and Searight, H.R. (1991) 'Family conflict and adolescent adjustment in intact, divorced and blended families', *Journal of Consulting and Clinical Psychology*, 59: 753–5.

Bowlby, J. (1969) *Attachment*. New York: Basic Books.

Brent, D., Perper, J., Maritz, G. and Allman, C. (1993) 'Bereavement or depression? The impact of the loss of a friend to suicide', *Journal of the American Academy of Child and Adolescent Psychiatry*, 32: 1189–97.

Briggs, J. (1992) 'Travelling indirect routes to enjoy the scenery: employing the metaphor in family therapy', *Journal of Family Psychotherapy*, 3: 39–52.

Bronzaft, A.L. and Dobrow, S.B. (1988) 'Noise and health: a warning to adolescents' (special issue on adolescence and the environment), *Children's Environments Quarterly*, 5: 40–5.

Brown, G.W., Summers, D., Coffman, B. and Riddell, R. (1996) 'The use of hypnotherapy with school age children: five case studies', *Psychotherapy in Private Practice*, 15: 53–65.

Browne, A. and Finkelhor, D. (1986) 'Impact of child sexual abuse: a review of the research', *Psychological Bulletin*, 99: 66–77.

Budman, S.H. and Gurman, A.S. (1992) 'A time sensitive model of brief therapy: the I–D–E approach', in S.H. Budman, M.F. Hoyt and S. Friedman (eds), *The First Session in Brief Therapy*. New York: Guilford Press. pp. 111–34.

Buhrmester, D. and Prager, K. (1995) 'Patterns and functions of self-disclosure', in K.J. Rotenberg (ed.), *Disclosure Processes in Children and Adolescents*. Cambridge: Cambridge University Press.

Burge, D., Hammen, C., Davila, J. and Daley, S. (1997) 'Attachment cognitions and college and work functioning two years later in late adolescent women', *Journal of Youth and Adolescence*, 26: 285–301.

Calabrese, R.L. and Noboa, J. (1995) 'The choice for gang membership by Mexican-American adolescents', *High School Journal*, 78: 226–35.

Casper, R. and Lyubomirsky, S. (1997) 'Individual psychopathology relative to reports of unwanted sexual experiences as predictor of a bulimic eating pattern', *International Journal of Eating Disorders*, 21: 229–36.

Champagne, M.P. and Walker-Hirsch, L.W. (1982) 'Circles: a self organisation system for teaching appropriate social/sexual behaviour to mentally retarded/developmentally disabled persons', *Sexuality and Disability*, 5: 172–4.

Chapman, A.H. and Chapman-Santana, M. (1995) 'Humor as psychotherapeutic technique', *Arquivos de Neuro Psiquiatria*, 53: 153–6.

Chassin, L. and Barrera, M. (1993) 'Substance use escalation and substance use restraint among adolescent children of alcoholics', *Psychology of Addictive Behaviours*, 7: 3–20.

Clark, A.J. (1995) 'Projective techniques in the counselling process', *Journal of Counselling and Development*, 73: 311–16.

Clarkson, P. (1989) *Gestalt Counselling in Action*. London: Sage.

Colarusso, C. (1992) *Child and Adult Development: A Psychoanalytic Introduction for Clinicians*. New York: Plenum Press.

Comings, D. (1997) 'Genetic aspects of childhood behavioural disorders', *Child Psychology and Human Development*, 27: 139–50.

Compas, B.E., Malcarne, V.L. and Fondacaro, K.M. (1988) 'Coping with stressful events in older children and adolescents', *Journal of Consulting and Clinical Psychology*, 56: 405–11.

Connor, M.J. (1994) 'Peer relations and peer pressure', *Educational Psychology in Practice*, 9: 209–15.

Corey, G. (1996) *Theory and Practice of Counselling and Psychotherapy* (5th edn). Pacific Grove: Brooks/Cole.

Cox, A.D., Cox, D., Anderson, R.D. and Moschis, G.P. (1993) 'Social influences of adolescents' shoplifting: theory, evidence, implications for the retail industry', *Journal of Retailing*, 69: 234–46.

Crespi, T.D. and Generali, M.M. (1995) 'Constructivist developmental theory and therapy: implications for counselling adolescents', *Adolescence*, 30: 735–43.

Cutrona, C.E., Suhr, J.A. and Macfarlane, R. (1990) 'Interpersonal transactions and the psychological sense of support', in S. Duck (ed.), *Personal Relationships and Social Support*. London: Sage. pp. 30–45.

Dacey, J. and Kenny, M. (1997) *Adolescent Development*. Chicago: Brown & Benchmark.

Darke, S., Ross, J. and Hall, W. (1996) 'Overdose among heroin users in Sydney, Australia: responses to overdoses', *Addiction*, 91: 413–17.

DeGaston, J.F., Weed, S. and Jensen, L. (1996) 'Understanding gender differences in sexuality', *Adolescence*, 31: 217–31.

Dequine, E. and Pearson-Davis, S. (1983) 'Video-taped improvisational drama with emotionally disturbed adolescents: a pilot study', *Arts in Psychotherapy*, 10: 15–21.

Derlega, V.I., Metts, S., Petronio, S. and Margulis, S.T. (1993) *Self-disclosure*. Newbury Park, CA: Sage.

Desivilya, H.S., Gal, R. and Ayalon, O. (1996) 'Long term effects of trauma in adolescence: comparison between survivors of a terrrorist attack and control counterparts', *Anxiety, Stress and Coping: An International Journal*, 9: 135–50.

DiGiuseppe, R., Linscott, J. and Jilton, R. (1996) 'Developing the therapeutic alliance in child–adolescent psychotherapy', *Applied and Preventative Psychology*, 5: 85–100.

Divinyi, J.E. (1995) 'Story telling: an enjoyable and effective therapeutic tool', *Contemporary Family Therapy: An International Journal*, 17: 27–37.

Downey, V.W. and Landry, R.G. (1997) 'Self reported sexual behaviours of high school juniors and seniors in North Dakota', *Psychological Reports*, 80: 1357–8.

Dryden, W. and DiGiuseppe, R. (1990) *A Primer on Rational Emotive Therapy*. Champaign, IL: Research Press.

Dupre, D., Miller, N., Gold, M. and Rospenda, K. (1995) 'Initiation and progression of alcohol, marijuana and cocaine use among adolescent abusers', *American Journal on Addictions*, 4: 43–8.

Dusek, J.B. (1996) *Adolescent Development and Behavior*. Englewood Clifs, NJ: Prentice-Hall.

Earls, F., Smith, E., Reich, W. and Jung, K.G. (1988) 'Investigating psychopathological consequences of a disaster in children: a pilot study incorporating a structured diagnostic interview', *Journal of the American Academy of Child and Adolescent Psychiatry*, 27: 90–5.

Ebata, A.T. and Moos, R.H. (1991) 'Coping and adjustment in distressed and healthy adolescents', *Journal of Applied Developmental Psychology*, 12: 33–54.

Eddowes, E. and Hranitz, J. (1989) 'Educating children of the homeless', *Childhood Education*, 65: 197–200.

Ehrhardt, A.A. (1996) 'Our view of adolescent sexuality: a focus on risk behavior without the developmental context', *American Journal of Public Health*, 86: 1523–5.

Elkind, D. (1967) 'Egocentrism in adolescence', *Child Development*, 38: 1025–34.

Elkind, D. (1980) 'The origins of religion in the child', in J. Tisdale (ed.), *Growing Edges in the Psychology of Religion*. Chicago: Nelson-Hall.

Elliot, D.S., Wilson, W.J., Huizinga, D. and Sampson, R.J. (1996) 'The effects of neighbourhood disadvantage on adolescent development', *Journal of Research in Crime and Delinquency*, 33: 389–426.

Eltz, M.J., Shirk, S.R. and Sarlin, N. (1995) 'Alliance formation and treatment outcome among maltreated adolescents', *Child Abuse and Neglect*, 19: 419–31.

Epstein, N.B., Bishop, D.S. and Levin, S. (1980) 'The McMaster model of family functioning', *Advances in Family Psychiatry*, 2: 73–89.

Erikson, E. (1968) *Identity: Youth and Crisis*. New York: W.W. Norton.

Erikson, E. (1987) *Childhood and Society*. London: Paladin.

Eskilson, A. and Wiley, N.G. (1987) 'Parents, peers, perceived pressure and adolescent self-concept: is a daughter a daughter all of her life?', *Sociological Quarterly*, 28: 135–45.

Feindler, E.L. and Ecton, R.B. (1986) *Adolescent Anger Control: Cognitive-behavioral Techniques*. New York: Pergamon.

Fergusson, D.M., Horwood, L.J. and Lyndley, M.T. (1997a) 'The effects of unemployment on psychiatric illness during young adulthood', *Psychological Medicine*, 27: 371–81.

Fergusson, D.M., Lynskey, M.T. and Horwood, L.J. (1997b) 'The effects of unemployment on juvenile offending', *Criminal Behaviour and Mental Health*, 7: 49–68.

Finch, A.J., Nelson, W.M. and Ott, E.S. (1993) *Cognitive Behavioral Procedures with Children and Adolescents: A Practical Guide*. Boston, MA: Allyn & Bacon.

Finkelhor, D. and Berliner, L. (1995) 'Research on the treatment of sexually abused children: a review and recommendations', *Journal of the American Academy of Child and Adolescent Psychiatry*, 34 (11): 1408.

Fitzgerald, M. (1995) 'On the spot counselling with residential youth: opportunities for therapeutic intervention', *Journal of Child and Youth Care*, 10: 9–17.

Flavell, J. (1977) *Cognitive Development*. Englewood Cliffs, NJ: Prentice-Hall.

Fodor, I.G. (1992) *Adolescent Assertiveness and Social Skills Training: A Clinical Handbook*. San Francisco: Springer.

Ford, M. (1992) *Motivating Humans: Goals, Emotions and Personal Agency Beliefs*. Thousand Oaks, CA: Sage.

Forman, S.G. (1993) *Coping Skills Interventions for Children and Adolescents*. San Francisco: Jossey-Bass.

Fowler, J. (1981) *Stages of Faith*. Melbourne: Dove.

Frankl, V. (1973) *Psychotherapy and Existentialism: Selected Papers on Logo Therapy*. Harmondsworth: Penguin.

Fransella, F. and Dalton, P. (1990) *Personal Construct Counselling in Action*. London: Sage.

Frauenglass, S., Routh, D.K., Pantin, H.M. and Mason, C.A. (1997) 'Family support decreases influence of deviant peers on Espanic adolescents substance use', *Journal of Clinical Child Psychology*, 26: 15–23.

Frederick, C.J. (1985) 'Children traumatized by catastrophic situations', in S. Eth and R.S. Pynoos (eds), *Post-traumatic Stress Disorder in Children*. Washington, DC: American Psychiatric Press. pp. 71–100.

Friedman, H.L. (1993) 'Adolescent social development: a global perspective – implications for health promotion across cultures', *Journal of Adolescent Health*, 14: 588–94

Frydenberg, E. (1999) *Learning to Cope: Developing as a Person in Complex Societies*. Oxford: Oxford University Press.

Frydenberg, E. and Lewis, R. (1993) 'Boys play sport and girls turn to others: age, gender, and ethnicity as determinants of coping', *Journal of Adolescence*, 16: 253–66.

Furman, L. (1990) 'Video therapy: an alternative for the treatment of adolescents', *Arts in Psychotherapy*, 17: 165–9.

Gaoni, B., Kronenberg, J. and Kaysar, N. (1994) 'Boundaries during adolescence', *Israeli Journal of Psychiatry and Related Sciences*, 31: 19–27.

Garcia, P. (1992) 'The family effect on adolescent drug use: environmental and genetic factors', *The American Psychological Association*, 13: 39–48.

Garnefski, M. and Diekstra, R. (1996) 'Child sexual abuse and emotional and behavior problems in adolescents: gender differences', *American Academy of Child and Adolescent Psychiatry*, 36: 323–9.

Garralda, N.E. (1992) 'A selective review of child psychiatric syndromes with a somatic presentation', *British Journal of Psychiatry*, 161: 759–73.

Geldard, K. and Geldard, D. (2002) *Counselling Children: A Practical Introduction*. London: Sage.

Gerevich, J. and Bacskai, E. (1996) 'Protective and risk predictors in the development of drug abuse', *Journal of Drug Education*, 26: 25–38.

Gibson-Cline, J. (1996) *Adolescents: from Crisis to Coping – a Thirteen Nation Study*. Oxford: Butterworth-Heinemann.

Gilligan, C. (1983) 'New maps of developments: new visions of maturity', *Annual Progress in Child Psychiatry and Child Development*, 3: 98–115.

Gladding, S.T. (1991) *Group Work: A Counseling Specialty*. New York: Macmillan.

Glasser, W. and Wubbolding, R. (1995) 'Reality therapy', in R. Corsini and D. Wedding (eds), *Current Psychotherapies* (5th edn). Itasca, IL: F.E. Peacock. pp. 293–321.

Glod, C. and Teicher, M. (1996) 'Relationship between early abuse, post-traumatic stress disorder and activity levels in pre-pubertal children', *American Academy of Child and Adolescent Psychiatry*, 34: 1384–93.

Grigg, N., Bowman, J. and Redman, S. (1996) 'Disordered eating and unhealthy weight reduction practices among adolescent females', *Preventative Medicine*, 25: 748–56.

Grinder, J. and Bandler, R. (1976) *The Structure of Magic*, vol. 2. Palo Alto, CA: Science and Behavior Books.

Grossman, N. and Rowat, K.N. (1995) 'Parental relationships, coping strategies, received support, and wellbeing in adolescents of separated or divorced and married parents', *Research in Nursing and Health*, 18: 249–61.

Guerrero, L.K. and Afifi, W.A. (1995) 'What parents don't know: taboo topics and topic avoidance in parent–child relationships', in T.J. Socha and G. Stamp (eds), *Parents, Children, and Communication: Frontiers of Theory and Research*. Hillsdale, NJ: Lawrence Erlbaum. pp. 219–45.

Haan, N. (1977) *Coping and Defending: Processes of Self–Environment Organization*. New York: Academic Press.

Hall, R., Tice, L., Beresford, T., Willey, B. and Hall, A. (1989) 'Sexual abuse in patients with anorexia nervosa and bulimia', *Psychosomatics*, 30: 73–9.

Hammarstrom, A. (1994) 'Health consequences of youth unemployment: review from a gender perspective', *Social Science and Medicine*, 38: 699–709.

Handford, H.A., Mayes, S.D., Mattison, R.E., Humphrey, F.J., Bagnato, S., Bixler, E.O. and Kales, J.D. (1986) 'Child and parent reaction to the Three Mile Island nuclear accident', *Journal of the American Academy of Child Psychiatry*, 25: 346–56.

Harris, T.A. (1973) *I'm OK – You're OK*. London: Pan.

Havighurst, R.J. (1951) *Developmental Tasks and Education*. New York: Longman.

Heubeck, B.G., Tausch, B. and Mayer, B. (1995) 'Models of responsibility and depression in unemployed young males and females', *Journal of Community and Applied Social Psychology*, 5: 291–309.

Hoffman, L. (1993) *Exchanging Voices: A Collaborative Approach to Family Therapy*. London: Karnac.

Hoffman, M. (1988) 'Moral development', in M. Bornstein and M. Lamb (eds), *Developmental Psychology: An Advanced Textbook*. Hillsdale, NJ: Lawrence Erlbaum. pp. 497–548.

Holland, D. and Kipnis, A. (1994) 'Metaphors for embarrassment and stories of exposure: the not so egocentric self in American culture', *Ethos*, 22: 316–42.

Houser, R., Daniels, J., D'Andrea, N. and Konstan, V.A. (1993) 'A systematic behaviourally based technique for resolving conflicts between adolescents and their single parents', *Journal of Child and Family Behaviour Therapy*, 15: 17–31.

Hu, F.B., Flak, B.R., Hedeker, D. and Syddiqui, O. (1995) 'The influence of friends and parental smoking on adolescent smoking behaviour: the effects of time and prior smoking', *Journal of Applied Social Psychology*, 25: 2018–47.

Hurrelman, K., Enel, U. and Wideman, J.C. (1992) 'Impacts of school pressure, conflict with parents, and career uncertainty on adolescent stress in the Federal Republic of Germany', *International Journal of Adolescents and Youth*, 4: 33–50.

Ianni, F.A.J. (1989) *The Search for Structure: A Report on American Youth Today*. New York: Free Press.

Ives, R. (1994) 'Stop sniffing in the states: approaches to solvent misuse prevention in the USA', *Drugs, Education, Prevention and Policy*, 1: 37–48.

Ivey, M., Ivey, A. and Simek-Morgan, L. (1993) *Counseling and Psychotherapy: A Multi-cultural Perspective*. Needham Heights, NY: Simon & Schuster.

Jackson, S. and Bosma, H. (1990) 'Coping and self in adolescence', in H. Bosma and S. Jackson (eds), *Coping and Self-concept in Adolescence*. Berlin: Springer-Verlag. pp. 203–21.

Janis, I. and Mann, L. (1982) 'Counseling on personal positions', in I. Janis (ed.), *Counseling on Personal Decisions: Theory and Research on Short Term Helping Relationships*. New Haven, CT: Yale University Press.

Jenkins, J.E. (1996) 'The influence of peer affiliation and student activities on adolescent drug involvement', *Adolescence*, 31: 297–306.

Jensen, A.R., Cohn, S.J. and Cohn, C.M. (1989) 'Speed of information processing in academically gifted youth', *Personality and Individual Differences*, 6: 621–9.

Jolley, R. and Thomas, G. (1994) 'The development of sensitivity to metaphorical expression of moods in abstract art', *Educational Psychology*, 14: 437–50.

Josselson, R. (1987) *Finding Herself: Pathways to Identity Development in Women*. San Francisco: Jossey-Bass.

Jung, C.G. (1968) *Collected Works*, vol. 9, pt 1: *The Archetypes and a Collective Unconscious* (2nd rev. edn). Princeton, NJ: Princeton University Press.

Kaffman, M. (1995) 'Brief therapy in the Israel kibbutz', *Contemporary Family Therapy: An International Journal* (special issue on family therapy in Israel), 17: 449–68.

Kaplan, S., Pelcovitz, D., Salzinger, S. and Mandel, F. (1997) 'Adolescent physical abuse and suicide attempts', *Journal of the American Academy of Child and Adolescent Psychiatry*, 36: 799–808.

Kazdin, A.E. (1985) *Treatment of Anti-social Behavior in Children and Adolescents*. Chicago: Dorsey.

Kearney, C.A. and Silverman, W.K. (1995) 'Family environment of youngsters with school refusal behavior: a synopsis with implications for assessment and treatment', *The American Journal of Family Therapy*, 23: 124–32.

Keil, F. and Batterman, N. (1984) 'A characteristic-to-defining shift in the development of word meaning', *Journal of Verbal Learning and Verbal Behaviour*, 23: 221–36.

Kelly, G.A. (1955) *The Psychology of Personal Constructs*. New York: Norton.

Kendall, P.C. and Southam-Gerow, M.A. (1996) 'Long term follow up of cognitive behavioural therapy for anxiety disordered youth', *Journal of Consulting and Clinical Psychology*, 64: 724–30.

Kingsbury, S.J. (1994) 'Interacting within metaphors', *American Journal of Clinical Hypnosis*, 36: 241–427.

Knight, G., Dubro, A. and Chao, C. (1985) 'Information processing and the development of cooperative, competitive and individualistic social values', *Developmental Psychology*, 27: 37–45.

Kohlberg, L. (1968) 'The child as a moral philosopher', *Psychology Today*, 2: 25–30.

Kohlberg, L. (1984) *The Psychology of Moral Development: The Nature and Validity of Moral Stages*. San Francisco: Harper & Row.

Kroger, J. (1996) *Identity in Adolescence* (2nd edn). London: Routledge.

Kutcher, S.P. and Marton, P. (1990) 'Adolescent depression: a treatment review', in J.G. Simeon and B. Ferguson (eds), *Treatment Strategies in Child and Adolescent Psychiatry*. New York: Plenum Press. pp. 20–7.

Lazarus, J.D. and Folkman, S. (1984) *Stress, Appraisal and Coping*. New York: Springer.

Leavitt, R.S. and Pill, C.J. (1995) 'Composing a self through writing: the ego and the ink', *Smith College Studies in Social Work*, 65: 137–49.

Lincoln, C. and McGorry, P. (1995) 'Who cares? Pathways to psychiatric care for young people experiencing a first episode of psychosis', *Psychiatric Services*, 46: 1166–71.

Lo, L. (1994) 'Exploring teenage shoplifting behavior: a choice and constraint approach', *Environment and Behavior*, 26: 613–39.

Lovat, T.J. (1991) *Childhood into Adolescence: Perspectives and Issues for Teachers*. Wentworth Fall, NSW: Social Science Press.

Lowenfeld, M. (1967) *Play in Childhood*. New York: John Wiley.

Luntz, B. and Widom, C. (1994) 'Anti-social personality disorder in abused and neglected children grown up', *American Journal of Psychiatry*, 151: 670–4.

Mabey, J. and Sorensen, B. (1995) *Counselling for Young People*. Buckingham: Open University Press.

McBroom, J.R. (1994) 'Correlates of alcohol and marijuana use among junior high school students: family, peers, school problems, and psychosocial concerns', *Youth and Society*, 26: 54–68.

McCaulley, M.H. (1990) 'The Myers–Briggs type indicator in counseling', in C.E. Watkins Jr and V.L. Campbell (eds), *Testing in Counseling Practice*. Hillsdale, NJ: Lawrence Erlbaum. pp. 91–134.

McClellan, J., McCurry, C., Ronnei, M. and Adams, J. (1997) 'Relationship between sexual abuse, gender and sexually inappropriate behaviors in seriously mentally ill youth', *Journal of the American Academy of Child and Adolescent Psychiatry*, 367: 959–65.

McEvoy, A. and Erickson, E. (1990) *Youth and Exploitation*. Holmes Beach, FL: Learning Publications.

McGee, R., Wolfe, D. and Wilson, S. (1997) 'Multiple maltreatment experiences and adolescent behaviour problems: adolescent perspectives', *Development and Psychopathology*, 9: 131–49.

Madanes, C. (1981) *Strategic Family Therapy*. San Francisco: Jossey-Bass.

Madanes, C. (1984) *Behind the One-way Mirror: Advances in the Practice of Strategic Therapy*. San Francisco: Jossey-Bass.

Madonna, J. and Caswell, P. (1991) 'The utilisation of flexible techniques in group therapy with delinquent adolescent boys', *Journal of Child and Adolescent Group Therapy*, 1: 147–57.

Mann, D. (1991) 'Humor in psychotherapy', *Psychoanalytic Psychotherapy*, 5: 161–70.

Martin, A. (1997) 'On teenagers and tattoos', *Journal of the American Academy of Child and Adolescent Psychiatry*, 36: 860–1.

Mazurova, A. and Rozin, M. (1991) 'Family conflicts of counter cultural youth of the USSR and possible psychotherapeutic approaches', *American Journal of Family Therapy*, 19: 47–53.

Mead, M. (1975) *Coming of Age in Samoa*. New York: Morrow.

Meeus, W., Dekobic, M. and Iedema, J. (1997) 'Unemployment and identity in adolescence: a social comparison perspective', *Career Development Quarterly*, 45: 369–80.

Meier, S.T. (1989) *The Elements of Counseling*. Pacific Grove, CA: Brooks/Cole.

Meshot, C. and Leitner, L. (1993) 'Adolescent mourning and parental death', *Amiga Journal of Death and Dying*, 26: 287–99.

Michell, L. and West, P. (1996) 'Peer pressure to smoke: the means depends on the method', *Health Education and Research*, 11: 39–49.

Miller, Shirley M. (ed.) (1983) *Counseling and Psychotherapy with Children and Adolescents*. Tampa, FL: Mariner.

Mitchell, R. and Friedman, H. (1994) *Sand Play: Past, Present and Future*. London: Routledge.

Molidor, C.E. (1996) 'Female gang members: a profile of aggression and victimisation', *Social Work*, 41: 251–7.

Monsour, M. (1992) 'Meanings of intimacy in cross- and same-sex friendships', *Journal of Social and Personal Relationships*, 9, 277–95.

Morra, S., Caloni, B. and d'Amico, M. (1994) 'Working memory and the intentional depiction of emotions', *Archives of Psychology*, 62: 71–87.

Mortlock, J. (1995) 'Chloe: "Who cares for me": counselling with a disturbed and disturbing teenager', *Therapeutic Care and Education*, 4: 10–13.

Nader, K., Pynoos, R.S., Fairbanks, L. and Frederick, C. (1990) 'Children's PTSD reactions one year after a sniper attack at their school', *American Journal of Psychiatry*, 147: 1526–30.

Nelson, R.C. (1992) *On the Crest: Growing through Effective Choices*. Minneapolis, MN: Educational Media Corporation.

Neumark-Sztainer, D., Story, M., French, S. and Resnick, N. (1997) 'Psycho-social correlates of health compromising behaviours among adolescents', *Health Education Research*, 12: 37–52.

O'Keefe, M. (1996) 'The differential effects of family violence on adolescent adjustment', *Child and Adolescent Social Work Journal*, 13: 51–68.

O'Koon, J. (1997) 'Attachment to parents and peers in adolescence and their relationship with self image', *Journal of Adolescence*, 32: 471–82.

Oppenheimer, R., Howels, K., Palmer, R. and Chalomer, D. (1985) 'Adverse sexual experiences in childhood and clinical eating disorders: preliminary description', *Journal of Psychiatric Research*, 19: 357–61.

Palazzoli, S.N., Boscolo, L., Cecchin, F.G. and Prata, G. (1980) 'Hypothesising circularity neutrality: three guidelines for the conductor of the session', *Family Process*, 19: 3–12.

Parks, M.R. and Floyd, K. (1996) 'Meanings for closeness and intimacy in friendship', *Journal of Social and Personal Relationships*, 13: 85–107.

Patton, W. and Noller, P. (1990) 'Adolescent self-concept: effects of being employed, unemployed or returning to school', *Australian Journal of Psychology*, 42: 247–59.

Perry, M.J. and Mandell, W. (1995) 'Psychosocial factors associated with the initiation of cocaine use among marijuana users', *Psychology of Addictive Behaviours*, 9: 99–100.

Peters, M. and Weller, E. (1994) 'Resolved: several weeks of depressive symptoms after exposure to a friend's suicide is "major depressive disorder: negative"', *Journal of the American Academy of Child and Adolescent Psychiatry*, 33: 584–6.

Peters, T.C. (1990) 'Student graffiti and social class: clues for counsellors', *School Counsellor*, 38: 123–32.

Peterson, R.W. (1994) 'The adrenalin metaphor: narrative mind and practice in child and youth care', *Journal of Child and Youth Care*, 9: 107–21.

Piaget, J. (1948/1966) *Psychology of Intelligence*. New York: Harcourt.

Pierce, R.A., Nichols, M.P. and Du Brin, J.R. (1983) *Emotional Expression in Psychotherapy*. New York: Amereon.

Pierce, W., Lemke, E. and Smith, R. (1988) 'Critical thinking and moral development in secondary students', *High School Journal*, 71: 120–6.

Prochaska, J.O. (1999) 'How do people change, and how change to help many more people', in M. Hubble, B. Duncan and S. Miller (eds), *Heart and Soul of Change: What Works in Therapy*. Washington, DC: American Psychological Association.

Radkowski, M. and Siegel, L.J. (1997) 'The gay adolescent: stresses, adaptations, and psychosocial interventions', *Clinical Psychology Review*, 17: 191–216.

Raich, R.N., Rosen, J.C., Deus, J. and Perez, O. (1992) 'Eating disorder symptoms among adolescents in the United States and Spain: a comparative study', *International Journal of Eating Disorders*, 11: 63–72.

Raviv, A. and Maddy-Weitzman, E. (1992) 'Parents of adolescents: help seeking intentions as a function of help sources and parenting issues', *Journal of Adolescence*, 15: 115–21.

Readdick, C.A. (1997) 'Adolescents and adults at the mall: diadic interactions', *Adolescence*, 32: 313–22.

Reyes, B. (1994) 'Cultural symbols and images in the counselling process', *Pastoral Psychology*, 42: 277–84.

Robin, S.S. and Johnson, E.O. (1996) 'Attitude and peer cross pressure: adolescent drug and alcohol use', *Journal of Drug Education*, 26: 69–99.

Rogers, C.R. (1955) *Client-Centered Therapy*. Boston: Houghton-Mifflin.

Rogers, C.R. (1965) *Client-Centered Therapy: Its Current Practice, Implications and Theory*. Boston: Houghton-Mifflin.

Rosenbaum, R. (1994) 'Single session therapies: intrinsic integration?', *Journal of Psychotherapy Integration*, 4: 229–52.

Rotenberg, K.J. (1995) *Disclosure Processes in Children and Adolescents*. Cambridge: Cambridge University Press.

Rutter, V. (1995) 'Adolescence: whose hell is it?', *Psychology Today*, 28: 54–65.

Ryce-Menuhin, J. (1992) *Jungian Sand Play: The Wonderful Therapy*. New York: Routledge, Chapman & Hall.

Ryder, R.G. and Bartle, S. (1991) 'Boundaries as distance regulators in personal relationships', *Family Process*, 30: 393–406.

Safyer, A.W., Leahy, B.H. and Colan, N.B. (1995) 'The impact of work on adolescent development', *Families in Society*, 76: 38–45.

Salzman, J. (1997) 'Ambivalent attachment in female adolescents: association with affective instability and eating disorders', *International Journal of Eating Disorders*, 21: 251–9.

Sanders, B. and Giolas, M. (1991) 'Dissociation and childhood trauma in psychologically disturbed adolescents', *American Journal of Psychiatry*, 148: 50–4.

Sandler, I.N., Wolchik, S.A., MacKinon, D., Ayers, T. and Roosa, M.W. (1997) 'Developing linkages between theory and intervention in stress and coping processes', in A. Walchik and I. Sandler (eds), *Handbook of Children's Coping: Linking Theory and Intervention*. New York: Plenum Press. pp. 3–40.

Santrock, J.W. (1993) *Adolescence*. Madison, WI: Brown & Benchmark.

Schlossberg, N.K. (1989) 'Marginality and mattering: key issues in building community', *New Directions for Children's Services*, 48: 5–15.

Schmidt, M. (1991) 'Problems of child abuse with adolescents in chemically dependent families', *Journal of Adolescent Chemical Dependency*, 1: 9–24.

Schonert-Reichl, K.A. and Muller, J.R. (1996) 'Correlates of help seeking in adolescents', *Journal of Youth and Adolescence*, 25: 705–31.

Schrof, J. (1995) 'Unhappy girls and boys', *US News and World Report*, 119: 86–8.

Searight, H.R., Thomas, S.L., Manley, C.M. and Ketterson, T.U. (1995) 'Self-disclosure in adolescents: a family systems perspective', in K.J. Rotenberg (ed.), *Disclosure Processes in Children and Adolescents*. Cambridge: Cambridge University Press. pp. 204–25.

Seiffge-Krenke, I. (1995) *Stress, Coping, and Relationships in Adolescence*. Hillsdale, NJ: Lawrence Erlbaum.

Shave, D. and Shave, B. (1989) *Early Adolescence and the Search for Self: A Developmental Perspective*. New York: Praeger.

Shulman, S., Seiffge-Krenke, I., Levy-Shiff, R. and Fabian, B. (1995) 'Peer group and family relationships in early adolescence', *International Journal of Psychology*, 30: 573–90.

Sigler, R.T. (1995) 'Gang violence', *Journal of Health Care for the Poor and Underserved*, 6: 198–203.

Simeonsson, R.J. (1994) *Risk, Resilience and Prevention: Promoting the Well Being of All Children*. Baltimore, MD: Brookes.

Singer, M.I., Anglin, T.M., Song, L.Y. and Lunghofer, L. (1995) 'Adolescents' exposure to violence and associated symptoms of psychological trauma', *Journal of the American Medical Association*, 273: 477–82.

Slavin, J.H. (1996) 'Readiness for psychoanalytic treatment in late adolescents: developmental and adaptive considerations', *Psychoanalytic Psychology*, 13: 35–51.

Smith, C. (1997) 'Factors associated with early sexual activity among urban adolescents', *Social Work Journal*, 42: 334–46.

Sommers-Flanagan, J. and Sommers-Flanagan, R. (1996) 'The wizard of Oz metaphor in hypnosis with treatment resistant children', *American Journal of Clinical Hypnosis*, 39: 105–14.

Spinelli, E. (1996) 'The existential-phenomenological paradigm', in R. Woolfe and W. Dryden (eds), *Handbook of Counselling Psychology*. London: Sage. pp. 180–200.

Spirito, A., Stark, L., Grace, N. and Stamoulis, D. (1991) 'Common problems and coping strategies reported in childhood and early adolescence', *Journal of Youth and Adolescence*, 20: 531.

Steinberg, L. (1990) 'Autonomy, conflict, and harmony in the family relationship', in S.S. Feldman and G.R. Elliot (eds), *At the Threshold: The Developing Adolescent*. Cambridge, MA: Harvard University Press. pp. 255–76.

Steinberg, L. and Steinberg, W. (1994) *Crossing Paths: How Your Child's Adolescence Triggers your own Crisis*. New York: Simon & Schuster.

Steiner, H., Garcia, I. and Matthews, Z. (1997) 'Post-traumatic stress disorder in incarcerated juvenile delinquents', *American Academy of Child and Adolescent Psychiatry*, 36: 357–65.

Stoddard, F.J., Norman, D.K. and Murphy, J.M. (1989) 'A diagnostic outcome study of children and adolescents with severe burns', *Journal of Trauma*, 29: 471–7.

Story, N., French, S.A., Resnick, N.D. and Blum, R.W. (1995) 'Ethnic/racial and socioeconomic differences in dieting behaviours and body image perceptions in adolescence', *International Journal of Eating Disorders*, 18: 173–9.

Sussman, T. and Duffy, M. (1996) 'Are we forgetting about gay male adolescents in AIDS related research and prevention?', *Youth and Society*, 27: 379–93.

Swanson, M.S. (1991) *At Risk Students in Elementary Education: Effective Schools for Disadvantaged Learners*. Springfield, IL: Thomas.

Talmon, M. (1990) *Single Session Therapy: Maximizing the Effect of the First (and Often Only) Therapeutic Encounter*. San Francisco: Jossey-Bass.

Tharp, R. (1991) 'Cultural diversity and the treatment of children', *Journal of Consulting and Clinical Psychology*, 59: 799–812.

Tomori, M. (1994) 'Personality characteristics of adolescents with alcoholic parents', *Adolescence*, 29: 949–59.

Tubman, J.G., Windle, M. and Windle, R.C. (1996) 'Cumulative sexual intercourse patterns among middle adolescents: problem behavior precursors and concurrent health risk behaviors', *Journal of Adolescent Health*, 18: 182–91.

Tucker, R. (1989) 'Teen Satanism', paper presented at the Conference on Ritual Abuse: Fact or Fiction, The Institute for the Prevention of Child Abuse, Ontario.

Tyler, M. (1978) *Advisory and Counselling Services for Young People*. DHSS Research Report no. 1. London: HMSO.

USA Today Magazine (1997) vol. 125, no. 2622, p. 8.

Valliant, P. and Antonowicz, D.H. (1991) 'Cognitive behaviour therapy and social skills training improves personality and cognition in incarcerated offenders', *Psychological Reports*, 68: 27–33.

VanderMay, B. and Meff, R. (1982) 'Adult–child incest: a review of research and treatment', *Adolescence*, 17: 717–35.

Vernon, A. (1993) *Counseling Children and Adolescents*. Denver, CO: Love.

Vondracek, F.W. and Corneal, S. (1995) *Strategies for Resolving Individual and Family Problems*. Pacific Grove: Brooks/Cole.

Waiswol, N. (1995) 'Projective techniques as psychotherapy', *American Journal of Psychotherapy*, 49: 244–59.

Walter, J. and Peller, J. (1992) *Becoming Solution-focused in Brief Therapy*. New York: Brunner/Mazel.

Wang, A.Y. (1994) 'Pride and prejudice in high school gang members', *Adolescence*, 29: 279–91.

Wang, M.Q., Fitzheugh, E.C., Eddy, J.M. and Fu, Q. (1997) 'Social influences on adolescents' smoking progress: a longitudinal analysis', *American Journal of Health Behavior*, 21: 111–17.

Wardle, J., Bindra, R., Fairclough, B. and Westcombe, A. (1993) 'Culture and body image: body perception and weight concern in young Asian and Caucasian British women', *Journal of Community and Applied Social Psychology*, 3: 173–81.

Warner, R.E. (1996) 'Comparison of client and counsellor satisfaction with treatment duration', *Journal of College Students Psychotherapy*, 10: 73–88.

Warren, S., Huston, L., Edgeland, B. and Sroufe, L. (1997) 'Child and adolescent anxiety disorders and early attachment', *Journal of the American Academy of Child and Adolescent Psychiatry*, 36: 637–44.

Waterman, A. (1984) *The Psychology of Individualism*. New York: Praeger.

Waterman, A.S. (1992) 'Identity as an aspect of optimal psychological functioning', in R. Adams, T.P. Gulotta and R. Montemoyr (eds), *Adolescent Identity Formation*. Thousand Oaks, CA: Sage. pp. 50–72.

Webster, R.A., Hunter, M. and Keats, J.A. (1994) 'Peer and parental influences on adolescents' substance abuse: a path analysis', *International Journal of the Addictions*, 29: 647–57.

Weinhold, B.K. (1987) 'Altered states of consciousness: an explorer's guide to inner space', *Counselling and Human Development*, 20: 1–12.

Welch, S., Doll, H. and Fairburn, C. (1997) 'Life events and the onset of bulimia nervosa: a controlled study', *Psychological Medicine*, 27: 515–22.

West, D.J. (1982) *Delinquency: Its Roots, Careers and Prospects*. Cambridge, MA: Harvard University Press.

West, M.O. and Prinz, R.J. (1988) 'Parental alcoholism and childhood psychopathology', in S. Chess, A. Thomas and M.E. Hertzig (eds), *Annual Progress in Child Psychiatry and Child Development*. New York: Brunner/Mazel. pp. 278–314.

White, F.A. (1996) 'Parent, adolescent communication and adolescent decision making', *Journal of Family Studies*, 2: 41–56.

White, M. (1989) *Selected Papers*. Adelaide: Dulwich.

White, M. and Epston, D. (1990) *Narrative Means to Therapeutic Ends*. New York: Norton.

Widon, C.S. (1994) 'Childhood victimization and adolescent problem behaviors', in R.B. Kettellinus and N.E. Land (eds), *Adolescent Problem Behaviors*. Hillsdale, NJ: Lawrence Erlbaum. pp. 127–64.

Wilkes, T.C., Belsher, G., Rush, A.J. and Frank, E. (1994) *Cognitive Therapy for Depressed Adolescents*. New York: Guilford Press.

Wills, T.A., Pierce, J.T. and Evans, R.I. (1996) 'Large scale environmental risk factors for substance abuse', *American Behavioral Scientist*, 39: 808–22.

Winefield, A.H. and Tiggemann, M. (1990) 'Employment status and psychological well-being: a longitudinal study', *Journal of Applied Psychology*, 75: 455–9.

Winter, D.A. (1996) 'The constructivist paradigm', in R. Woolfe, and W. Dryden (eds), *Handbook of Counselling Psychology*. London: Sage. pp. 219–39.

Woolfe, R. and Dryden, W. (eds) (1996) *Handbook of Counselling Psychology*. London: Sage.

Word, W. (1996) 'Mortality awareness and risk taking in late adolescence', *Death Studies*, 20: 133–48.

World Health Organization (1994) *ICD-10 Classification of Mental and Behavioural Disorders: Clinical Descriptions and Diagnostic Guidelines*. Geneva: World Health Organization.

World Health Organization, Collaborating Centre for Mental Health and Substance Abuse (1997) *Treatment Protocol Project Management of Mental Disorders*. Sydney, Australia: World Health Organization.

Yarnold, B.M. and Patterson, V. (1995) 'Factors correlated with adolescent use of crack in public schools', *Psychological Reports*, 76: 467–74.

Young, R.A., Antal, S., Bassett, M.E., Post, A., DeVries, N. and Valach, L. (1999) 'The joint actions of adolescents in peer conversations about career', *Journal of Adolescence*, 22: 527–38.

Youniss, J. and Haynie, D.L. (1992) 'Friendship in adolescence', *Developmental and Behavioral Pediatrics*, 13 (1): 59–66.

Youniss, J. and Smollar, J. (1985) *Adolescent Relations with Mothers, Fathers and Friends*. Chicago: University of Chicago Press.

INDEX